MORAL | *Relativism*
MORAL | *Diversity*
&
HUMAN | *Relationships*

J. KELLENBERGER

MORAL | *Relativism*
MORAL | *Diversity*
& |
HUMAN | *Relationships*

THE PENNSYLVANIA STATE UNIVERSITY PRESS
UNIVERSITY PARK, PENNSYLVANIA

LIBRARY OF CONGRESS CATALOGING-IN-PUBLICATION DATA

Kellenberger, James.
  Moral relativism, moral diversity, and human relationships / J. Kellenberger.
     p.   cm.
  Includes bibliographical references and index.
  ISBN 978-0-271-02287-1 (pbk : alk. paper)
  1. Ethical relativism.   2. Interpersonal relations—Moral and ethical aspects.
  I. Title.
  BJ1012.K45 2001
  171'.7—dc21

                                                                2001021480

Copyright © 2001 The Pennsylvania State University
All rights reserved
Printed in the United States of America
Published by The Pennsylvania State University Press,
University Park, PA 16802-1003

It is the policy of The Pennsylvania State University Press to use acid-free paper for the first printing of all clothbound books. Publications on uncoated stock satisfy the minimum requirements of American National Standard for Information Sciences—Permanence of Paper for Printed Library Materials, ANSI Z39.48-1992.

To Anne

Contents

	Preface	ix
	Introduction	1
ONE	Forms of Relativism	11
TWO	Are There Universally Accepted Moral Values?	31
THREE	What Would the Existence of Universally Accepted Moral Values Signify?	43
FOUR	Some Proposed Root Bases of Morality	61
FIVE	Pluralism, Monism, and Relativism	75
SIX	Moral Diversity and Relationships	91
SEVEN	Moral Diversity and the Person/Person Relationship	113
EIGHT	What Is Right/Wrong About Moral Relativism?	171
NINE	Diversity and Morality	201
	Works Cited	225
	Index	233

Preface

In the title of this book I have put in juxtaposition a recurring philosophical ethical issue (moral relativism), an increasingly palpable world cultural fact (moral diversity), and an element of each of our individual lives (human relationships). However, I am not putting into one basket apples, oranges, and vegetables. The first two, though in different categories—one being an issue, the other being a phenomenon—are interconnected. The third bears on the first two as a means of our increased understanding of them and their interconnection.

Relationships between persons form the unifying thread of the book. In much of my discussion, I will trace how reflection on the moral significance of relationships between persons illuminates the complexity of human morality and its attendant issues. In particular, I will be concerned to show how relationships help us to understand the issue of moral relativism and the phenomenon of moral diversity. Among contemporary moral philosophers there is a dissatisfaction with the distance between ethical theory and practical morality. Several, if not many, of those who reflect on the nature of morality and why much of traditional ethical theory seems unfruitful are turning their attention to relationships. Some who have done so started from a feminist standpoint, some from the standpoint of environmental ethics, some from the standpoint of ecofeminism, and some from a theological standpoint. I mention several of these thinkers in my discussion. Some whom I do not mention in what follows, but who deserve mention, are Claudia Card, Christopher Gowans, J. Harvey, Judith Plaskow, Rosemary Radford Ruether, and H. Richard Niebuhr.[1]

These authors and those I will subsequently mention do not all appeal to relationships in the same way or to the same effect, and for some, relationships are not limited to relationships between human persons.[2] Yet each in some way recognizes the moral importance of relationships.

Not only contemporary moral philosophers, but many among those who daily make their moral way, I suspect, have a residual sense of the moral importance of relationships. So much is this so, that this book in time may be seen as setting forth only commonplace truths. That time is not now.

Some of the material in this book has appeared or been presented elsewhere. An earlier version of Chapter 3 was presented in a paper, "Ethical Relativity, Actions,

---

1. See, for instance, Claudia Card, "Gender and Moral Luck," in *Identity, Character, and Morality: Essays in Moral Psychology*, eds. Owen Flanagan and Amélie Oksenberg Rorty (Cambridge, Mass.: MIT Press, 1990); Christopher W. Gowans, *Innocence Lost: An Examination of Inescapable Moral Wrongdoing* (New York: Oxford University Press, 1994); J. Harvey, *Civilized Oppression* (New York: Rowman & Littlefield, 1999); H. Richard Niebuhr, *Christ and Culture* (New York: Harper & Row, 1951) and *The Responsible Self* (Louisville, Ky.: Westminster John Knox, 1963); Judith Plaskow, *Sex, Sin, and Grace* (Lanham, Md.: University Press of America, 1980); and Rosemary Radford Ruether, *Gaia and God: An Ecofeminist Theology of Earth Healing* (San Francisco: Harper, 1992). The moral importance that Niebuhr saw in relationships was drawn to my attention by Philip Rossi, among others.

2. While relationships between human persons form the unifying thread of this book and it is reflection on such human relationships that will illuminate both moral relativism and moral diversity, human relationships between human persons should not be thought to be the exclusive basis of morality. Certainly this exclusivity is not entailed by anything I claim. My discussion in the pages that follow leaves it open that there may be persons that are not human to whom we are morally related, that humans have relationships to nonhuman animals and to the environment that have moral implications, and that humans have various possible relationships to God or the Absolute that have general and special moral requirements. I have explored these other kinds of relationships in *Relationship Morality* (University Park: Penn State University Press, 1995).

and More," at Where the Action Is: A Conference in Honor of Frank Ebersole, held in Coos Bay, Oregon, in 1996. Some material in Chapter 3 appeared in "Ethical Relativity," in *The Journal of Value Inquiry* 13 (1979): 1–20, copyright held by Kluwer Academic Publishers, and used with kind permission form Kluwer Academic Publishers. Some material in Chapters 3 and 6 appeared in "Religious Moral Diversity," in *Ethics in the World Religions*, edited by Nancy M. Martin and Joseph Runzo, published by One World Press and used with permission.

In *Relationship Morality* (1995), I developed and defended the idea that relationships are foundational to morality. The present book draws upon much of the previous enquiry but develops it further and applies those earlier reflections on relationships to new concerns with moral relativism and moral diversity.

Several persons have helped me in the writing and preparation of this book. I am thankful for help from Dr. Leo Rain, in particular his help in locating a passage in the Talmud referred to by Rabbi Schulweis, but also his help in drawing to my attention discussions in medical ethics that address issues of moral diversity. I am grateful for help from Lynne Mastnak on Bosnian practices regarding mourning the dead and to Takashi Yagisawa for confirming a point about the use of first-person pronouns in Japanese.

I am pleased to thank Sanford Thatcher, John Kekes, and Michael Krausz, who read the manuscript as a whole, for various helpful suggestions and comments; Elizabeth Yoder for her careful copyediting of the manuscript; and my colleague, wife, helper, and friend, Anne, who suggested connections and examples.

Finally, I am grateful for research reassigned time received from California State University, Northridge, the College of Humanities, and the Department of Philosophy over several years, which allowed me to sustain my work on this book over this period, and to the University and College for a sabbatical in the fall of 1999, which allowed me to complete the book.

Introduction

I. Moral Relativism and Moral Diversity

The two main concerns of this book are moral relativism and moral diversity. Just how these two are related is open to question, but that they are in some manner related is certain. Perhaps moral relativism rests upon moral diversity as a thesis rests upon its support. Perhaps moral diversity predisposes us to think of morality in a relativistic way, while in fact providing no evidential support for it. Perhaps it provides some support, but not enough to prove it. One thing we can be clear about, however, is that moral relativism and moral diversity are in different categories: the first is a view of morality, a moral theory, whereas the second is a moral phenomenon. As a theory about morality, the first has given rise to an issue about its truth. As a moral phenomenon, the second is there to be observed in our multicultural world.

In this book I have three main goals: first, to come to an understanding of the theory and issue of moral relativism; second, to come to an understanding of the phenomenon of moral diversity; and third, to show how moral relativism and moral diversity are related. We shall begin with an effort to understand the theory and issue of moral relativism, although, partly because the theory of moral relativism is interwoven with the phenomenon of moral diversity and partly because what helps us to understand the theory also helps us to understand moral diversity, we cannot complete the first effort without addressing moral diversity. The issue that the theory of moral relativism gives rise to may be called "the problem of moral relativism." This problem and the controversy in which it is cloaked have been with us since antiquity.

II. The Problem of Moral Relativism

The problem of moral relativism—Is morality at its core relative or is it not?—is among those problems that die hard. It is, moreover, among those problems that will not stay dead once they have died. Such problems return, not to haunt us, but to take on a new life in a new form. The old issue of moral relativism (or ethical relativism, or moral or ethical relativity) has returned in one form or another since the time of Protagoras, sometimes drawing strength from observations of different customs, like those made by Herodotus and those made since the seventeenth century by modern anthropology. Most recently the issue has reemerged as the issue between communitarianism and universalism.[1]

Why does this philosophical issue, like others, linger? Do philosophical issues refuse to die because philosophers have an employment problem? Despite appearances, I am not inclined to think so. Basic philosophical problems do not belong to the philosophers: they have a life of their own, regardless of the consensus or

---

1. David Rasmussen, ed., *Universalism vs. Communitarianism: Contemporary Debates in Ethics* (Cambridge, Mass.: MIT Press, 1990). Cf. Onora O'Neill, "Justice, Gender, and International Boundaries," in *The Quality of Life*, ed. Martha Nussbaum and Amartya Sen (Oxford: Clarendon Press, 1993), 307–9. O'Neill contrasts communitarianism and its contextual and "relativised principles of justice" with "abstract liberalism" and its universalist "internationalist, cosmopolitan commitments." She goes on to argue for principles of justice that are "neither idealized nor relative to actual societies" (317–18).

needs of philosophers. The issue of moral relativism, in particular, ranges beyond the borders of philosophy into the area of the social sciences, and beyond the borders of the academic disciplines into nonacademic reflection.

Does the issue of moral relativism refuse to die because new data emerge periodically and require us to reexamine our thinking about moral relativity? I would say that nothing—rightly or wrongly—invigorates an intellectual tendency toward at least one form of moral relativism quite as much as the experience of the moral diversity of a multiculturalism in which one sees the confrontation of the different moral values and practices of different societies or cultures. When cultures that have been geographically separated from one another become intermixed in urban settings or come before one another through the various electronic media, as now happens regularly, the confrontation of different values and practices becomes nearly inevitable. Something similar can be said for the intracultural experience of diverse subcultures within a culture.

Perhaps what accounts for the durable and protean nature of the issue of moral relativism is that each generation of moral thinkers—philosophers and others— has to work through the issue in its own way. Even if the issue has been resolved, that resolution has to be appropriated by the thinker who faces the issue and contemplates its resolution. This may (or may not) be one of the ways philosophical issues are unlike some of their foreign cousins in the sciences. Philosophical reasoning goes on too long, as John Wisdom observed.[2]

However, it may be too hasty to suggest that the issue of moral relativism has been resolved, so that its resolution is available for appropriation. That it has not been resolved seems more likely, for the issue continues to return, though in different guises, in different trappings and formulations. The issue of moral relativism as an inveterate philosophical problem is not merely an intellectual one, we may say. It *is* an intellectual issue, to be sure, but it is hardly purely intellectual. It has other, affective, dimensions. So it is that some who reflect on the issue intuitively and pretheoretically react to it with the sense that of course morality is relative, whereas others react with just as strong a sense that morality cannot be relative. F. H. Bradley commented that "metaphysics is the finding of bad reasons for what we believe on instinct."[3] Regarding some philosophical issues, including some that are not metaphysical, Bradley may have been fairly close to the truth. The issue of ethical relativism may be just that sort of issue—the kind we come to with a fairly firm intuition in place, which drives our search for justification in one direction rather than another.

2. John Wisdom, "Philosophy and Psycho-analysis," in *Philosophy and Psycho-analysis* (Oxford: Blackwell, 1964), 175.
3. F. H. Bradley, *Appearance and Reality*, 2d ed. (Oxford: Clarendon Press, 1897), x.

That this is so is sometimes forthrightly acknowledged. One author and ethicist who makes such an acknowledgment is Gilbert Harman. He begins a paper he wrote a few years back with a section he calls "Confession," and his first sentence is "I have always been a moral relativist."[4] That sounds rather like "I have always been an alcoholic." But Harman's "confession" is not of a weakness or offense; it is more a confession of commitment. He is confessing his abiding sense that moral relativism is not just true, but luminously true. As he says, "As far back as I can remember thinking about it, it has seemed to me obvious that the dictates of morality arise from some sort of convention or understanding among people, that different people arrive at different understandings, and that there are no basic moral demands that apply to everyone." Harman goes on to recount how early in his academic career he assumed that objections to relativism came from a faulty definition being given to the view, and how he "naively" thought a paper he wrote would clear away these misguided objections. In his classes he discovered that some of his students were "instinctive moral relativists" but that many others were "instinctive absolutists." Meanwhile, he found that among the philosophers who were his friends many were moral absolutists who thought that moral relativism was "perverse," just as he thought the denial of relativism flew in the face of the obvious.[5]

In accord with Bradley's observation, Harman confesses his "instinct" that relativism is right—his strong sense of the nature of morality that is in place *before* he takes up his theoretical reflections, which gives his reflections their direction. The same may be said for many moral absolutists. They also follow their essentially pretheoretical "instincts." Perhaps this state of affairs is unavoidable and hence something that none of us should denounce.

This is not to say that Harman thinks there is nothing to be said in defense of moral relativism. The form of moral relativism that seems undeniably obvious to Harman appeals to "conventions" ("the dictates of morality arise from some sort of convention"); he goes on to tie moral relativism to naturalism and argues that "the more plausible versions of naturalism involve a moral relativism that says different agents are subject to different basic moral requirements depending on the moral conventions in which they participate."[6] Here we need not linger over a clarification of Harman's form of moral relativism (we shall look at a fuller statement of it in the first chapter), nor need we here examine Harman's defense (which we shall return to in a later chapter).

---

4. Gilbert Harman, "Is There a Single True Morality?" reprinted in *Relativism: Interpretation and Confrontation*, ed. Michael Krausz (Notre Dame: University of Notre Dame Press, 1989), 363.
5. Ibid., 363–64.
6. Ibid., 366ff.

Harman ends his essay with the comment that he sees "no knockdown argument for either side [relativism and absolutism]," and the observation that, although to him the relativistic (and "naturalist") position is more "plausible," others find the absolutist position more "plausible."[7] And that is just the way it is, we might say—except that "plausible" does not do justice to the tenacious energy that each side can exhibit.

Intuitions on either side can be strongly expressed. Clifford Geertz, in an article with the title "Anti Anti-Relativism," is not concerned to defend relativism, he tells us, but to attack anti-relativism.[8] His concern is with cultural relativism, but cultural relativism, as we shall see, is often taken to involve moral relativism. Geertz undertakes his attack with a vengeance in his pungent essay. Often it is specific anti-relativists who draw his fire. So it is that he characterizes W. Gass as "novelist, philosopher, *précieux,* and pop-eyed observer of anthropologists' ways" and describes his view as an "overheated vision of 'the anthropological point of view' rising out of the mists of caricatured arguments ill-grasped to start with."[9] Maybe Geertz has reason to complain, but what is to be noted is the rhetoric of his delivery. There is feeling here. Geertz has a mission—to oppose absolutism, or "anti-relativism." Harman's concern, by way of contrast, was to defend moral relativism. But both Geertz and Harman are drawing upon intuitions about relativism that connect to some deep recesses of concern.

I have chosen two writers sympathetic to moral relativism to illustrate the point that pretheoretical intuitions and the strong feelings they generate inform reflection on the issue of relativism. I could as well have chosen writers who espouse absolutism in morality. The issue between relativism and absolutism is a logical issue, but it is more than a logical issue. To refer to John Wisdom's comment again, philosophical discussion of it "goes on too long."

III. This Book's Approach to the Problem of Moral Relativism

William James tells a classic story about another discussion that went on too long. His story is about a "ferocious metaphysical dispute" that arose on a camping trip, and his account of the dispute is instructive. The setting is this. Imagine a squirrel

---

7. Ibid., 385.
8. Clifford Geertz, "Anti Anti-Relativism," reprinted in *Relativism: Interpretation and Confrontation,* 12.
9. Ibid., 16 and 17.

clinging to the trunk of a tree with a man on the opposite side of the tree. The man tries to catch sight of the squirrel by going around the tree. However, as he does so, the squirrel moves around the trunk, so that the tree is between the squirrel and the man. And of course every time the man moves around the tree, the squirrel moves around the trunk, so that the man never sees the squirrel. The "metaphysical problem," as James expresses it, is this: "*Does the man go round the squirrel or not?*"

In James's story two sides are disputing this issue, and each side is adamant in its position. James is appealed to by both sides when he appears on the scene, and he offers a resolution by drawing a distinction. He says: "If you mean [by 'going round' the squirrel] passing from the north of him to the east, then to the south, then to the west, and then to the north of him again, obviously the man does go round him. . . . [If] on the contrary you mean being first in front of him, then on the right of him, then behind him, then on his left, and finally in front again, it is quite as obvious that the man fails to go round him." So, says James, "Which party is right . . . depends on what you *practically mean* by 'going round' the squirrel." He concludes that they "are both right and both wrong" according to what is meant by "going round" the squirrel.[10]

Amélie Oksenberg Rorty begins an article on relativism with the following nearly Jamesian comment: "The controversy over cultural relativism, whether it be construed as a controversy about cross-cultural interpretation or about cross-cultural evaluation, is the kind of dispute that gives intellectuals a bad name among sensible people. Both sides are so bent on exaggeration that they seem to be displacing the real issues that divide them. The claims of relativists and their opponents are, when sanely and modestly construed, each plausible and mutually compatible." Relativists are right, she says, "to insist that even such dramatically basic activities as birth, copulation, and death . . . are intentionally described in [cultural] ways that affect phenomenological experience," and "antirelativists . . . rightly insist that there are events and facts—some of them intentionally described by reference to social practices—whose truth is not culturally determined."[11] Birth and death may have both a cultural significance and a significance not dependent on cultural determinants.

James's distinction and the resolution it offers are clear and sweet. The majority accept his resolution—but some do not. The "hotter disputants" continue to

---

10. William James, "What Pragmatism Means," in *Essays in Pragmatism,* ed. Albury Castell (New York: Hafner, 1954), 141–42 (James's emphasis).
11. Amélie Okensberg Rorty, "Relativism, Persons, and Practices," in *Relativism: Interpretation and Confrontation,* 418–19.

disagree. The hotter disputants who felt that the man *does* go round the squirrel in effect say, "All right, I see your distinction, but I still feel that *really* the man goes round the squirrel," and the hotter disputants on the other side continue to have the equally strong sense that really the man does not go round the squirrel. Similarly, moral relativists may say to Rorty, "I see your point, but the deeper truth is that culture determines the true moral significance of birth and death"; whereas absolutists may say, "The true moral significance of birth and death is not culturally determined."

James's "metaphysical issue," we may feel, is not all that serious, a mere diversion for intellectual exercise and hardly to be compared to the issue of moral relativism and its opposition to absolutism. There is something to this point, of course. My reason for reminding us of James's story is this: sometimes an issue can have or take on a significance that resists the kind of resolution James—or Rorty—offers. It may be that the disputants have come to invest too much in the issue, or it may be that the issue has deep roots in contrary intuitions. In James's example it is the former; in the case of the issue of moral relativism it may be that, in addition, the other element is involved. In each case something more than intellectual clarity is at stake. As James, the author of "The Will to Believe," might have observed, our "passional nature" may be involved in directing our belief. In any event, as a clear and sweet distinction did not settle James's issue about the squirrel, so too, I suspect, no such distinction will in itself settle the issue regarding relativism. Too much is at stake, too much that connects to other deep intuitions, too much that lies beneath the surface of articulate understanding.

Three approaches to the issue of moral relativism may be distinguished: (1) try to defend moral relativism; (2) try to defend its opposite, moral absolutism; and (3) try to find what is right and wrong about each. None of these quite fits the approach of this book. Of the three, the third is closest. One thing I shall try to do is to bring out the strengths and weaknesses of each side, for following the third approach will at least help to clarify the issue, or issues, revolving around moral relativism. But I do not harbor the illusion that doing this will resolve the issue, so I shall endeavor to delve into the divisive moral intuitions that give the issue of moral relativity its continuing life. The approach of this book, then, regarding the problem of moral relativism will be to add a fourth approach: (4) while bringing out what is right and wrong about moral relativism and moral absolutism, to go further and explain the grounding of those pretheoretical intuitions that peremptorily recommend each.

IV. Moral Diversity

Cultural diversity is a familiar fact of life at the beginning of the millennium. It expresses itself not only in a diversity of holidays and festivals but in the everyday attire and diet of different ethnic and religious groups. Cultural diversity may not yet be moral diversity, for there could be a diversity of dress and diet without any moral diversity. But often cultural diversity is accompanied by, or has within itself, moral diversity. In various traditional Muslim societies, not only will women be expected to wear a chador or to observe some level of *hejab,* or covering up, but husbands will be allowed to have two or even four wives. The contrast with, for instance, American "mainstream society" is evident.

The second main concern of this book is moral diversity. At an easily accessible descriptive level, moral diversity registers as both a diversity of moral beliefs, or what is regarded as morally right, and as a diversity of moral practice. Moral diversity may also be understood as a diversity of moralities—as opposed to what is merely *regarded* as moral. One question about moral diversity is whether there can be a diversity of moralities in this sense. The question is not whether there can be different types of morality in the way that a shame morality is different from a guilt morality.[12] The question is whether there are different moralities that operate in the same moral landscape of obligations, virtue, and rights with equal validity, whether the phenomenon of moral diversity consists of *this* diversity.

In our effort to understand moral diversity, we shall try to answer this last question. What helps us to understand the theory and problem of moral relativism, as we shall see, also helps us to understand whether moral diversity is not only a diversity of what is regarded as right, but a diversity of moralities as well. If moral diversity is also a diversity in this second sense, its being so is a part of the phenomenon and will be open to our adequately prepared observation. The themes of moral relativism and moral diversity are interwoven, and in much of the book I shall address the two of them simultaneously. If I succeed in addressing these two concerns, the third goal of this book—to show how moral relativism and moral diversity are related—will be attained as well as the first two.

---

12. For a discussion of different types of morality, see my *Relationship Morality,* chaps. 10–12.

V. Human Relationships

The title of this book is *Moral Relativism, Moral Diversity, and Human Relationships*. Moral relativism and moral diversity are the book's two main concerns. What of human relationships? Relationships between persons do not constitute a further concern of the book but rather provide an understanding of morality that allows us to address the book's two main concerns and thus to attain its goals. The relationships between persons to which I shall appeal have a moral significance (which is why they can give us an understanding of moral relativism and diversity). Although I shall appeal to several relationships, most of them are the simple personal relationships that are familiar to us all. Many are relationships like that between friend and friend, spouse and spouse, child and parent; but some are less familiar, like that between speaker and hearer and between a member of society and his or her society. One relationship to which I shall appeal is not commonly named by us in ordinary discourse, although in concept it is readily recognizable. It is the relationship between persons as persons, and I shall call it "the person/person relationship."

VI. Summary of the Book's Chapters

In the chapters that follow I do the following:

Chapter 1: "Forms of Relativism": In this first chapter, I distinguish moral relativism from nonmoral relativisms such as cognitive relativism and religious relativism, disentangle several different forms of moral relativism, and identify a usable definition of "moral relativism."

Chapter 2: "Are There Universally Accepted Moral Values?" Drawing upon the observations of anthropologists and others, I identify and examine candidates for universally shared moral values (such as prohibitions against the taking of human life) in various cultures and traditions, including such different religious traditions as Buddhism and Islam.

Chapter 3: "What Would the Existence of Universally Accepted Moral Values Signify?" What does the existence of universally accepted moral values mean for moral relativism? If, beyond there being some shared values, there is a unique ideal moral code acceptable to all cultures, does this mean that absolutism is correct? Here I want to develop and discuss the "Principle of Ascent," which is that ascending values tend toward universality, so that as actions are described with more generality, there is more agreement among cultures as to their moral rightness.

Chapter 4: "Some Proposed Root Bases of Morality": In this chapter I consider several candidates for "the root basis" of morality, for example, natural law and basic human needs.

Chapter 5: "Pluralism, Monism, and Relativism": Here relativism is distinguished from moral pluralism (in one form, pluralism is the view that there is a plurality of values, and they are conditional in that any one may at times override any other), and both will be distinguished from monism (the view that there is but one reasonable system of values).

Chapter 6: "Moral Diversity and Relationships": In this, the first of two pivotal chapters, I show how an understanding of relationships between persons—understanding how they are a source for, and give particular form to, obligations—explains the moral diversity we find in the world, and how that diversity can consist of actual moralities.

Chapter 7: "Moral Diversity and the Person/Person Relationship": The fundamental relationship between persons as persons, the *person/person relationship,* is introduced. How it relates to various subissues is explored. These include recurring basic values, transcultural values, and human rights.

Chapter 8: "What Is Right/Wrong About Moral Relativism": What in moral relativism strongly appeals to our deepest intuitions, and what in moral absolutism appeals to our intuitions? Relationships are shown to explain what is right in moral relativism and where it goes wrong. Why the Principle of Ascent applies to morality is explained.

Chapter 9: "Diversity and Morality": In this final chapter, the perils and the hope of moral diversity are explored, and different conceptions of the moral progress that is possible are examined.

ONE

Forms of Relativism

In this chapter I want to identify a usable definition of *moral relativism*. My effort will not be to bind the view in a narrow and arbitrarily confining definition. A narrow definition might hamper our efforts to work toward an understanding of what is right and wrong about moral relativism and its opposite, moral absolutism, and what attracts and repels our deepest intuitions regarding it and its opposite. Still, it will be useful to have before us a working definition, which, among other things, will serve to distinguish moral relativism from other forms of relativism, of which there are several.

Relativism, of whatever form, however, must be distinguished from other views with which it has a certain consanguinity. Skepticism is one. As Jack Meiland and Michael Krausz point out, although skepticism and relativism may both be a reaction to the same observations about diversity and the apparent lack of "an objective criterion acceptable to everyone," relativism, unlike skepticism, does not deny truth or deny that truth is knowable.[1] Relativism of various forms allows that there are truths to be known. In particular, moral relativism allows that there is moral truth and that in many instances it can be known; however, it is a *relative* moral truth that may be different for different persons. Similarly, relativism—and moral relativism in particular—should be distinguished from nihilism, the view that there are no values.

Relativism in various forms has claimed adherents since antiquity. In "contemporary culture," Meiland and Krausz observe, "relativistic attitudes are widespread and extremely influential"; and, they say, this is so "both in intellectual circles and in popular thought and action about moral and social problems."[2] However, only a few years before Meiland and Krausz wrote these words, Philippa Foot observed that, though the view of moral relativism is a "natural philosophical thought" that occurs to many, for some years moral relativism has been the subject of philosophical neglect. Why so? she asks. Because, she suggests, most philosophers thought that the view could easily be refuted or that this had already been done. In the period she is reflecting on, many beginning philosophy students thought moral relativism to be true, but their teachers were dismissive of the view and did not make it a "central topic" in their classes or writings.[3] Harman reports a similar experience during this time. As a student he thought moral relativism to be clearly correct and could not understand why his teachers set up and argued against misguided statements of the view.[4] Moral relativism has always seemed a "natural thought" to many and has always been a current in popular thought; but by the end of the twentieth century, the pendulum of intellectual acceptance had swung, and relativism—moral relativism in particular, but other forms too—had regained influence in intellectual circles.

Not that relativism's victory is complete. The problem of moral relativism is not a problem to be once and for all resolved. Even if relativism has regained intel-

---

1. Jack W. Meiland and Michael Krausz, eds., *Relativism: Cognitive and Moral* (Notre Dame: University of Notre Dame Press, 1982), 1–2.
2. Ibid., 4.
3. Philippa Foot, "Moral Relativism," in *Relativism: Cognitive and Moral*, 152–53.
4. Gilbert Harman, "Is There a Single True Morality?" in Krausz, *Relativism: Interpretation and Confrontation*, 363–64.

lectual acceptance, deep intuitions that relativism is wrong abide. Paul Tillich expresses his concern about the resurgence of relativism in the different "realms of thought and life," and he names "scientific relativism," "ethical relativism," and an "increasing relativism in the most sacred and perhaps most problematic of all realms, that of religion." Sir Karl Popper, in expressing his concern about what he sees as the rise of irrationalism, wrote: "In my view one of the main components of modern irrationalism is relativism (the doctrine that truth is relative to our intellectual background or framework . . .)."[5]

Intractable intuitions exist on both sides of the issue of moral relativism, and the point can be extended to other forms of relativism, although, as we shall see, one can be one kind of relativist without being every kind.

I. Some Forms of Nonmoral Relativism

Cognitive Relativism

It can be argued that cognitive relativism, or relativism regarding truth and knowledge, may itself take several forms.[6] However, it is not too much to say that the primary form of cognitive relativism is *conceptual relativism*. For this form of relativism, the truth of what we think or say is relative to our "conceptual schema," or framework of concepts. Such a conceptual schema constitutes a "world-view" for Joseph Runzo, who has recently formulated and discussed conceptual relativism. In his formulation, conceptual relativism is "the epistemological position that the truth of statements is relative to the conceptual schema(s) from within which they are formulated and/or assessed."[7] It is this view of the relativity of truth that concerns Popper and that he addresses in the quotation at the end of the last section.

For Runzo, conceptual schemas have an impact on our perceptual experience. He argues that "the possession of concepts is a necessary condition of all perceptual

---

5. Paul Tillich, *My Search for Absolutes* (New York: Simon & Schuster, 1964), 64–65. Sir Karl Popper, "The Myth of the Framework," in *The Abdication of Philosophy: Philosophy and the Public Good*, ed. Eugene Freeman (LaSalle, Ill.: Open Court, 1976), 25. Both are quoted by Meiland and Krausz in *Relativism: Cognitive and Moral*, 4–5.

6. Maurice Mandelbaum distinguishes "subjective relativism," "objective relativism," and "conceptual relativism" in his "Subjective, Objective, and Conceptual Relativisms," in *Relativism: Cognitive and Moral*, 35–36.

7. Joseph Runzo, *World Views and Perceiving God* (London: Macmillan; New York: St. Martin's, 1993), 67–68.

experience."[8] A "consequence of this conceptualist thesis," Runzo says, "is that persons possessing sufficiently different conceptual schemas would live in their own 'perceptual worlds.'"[9] As long as our concepts are pretty much the same, we will perceive more or less the same things—trees and tomatoes and so on—but if they are sufficiently different, we will see different things: where one sees a tree, another may see an animistic colony. So for Runzo, it is not that our perceptions shape our concepts, but that our concepts, our conceptual schemas, shape our perceptions.[10]

Clearly, as he readily acknowledges, there is a Kantian influence reflected in Runzo's conceptual relativism, as there is in cognitive relativism generally. Meiland and Krausz observe that those who developed modern forms of cognitive relativism retained the Kantian idea "that the mind provides basic concepts with which experience is organized and interpreted," but, in opposition to Kant, they allowed "that these concepts may change over time."[11] In Runzo's language, there can be, and are, various "conceptual schemas." In a way, as Meiland and Krausz note, Kant's influence on the development of cognitive relativism is paradoxical, for "Kant gives every indication of being himself an absolutist of the strictest sort."[12] What sort of absolutist was Kant? He is regarded as the paradigmatic *moral* absolutist.

It is to be noted that Runzo does not extend his conceptual relativism to morality, although this is not to say that he embraces Kant's deontological ethics. For Runzo there are "meta-criteria" that, he allows, can be applied to "any truth claims." These include "coherence, comprehensiveness [and] parsimony."[13] Moreover, there are "general moral standards," like "cruelty is wrong," that operate as "trans-worldview standards."[14] "Cruelty is wrong," then, is a trans-schema standard by which schemas can be tested and which, it seems, is true, but not by virtue of the concepts of some particular schema.[15]

---

8. Ibid., 23 (emphasis deleted).
9. Ibid., 40–41.
10. Ibid., 42.
11. Meiland and Krausz, *Relativism: Cognitive and Moral*, 7.
12. Ibid.
13. Runzo, *World Views and Perceiving God*, xviii and 136.
14. Ibid., 178–79.
15. In recent work, Runzo suggests what may be a slightly different view. He has gone on to argue that though "some ethical principles *are* universal . . . morality is relative." He goes on to say that morality is relative to "the moral point of view," which "entails universal moral truths." "Reply: Ethical Universality and Ethical Relativism," in *Religion and Morality*, ed. D. Z. Phillips (London: Macmillan; New York: St. Martin's, 1996), 172 and 180 (Runzo's emphasis). Here it seems "general moral standards" may be "trans-world-view standards" to some or many worldviews, but not to *all*, not if the "moral point of view" is one worldview and its rejection another.

If we allow that cognitive relativism is the view that *truth* is relative to a conceptual framework, then it would seem that cognitive relativism should be thought to extend to *moral* truth and to make it relative to a conceptual framework. On this thinking, cognitive relativism would entail moral relativism. Such a construction seems straightforward. But alternatively, certain moral principles can be understood as true independently of conceptual frameworks, so that cognitive relativism does not entail moral relativism and allows moral absolutism.

Religious Relativism

We can distinguish several forms of *religious relativism*. One form is that of Joseph Runzo and is a special application of his conceptual relativism. For Runzo, religious truth is "relative and plural" in that it is relative to the worldview shared by a community of religious adherents.[16] Again, there are implications for experience, in this case religious experience. "Corresponding to each distinct religious world-view, there is a different set of possible religious *experiences*. For what can be experienced depends on what *can be* real or unreal, and what can be real—i.e., what is possible—is determined by the percipient's world-view."[17] Thus, the Christian worldview shapes the experience of Christians, and so too for other religious adherents with their worldviews. Nevertheless, in his religious relativism, as in his wider conceptual relativism, for Runzo, general moral standards operate as trans-schema standards and can be used to test religious worldviews.

Another form of religious relativism is to be found in the thought of John Hick. Hick is a major religious thinker who has done much in the last several decades to call to the fore the problem of religious plurality: How do the world's religions relate to one another? The resolution that Hick proposes and argues for is "religious pluralism." He does not label his view "relativism," and Runzo distinguishes his own religious relativism from Hick's pluralism.[18] Nevertheless, Hick's view does amount to a certain kind of relativism, or, more circumspectly, contains a distinct strain of relativism. Hick's "pluralistic hypothesis" is that "the great world faiths embody different perceptions and conceptions of, and correspondingly different responses to, the Real [the Real *an sich*] . . . and that within each of them the transformation of human existence from self-centredness to Reality-centredness is taking place."[19] Following Kant and using Kant's distinction between noumenon and

---

16. Runzo, *World Views and Perceiving God*, 203 and 197.
17. Ibid., 209 (Runzo's emphasis).
18. Ibid., 197–212.
19. John Hick, *An Interpretation of Religion* (New Haven: Yale University Press, 1989), 239–40.

phenomenon in his own way, Hick suggests that "the Divine Reality is not directly known *an sich*" but is humanly experienced either as a personal God or as an impersonal Absolute, as one of a range of *personae* (such as the God of Israel, the Holy Trinity, Shiva, or Allah), or as one of a range of *impersonae* (such as Brahman or Nirvāna).[20] In each case, it is the Real that is experienced, but it is experienced differently in different religions. The "categories of religious experience" are "culture-relative," Hick says.[21]

Hick's pluralism is relativistic, then, regarding religious experience. Various forms of religious experience may equally be of the Real *an sich*, but different religious-cultural categories give, and must give, different phenomenal forms to these experiences. However, his pluralism is not relativistic regarding religious truth. Hick does not say that what is true religiously is determined by a conceptual schema, as Runzo does. In fact, although he does not think it is likely, he allows that it is "logically possible that some present set of dogmas (Catholic or Protestant, Mormon or Seventh Day Adventist, Sunni or Shia, Theravāda or Mahāyāna, advaitist or visistādvaitist) will turn out to correspond precisely with reality."[22] For Hick, eschatological experience (experience in a life to come) will decide which religious claims are true, and he sketches in possible experiences in the eschaton that would verify theism over atheism and that would verify advaita Vedanta.[23] At the same time, Hick's "pluralistic hypothesis suggests," he says, that a number of dogmas or "transhistorical beliefs"—such as the Buddhist belief in rebirth or the Christian belief that Jesus was the Son of God—may turn out to be true only as "myths," that is, as stories that help and inspire adherents to come to an appropriate "relation to the Real," although, as he says, his pluralism does not entail that any specific belief is of this kind.[24]

Hick's pluralist view, though it contains a religious relativism, rejects *moral* relativism. Hick allows that religions can be "graded," and the "basic criterion is the extent to which they promote or hinder the great religious aim of salvation/liberation," which is the state realized in "the transition from self-centredness to Reality centredness." Also we can morally judge the long traditions of the great world religions as systems of salvation by considering the "good and evil" they contain (i.e., the virtues of love, compassion, and forgiveness they espouse in contrast to the violence, war, oppression, exploitation, slavery, and more that they have

20. Ibid., 245.
21. Ibid., 244.
22. John Hick, *Problems of Religious Pluralism* (New York: St. Martin's, 1985), 100.
23. Hick, *An Interpretation of Religion*, 178–83.
24. Ibid., 370–71.

occasioned). Finally though, Hick concludes that "we cannot realistically grade the great world religions as totalities [f]or each . . . is so internally diverse, containing so many different kinds of both good and evil, that it is impossible for human judgement to weigh up and compare their merits as systems of salvation." And so we ought to say, "So far as we can tell, they are equally productive of that transition from self to Reality which we see in the saints of all traditions."[25] In Hick's thinking, however, this state of affairs arises from the complexity of the heritages of the different world religions, not from an inapplicability of the categories of good and evil, understood nonrelatively, to grading religious traditions.

Cultural Relativism

We turn now to a form of relativism related to those just discussed but distinguishable from them. Inspired by an appreciation of cultural diversity, *cultural relativism* is associated with anthropology and protoanthropology going back to the observations of Herodotus. John Ladd refers to cultural relativism as an "anthropological theory."[26] Understood one way, cultural relativism is a methodology. Mari Womack says, "Anthropologists have advocated the principle of cultural relativism, which has been widely interpreted as adopting a nonjudgmental framework toward the people being studied."[27] As a methodological recommendation, cultural relativism would not entail moral relativism. However, Womack goes on to say, "Historically, cultural relativism contains elements of both a methodology and a value system."[28]

In formulations that are not purely methodological, cultural relativism is closer to moral relativism. The anthropologist Melville J. Herskovits characterizes cultural relativism this way:

> *Cultural relativism* is in essence an approach to the question of the nature and rule of values in culture. It represents a scientific, inductive attack on an age-old philosophical problem, using fresh, cross-cultural data, hitherto not available to scholars, gained from the study of the underlying value-systems of societies having the most diverse customs. The

---

25. Hick, *Problems of Religious Pluralism*, 83–87.
26. John Ladd, ed., *Ethical Relativism* (Belmont, Calif.: Wadsworth, 1973), 2.
27. Mari Womack, "Studying Up and the Issue of Cultural Relativism," *NAPA Bulletin* 16 (1995): 48.
28. Ibid. 51.

principle of cultural relativism, briefly stated, is as follows: *Judgments are based on experience, and experience is interpreted by each individual in terms of his own enculturation.*[29]

In this statement cultural relativism does not seem to entail moral relativism. Nevertheless, it is often understood as *implying* moral relativism. At the very end of her *Patterns of Culture,* reflecting on the "recognition of cultural relativity," Ruth Benedict looked forward to our "accepting as grounds of hope and as new bases for tolerance the coexisting and equally valid patterns of life which mankind has created for itself from the raw materials of existence."[30] Meiland and Krausz say that "cultural relativism is the position that begins with value relativism," and I. C. Jarvie observes that cultural relativism is "conventionally divided into cognitive relativism and moral relativism."[31] For that matter, Herskovits himself goes on to affirm as continuous with cultural relativism a societal form of moral relativism: "Cultural relativism is a philosophy that recognizes the values set up by every society. . . . The relativistic point of view brings into relief the validity of every set of norms for the people who have them, and the values these represent."[32]

John Ladd regards cultural relativism as a "descriptive theory" of anthropology. He finds that it consists of two distinguishable theses. One, the diversity thesis, "asserts that there is a diversity of moral opinions from one society to another and hence that there is no *consensus gentium* concerning morals: what is regarded as right in one society is regarded as wrong in another." The second, the dependency thesis, "maintains that the character of people's moral opinions is to be explained by cultural and social factors of some sort, such as linguistic structure, economic determinants, psychological conditioning, psychoanalytic mechanisms, historical factors, or the unique pattern of culture of the society in question." For Ladd cultural relativism is "neutral as far as evaluations are concerned," although he allows that it may be "relevant to ethics and evaluations in general."[33]

In another discussion of these two theses, Ladd characterizes them differently. There he says that the dependency thesis "asserts that the moral beliefs, rules, and

---

29. Melville J. Herskovits, "Cultural Relativism and Cultural Values" (chap. 19 of *Cultural Anthropology*), reprinted in Ladd, *Ethical Relativism,* 61 (Herskovits's emphasis).
30. Ruth Benedict, *Patterns of Culture* (Boston: Houghton Mifflin, 1934), 278.
31. Meiland and Krausz, *Relativism: Cognitive and Moral,* 7. I. C. Jarvie, *Rationality and Relativism* (Boston: Routledge and Kegan Paul, 1984), 68.
32. Herskovits, "Cultural Relativism and Cultural Values," 74.
33. John Ladd, "The Issue of Relativism," in Ladd, *Ethical Relativism,* 109.

practices of a society are necessarily and invariably dependent for their validity on other facets of the culture—for example, its institutions, its language, or its cultural pattern." Here his language is that of Ruth Benedict, and the thesis states that the "validity" of the moral beliefs and rules of a society depends on societal or cultural factors. In connection with this formulation, Ladd says that "cultural relativism implies ethical relativism."[34] In the other formulation the dependency thesis said only that moral opinions are to be "explained by cultural and social factors," and the diversity thesis said that what is "regarded as right in one society is regarded as wrong in another." So formulated, neither of these theses, nor both together, seem to imply moral relativism (since *explanations* of moral opinions need not justify them, and what one *regards* as right may be wrong and conversely).

Perhaps what appears to be Ladd's ambivalence about the implications of cultural relativism for moral relativism simply reflects the present intellectual status of cultural relativism. Clyde Kluckhohn, who was an anthropologist with strong reservations about moral relativism, observed some years ago: "Few anthropologists would today defend without important qualifications Ruth Benedict's famous statement: '. . . the coexisting and equally valid patterns of life which mankind has carved for itself from the raw materials of existence.'"[35] He goes on to identify what he regards as the "central and dominant anthropological view": "The simplest self-contained unit of conduct, which can justify or render intelligible a final moral judgment, is a way of life as a whole, or at least a very substantial part of such a way of life."[36]

Assuming that this "anthropological view" is a formulation of cultural relativism, then—because of the disjunction, "justify or render intelligible"—this expression seems to allow us to regard cultural relativism either as implying moral relativism or as not implying moral relativism. As Kluckhohn says, "[Cultural relativity] has been employed by anthropologists in importantly different senses," although he also insists that "no anthropologist . . . doubts that the theory of cultural relativity is in some sense forced by the facts and meaningful."[37] Yes, in "some sense." What emerges, then, is that cultural relativism may or may not be conjoined with moral relativism in a cultural relativist's approach; in some forms cultural relativism may entail moral relativism, but not in all.

---

34. "Introduction," in Ladd, *Ethical Relativism*, 3.
35. Clyde Kluckhohn, "Ethical Relativity: *Sic et Non*," reprinted in Ladd, *Ethical Relativism*, 78.
36. Ibid., 85. Kluckhohn is quoting Alexander MacBeath, from his *Experiments in Living*.
37. Ibid., 84–85 and 85.

Ethnocentrism

Ethnocentrism is not itself a form of relativism, and, depending on how it is formulated and unfolded, it may be in opposition to relativism. In fact, I think that most often ethnocentrism is regarded as opposed to relativism in such a way that relativism is its antidote, although there are other ways to understand ethnocentrism. A fairly typical formulation of ethnocentrism presents it as "the belief that our ways, because they are ours, must be closer to truth, goodness, and beauty than are the ways of others." In the face of such an expression of ethnocentrism, it is understandable that in their classes anthropologists might be "eager to raise to consciousness that presumption and to banish it through schooling," as Richard Shweder observes anthropologists have been eager to do.[38] Herskovits' characterization of ethnocentrism is similar: "Ethnocentrism is the point of view that one's own way of life is to be preferred to all others."[39] Given such definitions of ethnocentrism, it is not surprising that Geertz would refer to an "ethnocentric bias."[40]

However, Richard Rorty, who has been regarded as a relativist, embraces ethnocentrism and hardly regards it as an ethically deplorable "bias." He identifies three views that are "commonly referred to by [the name 'relativism']." One is that "every belief is as good as every other." Another is the view that "'true' is an equivocal term, having as many meanings as there are procedures of justification." And the third view is the pragmatist's ethnocentrism, which affirms "that there is nothing to be said about either truth or rationality apart from descriptions of the familiar procedures which a given society—*ours*—uses in one or another area of inquiry." Rorty rejects the first two views but, as a pragmatist, accepts the third. However, he argues that the pragmatist's ethnocentrism should not be called "relativism." It is wrongly called relativism by "realists"—those who seek to ground "solidarity" or agreement in "objectivity" and "construe truth as correspondence to reality," indeed, "correspondence . . . to the intrinsic nature of things." But it really is not relativism, for the pragmatist holds no "theory . . . that something is relative to something else."[41]

---

38. Richard A. Shweder, "Post-Nietzschean Anthropology: The Idea of Multiple Objective Worlds," in *Relativism: Interpretation and Confrontation,* ed. Michael Krausz (Notre Dame: University of Notre Dame Press, 1989), 99–100.
39. Herskovits, "Cultural Relativism and Cultural Values," 66.
40. Clifford Geertz, "Anti Anti-Relativism," in *Relativism: Interpretation and Confrontation,* 24.
41. Richard Rorty, "Solidarity or Objectivity?" in *Objectivity, Relativism, and Truth, Philosophical Papers,* Vol. 1 (Cambridge: Cambridge University Press, 1991), 22–24. Rorty's paper is also in *Relativism: Interpretation and Confrontation.*

For Rorty, we face a "dilemma formed by ethnocentrism on the one hand and relativism on the other." And he says that "we pragmatists must grasp the ethnocentric horn of this dilemma" and acknowledge that "we must, in practice, privilege our own group."⁴² "To be ethnocentric," Rorty continues, "is to divide the human race into the people to whom one must justify one's beliefs and the others." The first group, "our own group," is one's *ethos* and consists of "those who share enough of one's beliefs to make fruitful conversation possible." Everybody in actual practice does this—makes this division—as Rorty sees it, so "everybody is ethnocentric when engaged in actual debate."⁴³

It seems that for Rorty, and for anthropologists like Herskovits as well, there is, to use Rorty's term, a "dilemma" between relativism and ethnocentrism: one must choose one or the other, and to choose one is to reject the other. Of course, in practice, "in actual debate," we are all ethnocentrists for Rorty; so at the practical level, Rorty sees ethnocentrism as unavoidable. Herskovits and other anthropologists see ethnocentrism as *nearly* unavoidable—Herskovits says that ethnocentrism "characterizes the way most individuals feel about their own culture."⁴⁴ But this is before the lessons of anthropology are learned. Thus, there is room for the anthropological effort we noted to "banish" ethnocentrism. Moreover, Herskovits and Rorty have different attitudes about ethnocentrism.

For Herskovits and other anthropologists, the time has come to cease judging other societies by our standards, for each society has its own set of valid "norms." For Rorty, the time has come to recognize that "fruitful conversation" is possible only with those in our own *ethos*. For Herskovits and others, ethnocentrism is to be rejected in favor of relativism. For Rorty, relativism is to be rejected in favor of ethnocentrism. For Rorty, "there is *no* truth in relativism, but this much truth in ethnocentrism: we cannot justify our beliefs (in physics, ethics, or any other area) to everybody, but only to those whose beliefs overlap ours to some appropriate extent."⁴⁵

Relativism comes in for Herskovits when he affirms societal moral relativism, as we have seen he does. Rorty, like Herskovits, opposes ethnocentrism to relativism, and he chooses the ethnocentric horn. But is he right that he has avoided relativism? Perhaps not. Relativism would come in for Rorty if he affirmed that there *are* people to whom we cannot "justify our beliefs" because their "beliefs" do

---

42. Ibid., 29.
43. Ibid., 30.
44. Herskovits, "Cultural Relativism and Cultural Values," 66.
45. Rorty, "Solidarity or Objectivity?" 31 n. 13 (Rorty's emphasis).

not "overlap ours to some appropriate extent," but *they* can "justify" their beliefs to themselves by appealing to *their* background beliefs. If the different background beliefs of those outside our "group" cannot be addressed and evaluated by us (and cannot be evaluated by others in other "groups"), then there is in Rorty's background thinking the counterpart of Herskovits' equally valid but different sets of "norms"—and if some of these beliefs are moral beliefs, then there is moral relativism in Rorty's background thinking.

It seems, then, that ethnocentrism is opposed to relativism if it says that one society embodies standards or norms that may appropriately be used to judge the beliefs and norms of other societies. But it is not opposed to relativism if it says that we can justify our beliefs, moral and otherwise, only to those in our own society—and goes on to affirm that this holds as much for others in their respective societies as it does for us, where this is taken to deny a trans-society "objective" basis for judgment. So it looks as though under some constructions of ethnocentrism one can be a moral relativist *and* an ethnocentrist, although under other constructions one cannot be both. (A question I have not addressed is this: Need one embrace relativity in order to avoid ethnocentrism? I shall leave this question open for now.)

To sum up: *cognitive relativism,* and *conceptual relativism* in particular, may or may not include moral relativism. *Religious relativism* need not include moral relativism. *Cultural relativism* may or may not include moral relativism, and *ethnocentrism* may or may not include relativism of different forms, moral relativism being one form that may or may not be included.[46]

II. Subissues Within the Issue of Moral Relativism

Moral relativism, as relativism regarding morality, may yet have one of several foci. Morality—the phenomenon of human morality, which is no less than our moral lives—is complex. True, if we take our guidance from philosophical reflection on "theories of obligation," we might get the idea that morality is essentially a matter of right (and wrong) *action*. Usually when "norms" or moral rules or moral beliefs, principles, or criteria are treated, the focus is on moral action: right and wrong

---

46. This list of types of relativism is not intended to be exhaustive or definitive. Different categories are possible. Cf. Rom Harré and Michael Krausz, *Varieties of Relativism* (Oxford: Blackwell, 1996), 3–7 and 23–25.

action or "behavior." Such a focused concern is not illegitimate, but it is not the whole story. Morality also includes other connected areas of concern: virtue, moral goods, and moral rights, to name a few. This means that there could be forms of moral relativism regarding virtue or moral goods or moral rights, as opposed to right action; and there are.

There is, for instance, a form of moral relativism relating to *virtue*. In ethics it was virtue that primarily concerned Plato and Aristotle, and there is a tradition of philosophical and religious thought about virtue going back to the Greeks. One strain of this reflection involves a form of relativism, even though others that may seem to involve relativism do not, I think. A strain of reflection on the virtues that does not involve relativism, as I see it, is a form of psychological reflection on the nature of the virtues and their opposites. Traditionally the four cardinal virtues are courage, temperance, wisdom, and justice, along with such other traditional virtues as honesty and generosity. What is the opposite of courage? Clearly it is cowardice, one might think. This is what Aristotle said (or rather, for Aristotle, cowardice is one of the states opposed by courage—its deficiency—whereas its excess is rashness).[47] In "The Parson's Tale" in Chaucer's *The Canterbury Tales*, however, the virtue of courage ("*fortitudo* or strengthe") is the remedy for "accidie" (acedia or sloth). Perhaps cowardice is a kind of spiritual sloth: a connection we may not have contemplated. In "The Parson's Tale," in fair accord with tradition, gluttony has the remedy of abstinence (pursued with a proper motive, not just for the sake of good health), and lechery or lust has the remedy of chastity and continence. But the remedy for avarice is not generosity, as one might think, but pity. So Chaucer invites us to consider whether underlying the habit of graspingness is a lack of sympathetic feeling toward others.[48]

So far, it seems to me, there is no moral relativism regarding the virtues. But there is in the contemporary thinking of Alasdair MacIntyre. MacIntyre comments on five different "conceptions of a virtue." These different conceptions result in different "catalogues" of the virtues, and each of these different lists is the product of "a different theory about what a virtue is." Briefly, the five theories MacIntyre cites are these: (1) The theory or conception of the virtues implicit in the Homeric poems, according to which a virtue is a quality that enables one to do what one's social role requires. Accordingly, in Homer's epics physical strength was counted a virtue. (2) Aristotle's theory of virtue. For Aristotle the end or *telos* of humanity

---

47. *Nicomachean Ethics* 1116a6–9.
48. Chaucer, "The Parson's Tale," *The Canterbury Tales in the Works of Geoffrey Chaucer*, ed. F. N. Robinson, 2d ed. (Boston: Houghton Mifflin, 1957), 251, 255, 258, and 254.

determines virtue, friendship (as Aristotle understood it) is a virtue, and the intellectual virtue of *phronēsis,* or practical wisdom, is necessary for the possession of the other virtues. (3) The New Testament conception of virtue. Here, too, for MacIntyre, a *telos* determines virtue—a "supernatural" *telos*—and virtues not on Aristotle's list emerge: faith, hope, and charity. Furthermore, what Aristotle counted as a vice—namely, humility—emerges as a virtue. (4) A theory that MacIntyre finds in the writings of Jane Austen, according to which "constancy" is a virtue. And (5) the theory of Benjamin Franklin, which is "utilitarian" and which counts as virtues "cleanliness, silence, and industry."[49]

MacIntyre concludes that there are "at least three very different conceptions of virtue": one looks to the fulfillment of social roles; another looks to a *telos;* and a third is utilitarian. At the same time, there is a "core concept" to virtue. Virtues are qualities that tend to enable us to attain certain important human goods that are internal to human "practices," a "socially established cooperative human activity through which goods internal to that form of activity are realized." Virtues are to be understood in terms of the achievement of *goods* through the use of some such practice. In different "traditions" there can be different conceptions of "human goods," so there can be different conceptions and catalogues of the virtues. Traditions—an example is the "Aristotelian moral tradition"—can be internally judged, and rival traditions can judge one another if they share a conception of human goods. But there is no trans-traditional standard for such judgments across traditions that do not share a conception of human goods. In this way MacIntyre ends up with a form of moral relativism relating to virtue and perhaps to the good as well.[50]

Michael Walzer also suggests a moral relativism regarding goods: "All the goods with which distributive justice is concerned are social goods," he affirms, and "goods in the world have shared meanings because conception and creation are social processes." For Walzer "there is no single set of basic goods across all moral and material worlds." To use Walzer's example, although it is true that all may value having food, what will be counted as food will vary socially: *food* "carries different meanings in different places."[51] Walzer, along with Alasdair MacIntyre, is said by Alessandro Ferrara to have a "communitarian orientation," which is to say that he has an orientation that exhibits a "genuine acceptance of the pluralism of life forms" and appreciates the "contextuality" of values.[52]

---

49. Alasdair MacIntyre, *After Virtue: A Study in Moral Theory,* 2d ed. (Notre Dame: University of Notre Dame Press, 1984), 181–85.
50. Ibid., 272–77.
51. Michael Walzer, *Spheres of Justice* (New York: Basic Books, 1983), 7–9.
52. Alessandro Ferrara, "Universalism: Procedural, Contextualist, and Prudential," in Rasmussen, *Universalism vs. Communitarianism,* 12–13.

Finally, we should note in this section how a form of moral relativism could arise regarding moral rights. Such a relativism would see the rights persons have as relative to their society or state or governmental system. Such a view might or might not equate moral and legal rights, but almost certainly would oppose the idea that there are universal human rights that human beings have by virtue of being human persons.

III. Different Formulations of Moral Relativism

More than thirty years ago, in his *The Concept of Morals,* Walter Stace defined moral relativism or ethical relativity this way: "Any ethical position which denies that there is a single moral standard which is applicable to all men at all times may fairly be called a species of ethical relativity. There is not, the relativist asserts, merely one moral law, one code, one standard."[53] At about the same time, Richard Brandt formulated moral relativism as the thesis that "there are conflicting ethical opinions that are equally valid."[54] These two definitions are different, but they are alike in that they were applied by their authors primarily, if not exclusively, to moral action. Brandt's is broad enough that it could cover other aspects of morality, such as virtue; but in his discussion of moral relativism, he focuses on action almost exclusively.

A feature of Brandt's formulation, as he points out, is that "it does not say that no ethical opinions are valid for everybody."[55] Richard Rorty, we will recall, identifies three views that he says are commonly called "relativism." The first of these is that "every belief is as good as every other." If we apply this formulation to morality, we obtain a severe form of moral relativism, which would, in Brandt's language, affirm that every ethical opinion is equally valid. Brandt's definition shows us that moral relativism does not have to go this far.

For John Kekes, relativism is the moral position that values are "context-dependent." However, he distinguishes three versions of moral relativism: *Radical relativists* "think that all moral judgments are relative to the particular conception of morality that has emerged in a specific historically, culturally, and socially conditioned

---

53. W. T. Stace, *The Concept of Morals* (New York: Macmillan, 1962), 8.
54. Richard B. Brandt, *Ethical Theory: The Problems of Normative and Critical Theories* (Englewood Cliffs, N.J.: Prentice-Hall, 1959), 272.
55. Ibid., 272.

setting." *Conventionalists* "concede ... that all reasonable conceptions of morality must recognize that some values are primary and that these values depend on human nature.... [They] claim that only secondary values are relative ... to the conventions of particular traditions, [but say] some of these conventions prescribe the acceptable interpretations of primary values." *Perspectivists* accept "that human nature and traditions require the recognition of both primary and some secondary values, but ... [hold] that what other values are regarded as secondary is relative to the conception of a good life of the agent."[56] Primary values are "universally human" and are not context-dependent, but instead derive from "human nature"; primary values have "associated benefits and harms" that may be "physiological (e.g., food and torture), psychological (e.g., love and humiliation), and social (e.g., respect and exploitation)." Secondary values derive from, for instance, our various social roles, aspirations, and preferences.[57]

Note that Kekes's formulations are not in terms of action, but in terms of "values." Moreover, two of his forms of relativism recognize some values that are not context-dependent: conventionalism allows the "universality and objectivity of primary values," and perspectivism allows the "objectivity of some secondary values" as well.[58] Relativism need not contend that all moral values are relative. Furthermore, for radical relativism and conventionalism, relative values are relative to societies and traditions; whereas for perspectivism, relative values are relative to an individual's conception of a good life. In this dimension—society vs. individual—there arises a significant division between forms of moral relativism.

The significance of societal or group forms of relativism can hardly be overestimated. It is to this kind of moral relativism that anthropological observations lead many. When Herskovits states the view of cultural values that cultural relativism endorses, he expresses a form of societal moral relativism in which values are "set up" by every society and "every set of norms" has validity for those who have those norms. When Gilbert Harman "confesses" his moral relativism, he confesses that it has always seemed to him that morality arises from "some sort of convention" (as we noted in the Introduction). John Kekes recognizes the role of convention and societal settings in two of the three forms of moral relativism he identifies, one of which he calls "Conventionalism."

---

56. John Kekes, *The Morality of Pluralism* (Princeton: Princeton University Press, 1993), 48.
57. Ibid., 18 and 38–39. For a cognate distinction, see Ralph D. Ellis, "Moral Pluralism Reconsidered: Is There an Intrinsic-Extrinsic Value Distinction?" *Philosophical Papers* 21 (1992): 51.
58. Kekes, *The Morality of Pluralism*, 48.

On the other hand, there can be forms of individual moral relativism, according to which morality is relative to individual attitudes or beliefs. Bimal Krishna Matilal identifies two forms of societal or group moral relativism, cultural and intracultural, and distinguishes both from "subjectivism," by which he means an individual form of moral relativism. He prefers not to count it as a form of moral *relativism*, a term he reserves for the group forms.[59] Nevertheless it is a relativistic form in that it makes morality relative to the individual. It is against such a form that Herskovits reacts when he says that cultural relativism "must be sharply distinguished from concepts of the relativity of individual behavior, which would negate all social controls over conduct."[60] It is this form of moral relativism that Runzo argues against when he argues against "the moral anarchy of subjectivism."[61] However, these thrusts in themselves indicate a target. Stace's classical definition of ethical relativity as the denial of "a single moral standard" clearly allows such a form of moral relativism, as does Brandt's. Philippa Foot allows at least the inchoate formulation of a moral relativism in which the truth of moral judgments is relative to "the standards of the individual."[62] Perhaps Jean-Paul Sartre held such a view of morality, and perhaps C. L. Stevenson did as well.[63] In any case, such a form of moral relativism is available to invite our intuitions, even though those attracted to the societal form may find it objectionable. It emerges that just as one can be a relativist without being a moral relativist, so one can be one kind of moral relativist without being every kind of moral relativist.

Other distinctions between forms of moral relativism have been suggested. For instance, Matilal draws a distinction between "soft relativism" and "hard relativism." Soft relativism allows that different cultural moral norms are mutually comprehensible but denies that there are transcultural standards of evaluation. Hard relativism sees cultural norms as both incommensurable and mutually incomprehensible.[64] But now let us try to characterize moral relativism in a way that will serve our purposes and yet respect its intuitive roots.

---

59. Bimal Krishna Matilal, "Ethical Relativism and Confrontation of Cultures," in Krausz, *Relativism: Interpretation and Confrontation,* 340.
60. Herskovits, "Cultural Relativism and Cultural Values," 76.
61. Runzo, *World Views and Perceiving God,* 179.
62. Philippa Foot, "Moral Relativism," 157.
63. Jean-Paul Sartre, *Being and Nothingness,* trans. Hazel E. Barnes (New York: Philosophical Library, 1956); and Charles L. Stevenson, *Ethics and Language* (New Haven: Yale University Press, 1944).
64. Matilal, "Ethical Relativism and Confrontation of Cultures," 340.

IV. Conclusion: A Fair Characterization of Moral Relativism

David Wong considers several claims that moral philosophers who see morality as "objective" would be inclined to accept and that moral relativists would be inclined to reject. However, one of these claims seems to him to be critical: "There is a single true morality." Moral relativists, he suggests, are those who reject this crucial claim. Put positively, moral relativists are those who hold that *there is no single true morality*.[65] Wong defends relativism; and Harman, who also is a moral relativist, agrees with Wong's formulation in his own defense of moral relativism. So it is that Harman gives the paper I referred to in the Introduction the title "Is There a Single True Morality?"—to which his implicit answer is no. More recently, in the same vein, he expresses the claim of moral relativism as: "There is no single true morality. There are many different moral frameworks, none of which is more correct than the others."[66]

However, I think that those who oppose moral relativism can also accept this formulation. To the extent that moral absolutists believe, as Stace put it, "that there is a single moral standard which is applicable to all men at all times," Wong's formulation seems to respect their position. Absolutism can take other forms, however, and Wong's formulation of relativism, we might observe, opposes signal forms of relativism's antithesis. One form of absolutism expresses itself in the claim that *the rules of morality are exceptionless*. Another form asserts that *there is a universal moral standard*. These claims are clearly different, although an absolutist may accept both. On the other hand, one may accept either without accepting the other. John Stuart Mill, who held the second and identified the universal standard as the Principle of Utility, rejected the first. If moral relativism in Wong's definition is true, then absolutism in both these versions would turn out to be false. In the same way, there may be logical room for a noncognitivist form of absolutism—owing to Hume in inspiration—which would deny that there is a single true morality consisting of moral truths but would affirm a single true morality consisting of shared feelings of approval and disapproval. If moral relativism in Wong's definition is true, then absolutism in this form too would be false.

Beyond its succinctness, Wong's characterization of moral relativism has several virtues:

---

65. David B. Wong, *Moral Relativity* (Berkeley and Los Angeles: University of California Press, 1984), 1 and 4.
66. Gilbert Harman, "Moral Relativism," in Gilbert Harman and Judith Jarvis Thomson, *Moral Relativism and Moral Objectivity* (Cambridge, Mass.: Blackwell, 1996), 5.

1. It is broad enough to cover virtues, rights, obligations, and right and wrong action, while allowing a concentration on, say, actions.
2. It allows both societal or group forms and individual forms of moral relativism.
3. It is vague in a fruitful way so that it leaves it open what the further character of morality is (beyond its being not singular) and so allows some latitude in just what the character is of the single "true" morality that it denies.
4. It allows gradations of less and more moderate relativisms of the forms Kekes identifies.
5. It is incisive enough to elicit initial intuitive reactions, one way or the other, from both those with relativist inclinations and those with absolutist inclinations.

This characterization of moral relativism will serve us as we begin our enquiry. Later (in Chapter 3), in order to address adequately the import of universal moral values, we will find it necessary to make explicit an element we here leave implicit. For now let us allow that relativists are those who tend to find something insightful in the claim that there is no single true morality, whereas absolutists are those who tend to find this claim misguided.

TWO

Are There Universally Accepted Moral Values?

Are there moral values that are accepted by all human beings? This question asks whether there are values that are transcultural, that are not limited by societal boundaries or by the conventions of any group, and that are not limited by the attitudes or choices of particular individuals. It asks whether there are panhuman values. The question of this chapter is whether there are values that are *recognized* or *acknowledged,* implicitly or explicitly, as holding for all human beings. In our pursuit of this question, we shall clearly want to consider the views of anthropologists and others who have reflected on the values that are shared by cultures and groups. Also, however, we shall want to consider claims about universal values that arise within particular traditions, such as religious traditions.

Our concern, of course, is with universal *moral* values. There may be a variety of cultural or social values relating to food preparation and seasoning, dress, style of expression, and more, that are not moral values, even though they have their own kind of significance. In the same way, individuals may have values that are personal preferences, and these too should be distinguished from moral values. In principle, this distinction between values of social and individual preference on the one hand, and moral values on the other hand, is available to both those who are inclined toward moral relativism and those who are inclined to reject it, although they may draw the distinction differently. Thus, how close you stand to people when you speak to them or whether you use your handkerchief in public may be a social value but not a moral value. Similarly, whether one prefers to dine on linen, or whether one prefers classical or romantic or rock music may be an individual value but not a moral value.

Of course, there may be no hard line between these categories. For one thing, there may be moral implications of an individual value like one's preferring to dine on linen. Perhaps the only linen available comes from sweatshops. Moreover, there may be moral issues relating to the observance of social and individual values. If I insist on using my handkerchief in public in a way that goes counter to the social values of the culture in which I am visiting, I may exhibit an insensitivity to the feelings of my hosts that is morally blameworthy: at times when in Rome it may be wrong not to do what the Romans do. However, these points do not impugn the distinctions I have suggested. In any case, for the purposes of this chapter, we should keep our focus on issues and values that are unproblematically moral.

I. Proposed Universal Values

Social scientists, philosophers, and other authors regularly name values that they identify as universal values. Here are some examples.

Harvard political scientist Samuel P. Huntington argues that although it may be that various cultures of the world are becoming modernized, in the sense that they are more and more consuming a range of goods produced in the West, these civilizations still retain their own values: they are becoming modernized without becoming Westernized. However, at the same time, he affirms that "human beings in virtually all societies share certain basic values, such as murder is evil, and certain basic institutions, such as some form of the family." "Most people in most societies," he says, "have a similar 'moral sense,' a 'thin' minimal morality of basic concepts of what is right and wrong."[1]

The anthropologist Clyde Kluckhohn observes that "every culture has a concept of murder, distinguishing this from execution, killing in war, and other 'justifiable homicides.'" He goes on to say that "incest . . . prohibitions upon untruth . . . restitution and reciprocity [and] mutual obligations between parents and children—these and many other moral concepts are altogether universal."[2]

Kluckhohn offered his reflections on these universal "moral concepts" in 1955. A few years later, the philosopher Richard Brandt added to Kluckhohn's list. "There are," says Brandt after quoting Kluckhohn, "other universals we could mention: disapproval of rape, the ideal for marriage of a lifelong union between spouses, the demand for loyalty to one's social group, the recognition that the interests of the individual are in the end subordinate to those of the group."[3]

In ethics and international relations, Frances Harbour affirms that "a shared core of human moral values does exist, but only at the most basic level: approval of beneficence, justice, courage and so on." She goes on to formulate a tentative list of such shared "primary moral values." Her list: approval of "justice, special beneficence to kin/compatriots, subordinating interests of individual to group, good faith and veracity, courage, [and] self-control"; and disapproval of "murder and incest or rape." Harbour's list is compounded from the reflections of Kluckhohn, Brandt, the philosopher and religious thinker C. S. Lewis, and the social psychologists Shalom Schwarz and Wolfgang Bilsky. Counting Kluckhohn/Brandt, Lewis, and Schwarz/Bilsky as three sources, each "primary value" she puts on her list is recognized as such by at least two of these three sources. Harbour's list is tentative, and she does not claim that it is exhaustive.[4]

1. Samuel P. Huntington, *The Clash of Civilizations and the Remaking of World Order* (New York: Simon & Schuster, 1996), 56, 58, 78.
2. Clyde Kluckhohn, "Ethical Relativity: *Sic et Non*," in Ladd, *Ethical Relativism*, 89.
3. Richard B. Brandt, *Ethical Theory*, 286.
4. Frances V. Harbour, "Basic Moral Values: A Shared Core," *Ethics and International Affairs* 9 (1995): 156 and 163. Harbour cites Alfred Louis Kroeber and Clyde Kluckhohn, "Culture," in *Choice and Action: An Introduction to Ethics*, ed. Charles L. Reid (New York: Macmillan, 1981); Richard B. Brandt, "Relativism and Ultimate Disagreements about Ethical Principles," in *Philosophical Ethics: An Introduction to Moral Philosophy*, ed. Tom Beauchamp (New York: McGraw-Hill, 1982); C. S. Lewis, *The Abolition of Man* (New York: Macmillan, 1947); and Shalom H. Schwarz and Wolfgang

The social and moral philosopher John Kekes, as we saw in the last chapter, also uses the category of "primary values." For Kekes primary values, unlike secondary values, are "universally human." They are primary in that their being realized is "a minimum requirement of all good lives, quite independently of how such lives are conceived by individuals or by traditions."[5] Food is one such primary value, but there are also psychological and social primary values, Kekes allows, such as love and respect. For Kekes there are indeed such primary values, and though no one of them is "absolute" or always "overriding," they are universal in that they "derive from aspects of human nature that all normal members of our species share."[6]

That there are basic or primary values shared by human beings by virtue of their common humanity or elements of a shared human nature is an understandable and widespread notion. A variant of this idea is that primary values are determined by the basic needs of human beings, either as individuals or in societies. The anthropologist Ralph Linton suggests that "associated with the satisfaction of the basic needs of individuals, both physical and psychological, and the functioning of societies [are values that] may be termed *basic values*," and "the *basic values* of all societies include many of the same elements."[7]

II. Values from Various Religious Traditions That Are Regarded as Universal

The idea that God has established common moral values for all human beings through his commands is at home in the Western theistic traditions, but the general religious idea that there are universal moral values holding for all persons in all cultures is not limited to Western traditions. This section will not attempt to canvas every religion or even every "world religion." Rather, we shall look at several religious traditions, noting the moral values and obligations they recognize as universal and the points of moral agreement among these traditions.

Bilsky, "Toward a Theory of the Universal Content and Structure of Values: Extensions and Cross-Cultural Replications," *Journal of Personality and Social Psychology* 58 (1990).

5. Kekes, *The Morality of Pluralism*, 32.
6. Ibid., 32.
7. Ralph Linton, "Cultural Relativity," October 1951, a mimeographed report; quoted in Brandt, *Ethical Theory*, 287.

Buddhism

In the Buddhist tradition, where the final goal is *Nirvāna* (or *Nibbāna*), much importance is given to such states as *mettā* (loving-kindness) and *karunā* (compassion). There is a recognition of the importance of such virtues as self-restraint and justice, as well as a recognition of the moral significance of such internal actions as willing to slander or use hurtful language before any overt action.[8] Moreover, in Buddhism there are a large number of scriptural precepts, many of these relating to the life of the *bhikku* (sometimes *bhikkhu*), or monk (for whom there are 227 precepts).[9] Other precepts relate to the Buddhist layman. There are Five Precepts of Buddhism that are binding on all Buddhists. They are (1) "to abstain from the taking of life"; (2) to abstain from taking "that which is not given"; (3) "to abstain from misconduct in sensual actions," that is, sexual misconduct; (4) "to abstain from false speech"; and (5) "to abstain from liquor that causes intoxication and indolence."[10] There are other Buddhist precepts as well. There are the Eight Precepts for laymen on special days. The Eight Precepts include the Five Precepts and three others, such as the precept against dancing, singing, and music; however, these are not lifelong but only periodical prohibitions that obtain on special days. And there are the Ten Precepts for the "more pious of the laity who could remain unattached to their families."[11]

The Five Precepts remain, within Buddhist thought, as universally binding on Buddhists. But for some commentators, the scope of these prohibitions is wider than the Buddhist community. Referring to the first four of the Five Precepts—"those forbidding murder, stealing, lying, and sexual misconduct"—Damien Keown observes that "there is little doubt the Buddha intended these four basic precepts, at least, to be absolutely and universally respected," where by "universal" he means "applying to all rational beings," not Buddhists only, and by "absolute" he means "applicable in all circumstances."[12]

Another commentator, Bhikkhu Chao Chu, a Buddhist monk, observes: "Most societies that base their morals and ethics on revealed traditions share basic prohibitions against such acts as killing, stealing, and lying," and these same prohibitions tend to survive in "a secular society that no longer believes in revelation."

---

8. H. Saddhatissa, *Buddhist Ethics* (London: George Allen & Unwin, 1970), 90 and 182; and S. Tachibana *The Ethics of Buddhism* (London: Oxford University Press, 1926), 95 and 69.
9. Tachibana, *The Ethics of Buddhism*, 80.
10. Saddhatissa, *Buddhist Ethics*, 87; cf. Tachibana, *The Ethics of Buddhism*, 59.
11. Tachibana, *The Ethics of Buddhism*, 63–65, and Saddhatissa, *Buddhist Ethics*, 110–12.
12. Damien Keown, *The Nature of Buddhist Ethics* (New York: St. Martin's Press, 1992) p. 232.

Although Bhikkhu Chao Chu does not say so, these three prohibitions correspond to three of the Five Precepts. As he sees it from a Buddhist perspective, there is reflected in these various societies a "knowledge of moral values," and "the reason why different people, whose respective revelations disagree in various ways, tend to agree about prohibitions against such actions as killing, stealing, and lying is because they all perceive, however dimly, the same universal laws inherent in the world itself."[13]

Christianity

Although many Christians would follow St. Thomas Aquinas and reject the Divine Command Theory (the religious and ethical view that those actions that are right or wrong are so precisely because God commands what he does), many Christians believe that the moral order is established by God and applies to human beings universally. A central moral teaching of Christianity is the Golden Rule, which in a familiar phrasing is: "Do unto others as you would have them do unto you" (after Matt 7:12). Most Christians would understand actions based on such concern for others to be what ought to be done, not by Christians alone, but universally. However, as John Hick has argued, it is not Christians alone who have this understanding of the universal applicability of the Golden Rule; rather its principle in some formulation, positive or negative, is found in all the major religions. Thus, to cite one or two of Hick's examples, in Confucianism we find "Do not do to others what you would not like yourself"; and in the Hadith of Islam, there are Mohammed's words, "No man is a true believer unless he desires for his brother what he desires for himself."[14]

Hinduism

There are different forms of Hinduism, some devotional and theistic, some meditative and not devotional or theistic. However, in the heritage of Hindu thought, there is a distinction that bears on our current concern. For Indian ethicists, Bimal Krishna Matilal points out, there are, on the one hand, "group-relative *dharmas*" or duties (*viśesa dharmas*), and on the other hand, there is a "culture-neutral side

---

13. Bhikkhu Chao Chu, "Buddhism and Dialogue Among the World Religions: Meeting the Challenge of Materialist Skepticism," in *Ethics, Religion, and the Good Society*, ed. Joseph Runzo (Louisville, Ky.: Westminster John Knox, 1992), 167–68.

14. John Hick, *An Interpretation of Religion*, 313.

of morality" with its duties (*sādhārana dharma*).¹⁵ Duties that one has by virtue of one's caste or station are associated with the first kind of *dharma*. In the second category, observes Cromwell Crawford, are "generic duties . . . independent of caste and station in life . . . binding upon man as man."¹⁶ "To articulate [the] culture-neutral side of morality is not an easy task," suggests Matilal, and, he continues, "these values or value-experiences may not be totally immutable across cultures or over time."¹⁷ Crawford suggests that importantly embodied in *sādhārana dharma*, in Hindu thinking, are a sense of life's sacredness and gratitude for life, the first arising from a sense of the unity of life, and the second leading to service to the community and the universal good.¹⁸ Whatever difficulties there may be in an articulation of the exact moral requirements of *sādhārana dharma*, for Hinduism there is this universal aspect of morality.

Islam

Writing on Islamic ethics, Isma'il R. al Faruqi observes, "Islām has always been universalist. . . . The religion, as represented by its supreme authority, the divine word or the Qur'ān, speaks with utmost emphasis and clarity. 'O mankind, We have created you of one pair, male and female, and constituted you in tribes and peoples that you may complement one another. Nobler among you is only the more righteous.' [Qur'ān, 49:13]." He continues, "The ethical principles constitutive of Islāmic humanism are not denied of any human being even though he may belong to another faith; to another culture, civilization or age."¹⁹

Muzammil H. Siddiqi says this: "There are two interesting ethical terms of Islam that frequently occur in the *Qurān*: *Ma'rūf* (good, virtue, etc.) and *Munkar* (bad, evil). *Ma'rūf*. . . means an action that is generally recognized and known to people as acceptable, good, and hence virtuous. *Munkar* on the other hand . . . is an action that is generally unacceptable to people and hence bad and evil. Thus the *Qur'ān* seems to have recognized a general and common standard of virtue and evil."²⁰

"The *sharī'ah*, or law of Islam," says Faruqi, "is a complete system of desiderata, principles, rules, and laws regarding human activity. . . . The life that is worthy

---

15. Matilal, "Ethical Relativism and the Confrontation of Cultures," 352–53.
16. Cromwell Crawford, "Hindu Ethics for Modern Life," in *World Religions and Global Ethics*, ed. Cromwell Crawford (New York: Paragon House, 1989), 11.
17. Matilal, "Ethical Relativism and Confrontation of Cultures," 353.
18. Cromwell, "Hindu Ethics for Modern Life," 12.
19. Isma'il R. al Faruqi, "Islamic Ethics," in *World Religions and Global Ethics*, 224.
20. Muzammil H. Siddiqi, "Global Ethics and Dialogue Among World Religions: An Islamic Viewpoint," in *Ethics, Religion, and the Good Society*, 181.

of man is one totally dedicated to the pursuit of the divine will in all its detail. Observance of the laws of traffic is as religious as that of the laws affecting property, life, worship, or war and peace. The sanctity of life is inseparable from its unity, and its unity, inseparable from the will of the Creator of all life."[21]

It seems, then, that in more than one religious tradition there is the abiding sense that there are at least *some* universally shared moral values. In fact, it is arguable that what appear to be different values in different religious traditions may not be different after all. Huntington, as we have seen, affirms that "most people in most societies" share "certain basic values." For instance, people in "virtually all societies" condemn murder as wrong. But in *The Clash of Civilizations* he also conveys reports that some basic values of Asian societies are different from basic "Western" values. Various Asians, he observes, have argued that there are common values, mainly Confucian, shared by Asian societies, which are different from Western values and greatly responsible for the recent economic rise of Asian countries. "From Lee Kuan Yew on down," writes Huntington, "Singaporean leaders [in the early 1990s] trumpeted the rise of Asia in relation to the West and contrasted the virtues of Asian, basically Confucian, culture responsible for this success—order, discipline, family responsibility, hard work, collectivism, abstemiousness—to the self-indulgence, sloth, individualism, crime, inferior education, disrespect for authority, and 'mental ossification' responsible for the decline of the West."[22]

Here is the idea that Asian, or Confucian, values embrace order and discipline, whereas Western—and so Christian-influenced—values do not. Amartya Sen speaks to this point. One thing he observes is that there is a diversity of Asian traditions and that in the Buddhist tradition great importance is attached to "freedom." Furthermore, even Confucius "does not forego the recommendation to oppose a bad government" if it is done tactfully—as when he says, "When the state has lost the way, act boldly, and speak softly." As for order and discipline, these values are championed in the West as well, Sen observes, and "Confucius is no more authoritarian than, say, Plato or Augustine."[23] In short, if we mean *acknowledged* values, the differences between Asian Confucian values of order and discipline and Western values may not be great, and, in fact, closer scrutiny may reveal that these values are shared.

---

21. Faruqi, "Islamic Ethics," 226 and 227.
22. Huntington, *The Clash of Civilizations*, 108.
23. Amartya Sen, "Human Rights and Asian Values," *New Republic*, 14–21 July 1997, 36 (a revised version of his Morgenthau Memorial Lecture, Carnegie Council on Ethics and International Affairs, 1 May 1997).

One of the values recognized by Singaporean leaders like Lee Kuan Yew and others is *hard work*. But this same value is regarded as a Western or American value. Timothy Tseng and David Yoo observe that hard work, along with "rugged individualism," is an "American value" often found in refugees from Vietnam as well as in migrant workers from Mexico.[24]

Another value that initially appears to have a different status in Asian and Western cultures is "transparency." Transparency in decision making is sometimes named as a Western value that is disparaged in Asian cultures, where decisions are often made through personal contacts behind closed doors. True enough, Western commentators reflecting on international monetary negotiations have called for transparent political processes.[25] But is transparency a Western value? It is espoused, of course; so it is an *acknowledged* value. But a moment's reflection on business decisions, personnel decisions of all kinds, and political decisions, as they are made in the West, is enough to suggest that the difference between Western acceptance of the value of transparency and Asian rejection of it, in practical terms, may not be that great.

III. Exceptions to Universals

In the next chapter we shall take up the question of the significance of there being universal moral values, allowing that such shared values do exist. Just here we may raise a lesser issue: Are there, after all, exceptions to the strong candidates for universal moral values being regarded as universals? Although we cannot canvas all those values proposed, we can consider one or two. As we take up this question, let us keep our eyes on *moral* values as best we can, and not mere social values about such matters as food seasoning. And let us focus on some of the strong candidates—those moral values that readily strike us as not admitting exceptions. I want to do this, in part, to show that exceptions can and have been offered to values that for many of us look to be near the core of shared inner values.

Take the prohibition against causing needless suffering to people or to animals. It seems evident to most people that, although at times it may be necessary to cause

---

24. Timothy Tseng and David Yoo, "The Changing Face of America," *Sojourners*, March–April 1998, 28.
25. Marie Dennis, "For a Dignified Life: The Worldwide Movement for Debt Relief is Rooted in Jubilee," *Sojourners*, May–June 1998, 34.

incidental pain to a person or animal, inflicting gratuitous or avoidable pain is not morally allowable. Though there may be disagreement about when causing pain is "necessary," the principle that inflicting pain unnecessarily is wrong strikes us as one that surely would be universally recognized. Richard Brandt, however, draws to our attention what amount to counterexamples. His concern is not to present an exception to a principle taken to be a universal, but rather to show how there can be an "ultimate disagreement" of ethical opinion. The cases he presents arguably do both.

Brandt invites us to consider two cases. One is the practice of plucking chickens while they are alive (with the thought that doing so makes them more succulent); this is often done in Latin America, Brandt tells us. The other case is the "chicken pull," a kind of game played by the Indians of the Southwest, the Hopi and the Navaho (but learned from the Spaniards, Brandt believes). "In this 'game,'" Brandt tells us, "a chicken is buried in the sand up to its neck. The contestants ride by on horseback, trying to grab the chicken by the neck and yank it from the sand. When someone succeeds in this, the idea is then for the other contestants to take away from him as much of the chicken as they can. The 'winner' is the one who ends up with the most chicken."[26]

One other example of a strong candidate for a moral universal that suffers an exception: the moral principle that inflicting harm is wrong. It is this principle that Socrates reminds Crito they earlier agreed upon, from which he traces the implication that it is never right to inflict an injury, not even in return for an injury suffered (a moral implication that is rejected by the majority, says Socrates).[27] It is this principle that stands behind the motto "Two wrongs do not make a right" and that requires us to distinguish morally justifiable punishment from harm.

Gilbert Harman, however, in effect proposes an exception. "There is no prohibition on harm to outsiders in the criminals' morality," he reflects. Harman apparently is alluding to the practice of criminal "gangs" and "mobs" of inflicting bodily harm and even death on rivals and victims without any moral qualms. He is making the point that, although not caring about or respecting others may be a moral reason in some other morality against harming others, it does not give the criminal, who does not accept that morality, "a sufficient reason to do anything."[28] Without here and now concerning ourselves with Harman's point, we can observe that he has at a minimum presented us with an instance of certain individuals—his "criminals"—not accepting the seemingly universal principle that it is wrong

---

26. Brandt, *Ethical Theory*, 102; and *Hopi Ethics* (Chicago: University of Chicago Press, 1954), 213 and 361 n. 6.
27. *Crito* 49a–e.
28. Harman, "Is There a Single True Morality?" 375.

to harm others. For his criminals allow that it is perfectly all right to harm at least *some* others—those outside their group.

Of course, admitting that there are exceptions to even such seemingly central moral universals as these is compatible with claiming that there are *some* universals—such as the moral prohibition against murder and the positive value of courage.

IV. Human Rights

Finally, let me add this comment on human rights: the moral rights that human beings are said to have by virtue of being human beings. If there are such rights, they clearly are universal rights possessed by every human being. Several questions present themselves.

Are there such *human* rights—universal rights grounded in the condition of being human—or are there only those rights recognized in this or that culture? If we say that there are human rights—universal human rights—what are they? We may agree that there are such rights and yet disagree about what they are. Given that we agree there are human rights, and what they are, we can still disagree about what overrides those rights, or this or that particular right; and we can still disagree about the kind of moral claim such rights put on others.

Nevertheless, if there are human rights, then by definition they are culture-neutral in the sense that they exist by virtue of what is common to all human cultures. As Sen observes, "The notion of human rights builds on our shared humanity."[29] Though such rights are not affirmed in all cultures and are most at home only in some cultural traditions, they and the duties they entail would be universally binding even if not universally accepted.

V. Conclusion

There are some candidates for universal values that recur with some regularity on the lists of anthropologists, political scientists, and moral philosophers. Universal values, for some, include a prohibition against murder, the value of the family, and truth telling. For Kekes a "primary value" is food, and another is love. In religions,

29. Sen, "Human Rights and Asian Values," 39.

again, there often are prohibitions against killing and stealing, and the value of treating others as one wants to be treated seems to recur in various traditions.

The belief in universal—that is, universally accepted—moral values is widely held. Even the allegedly great difference between Western and Asian values may distil to a residue of shared values in many instances, as we illustrated with the value of hard work. At the same time, some have argued that the seemingly most inviolate values are not universal in that some persons reject even them.

Human rights, *if* there are human rights, we observed, would seem to establish values that ought to be acknowledged independently of one's society. We shall return to the issue of human rights in Chapter 7. In the next chapter we shall take up the question of the import of there being universally shared moral values, under the assumption that there are such shared values.

THREE

What Would the Existence of Universally Accepted Moral Values Signify?

Richard Brandt, as we saw in the last chapter, presents cases that look like exceptions to strong candidates for universally shared values. On the basis of such cases, he allows that "ethical relativism may be true in the sense that there are *some* cases of conflicting ethical judgments that are equally valid." But, he says, "it would be a mistake to take it as a truth with a pervasive scope." Relativism "draws our attention away from the central identities, from widespread agreement on the forms we care most about."[1]

---

1. Brandt, *Ethical Theory*, 288 (Brandt's emphasis).

In the last chapter we saw that various values are recognized or strongly recommended as universal moral values, including the prohibition against murder and the recognition of family obligations. Let us allow that there are universally accepted moral values. What does the existence of such universal values mean for moral relativism? A second and perhaps more important question relates to the content of universal moral values: Does the content of shared moral values remain the same from culture to culture and from era to era? Finally, in this chapter I want to introduce for a first reading a principle that reflects the scope of moral approval for actions across groups and cultures: the Principle of Ascent.

I. The Import of Universally Accepted Moral Values

Universal moral values have either no or comparatively little import for the truth of moral relativism. Even if it is clear that there are some universally shared moral values, their existence does not entail that moral relativism is false. Nor, for that matter, would a vast number of shared moral values. What if there should be, or there should come to be, a single worldwide "moral code," so that virtually all moral values are shared by virtually all societies and all persons? Not even this turn of events would show that moral relativism is false. Harman observes that there could be "a unique ideal moral code of such and such a type" to which relativists and absolutists agree. It might be "ideal" in the sense that everyone "ought to follow it," meaning that it would be "a good thing" if everyone followed it, and yet such an ideal code would not deny relativism if it remained that not everyone would have "a sufficient reason to follow it," as Harman believes could well be the case.[2] Without here addressing the particular way that Harman understands moral relativism (something we shall do later), we should acknowledge that he is surely right that the existence of such a unique ideal moral code—ideal in any of various senses—would not disprove relativism.

Why this is so is implicit in our working definition of moral relativism: "There is no single true morality." What this definition opposes is the absolutist idea that there is a "single true morality," that is, a single true morality that all *ought* to follow—not merely in the sense that it would be a "good thing" or useful to follow it—but in the sense that it is morally binding on all. Moral relativism, then,

---

2. Harman, "Is There a Single True Morality?" 370–71.

allows that many or even all may share moral values, but denies that there is a morally binding reason for them to do so. (Henceforth I shall leave implicit this element of our definition of moral relativism and express it simply as "There is no single true morality" and express the opposing absolutist view as "There is a single true morality").

Granting that the existence of universally shared moral values would not show that moral relativism is false, would it provide at least some evidence against it? Harbour, observing that there are "a few shared moral values," reflects that "this fact is consistent with, and indeed suggestive of some underlying objective causal factor."[3] Such an "underlying objective causal factor" might in turn be taken to provide support for moral absolutism. On the other hand, Paul Taylor argues that such shared moral values do not provide any evidence against moral relativism. For Taylor "pan-human values" do not "imply or support or confirm" "ethical absolutism," and the universality of values is irrelevant to the dispute over whether there are "absolute, cross-cultural moral norms."[4] How so?

It is now widely acknowledged that differences in moral beliefs do not entail moral relativism. Stace argued this point some sixty years ago.[5] Taylor's point is that just as cultural differences do not argue for moral relativism, so cultural agreement does not argue against moral relativism.[6] It might seem that universally shared values would support the absolutist's claim that there is one true morality with absolute and nonrelative norms. For after all, wouldn't the existence of absolute norms explain the existence of universal values? It would, but so would the convergence or overlap of several relative moralities. Just as differences can be explained on a nonrelativistic view (at least some moral beliefs are in error), so shared moral values can be explained on a relativistic view (though there are values shared across moralities, this is due, not to a common absolute standard, but to factors like communication between groups, leading to overlap). Nor is this point—that universal values are compatible with moral relativism—unappreciated by anthropologists. Many, including Elvin Hatch, but others as well, realize that universal values and relativism "are not necessarily mutually contradictory."[7]

However, there may be one way in which shared values are relevant to the wider issue of moral relativism. If they are not relevant to the truth of moral relativism

---

3. Harbour, "Basic Moral Values: A Shared Core," 157.
4. Paul W. Taylor, "Social Science and Ethical Relativism," in Ladd, *Ethical Relativism,* 103 and 104.
5. Stace, *The Concept of Morals,* 15.
6. Taylor, "Social Science and Ethical Relativism," 96.
7. Carole Nagengast and Terence Turner, "Introduction: Universal Human Rights Versus Cultural Relativity," *Journal of Anthropological Research* 53 (1997): 272.

or as support for absolutism, they may still have an impact on what impresses many of us as in some way pointing toward moral relativism as a truth in our culturally diverse world. Traditionally, when relativists have argued for their view on the basis of the comparison of societal values, they have cited differences in moral values that anthropologists have observed, not points of agreement. To the extent that there is a correspondence among societal moral codes, anthropological observations are not thought to provide any support for the societal form of moral relativism. From Herodotus onward, it has been observed differences among cultural values that have encouraged us to think that moral relativism is correct. Societal moral relativism tends to insist that there are, in fact, some acts that are right in one society and wrong in others—while allowing that in time there *could* be but one moral code. To the extent that shared values are recognized, the differences decrease, and the scope of this sort of anthropological encouragement for societal forms of moral relativism diminishes.

II. Problems with the Idea of Universally Accepted Values

Now let us take up the second question to be addressed in this chapter: Does the content of shared universal values remain constant? The candidates for shared universal values that we have seen proposed by Kluckhohn, Brandt, and Harbour include prohibitions against untruth and against murder and incest, and the positive recognition of family obligations, group loyalty, veracity, and courage. Such values Harbour calls "primary moral values." The anthropologist Ralph Linton terms them "basic values," and for him they "are usually associated with the satisfaction of the basic needs of individuals, both physical and psychological, and the fulfillment of the conditions necessary for the continuation and effective functioning of societies." As basic values they are at the far extreme from "superficial values" relating, for instance, to "a particular style of clothing while it was in fashion."[8]

Primary, or basic values penetrate deeply into our lives, we may say; and unavoidably they seriously affect our lives as individuals and as members of a society. Granting this, however, there still can be a question about the *content* of these shared values. After affirming that there is a "shared core of moral values," Harbour

---

8. Ralph Linton, "Cultural Relativity"; quoted by Brandt, *Ethical Theory,* 287.

goes on to say that "secondary and tertiary moral values differ between societies because cultures build upon these basic, shared building stones in different ways." She continues:

> Secondary values are elaborations and specifications of the general values in the form of culturally shaped definitions and principles of conduct. For example, is there a moral difference between murder and killing in war? Am I bound by my promises in business transactions? The definitions or intermediate-level principles, in turn, are used to construct specific codes of behavior at a tertiary level. What is the just punishment for murder? May I kill male noncombatants in war? Am I bound by contracts with foreigners?[9]

What she does not say is that, if she is right about "secondary" and "tertiary" values, then the claim about primary values may be vitiated or at least qualified in that the content of a shared value may change from one culture to another. Take the prohibition against murder. Although everyone may agree that murder, as wrongful killing, is wrong by definition, there may be a vast disagreement about what counts as murder. Is killing in war murder? Is the killing of noncombatants in war murder? And to these questions, raised by Harbour, we may add: Is the killing of a slave murder? Is abortion murder? If societies or individuals answer these questions differently, then to that extent they arguably do not share a moral value prohibiting murder.

The difference between groups regarding what appears to be a shared value against murder comes out in an examination of what those groups are and are not prepared to allow as a justification for killing. A variation on this point is brought out by reflecting on forms of religious hypocrisy. Thomas Kasulis has argued that in trying to discern the differences between two religious traditions it is more useful to compare the forms of hypocrisy in those traditions than to compare exemplars or saints in those traditions. Buddhist and Christian saints may be essentially indistinguishable, but Buddhist and Christian hypocrites are distinctly different. "Buddhist hypocrites," Kasulis observes, "are simply not like Christian hypocrites. In the name of strengthening Christianity, Christian hypocrites have sometimes killed for Christ, for example. Buddhists—even hypocritical Buddhists—do not kill for the Buddha. Hypocritical Buddhists, on the other hand, have in the name of Buddhism sometimes turned their backs on the pain of others. Christians—even

---

9. Harbour, "Basic Moral Values: A Shared Core," 156.

hypocritical Christians—do not typically argue that to refuse to help people in need is good Christianity."[10]

Let us focus on the Christian hypocrites that have "killed for Christ." As Christians, they accept the Christian prohibition against killing, and, as there is also a Buddhist prohibition against killing, it would seem that they and Buddhists share a moral value. But, Kasulis argues, such Christian hypocrites get around this prohibition and the Christian teachings that we should love our enemies and avoid violence by saying that they are "not killing their enemies, but the enemies of the Church." And they urge that they are, in fact, practicing Christian charity in inquisitorial torture, the military conquest of non-Christian populations, and the forcing of baptism; for, they argue, these extreme measures are necessary to save souls for eternity.[11] These Christian hypocrites, Kasulis wants us to appreciate, are not arguing that their killing is excusable; they are arguing that Christian charity requires it. They kill *for* Christ, as no Buddhist kills for the Buddha.

Thus, what counts as justified killing in some strains of the Christian tradition does not have a counterpart in the Buddhist tradition. To be sure, for Kasulis these Christians are hypocrites. Without denying this point, we should observe that Kasulis's own examples of such hypocrites historically embrace very many who were Christians in good standing in their time (the inquisitorial persecutors of heretics and witches, the military supporters of Christian missionary efforts in the Americas). To the extent that the justifications for killing proffered by these Christians shed light on the content on their understanding of the prohibition against murder, it would appear that the content of the value prohibiting killing that they embraced is different from the content of the Buddhist value prohibiting killing.

The distinction between "primary" and "secondary" values, or some cognate distinction, is fairly widely recognized. Consequently, to the extent it is allowed that different secondary values differently interpret shared primary values, it must be equally widely acknowledged that the content of shared primary values varies.

For John Kekes, as we saw in Chapter 1, there are "primary values" that are physiological (food) or psychological (love) or social (respect), and there are "secondary values." Now may be the time to say more about his conception of secondary values. Kekes allows that secondary values "vary with persons, societies, traditions, and historical periods." There are two reasons for this variability. First, the "conceptions of a good life" can vary, incorporating different values deriving

---

10. Thomas P. Kasulis, "Hypocrisy in the Self-Understanding of Religions," in *Inter-Religious Models and Criteria*, ed. J. Kellenberger (New York: St. Martin's, 1993), 155.
11. Ibid., 156.

from different social roles, the work by which one earns a livelihood, special aspirations one has, and simply different preferences. Second, "although the benefits and harms encapsulated in primary values are normally universal, the forms and ways in which the benefits are sought and the harms are avoided allow for enormous difference."[12]

Michael Walzer, like Harbour and Kekes, in effect distinguishes between primary and secondary values, although he does not use these terms. He uses different language, distinguishing between "thin" and "thick" morality. Thin morality "consists in principles and rules that are reiterated in different times and places."[13] Thick morality requires a particular moral culture. Moral terms like "justice" and "truth" (the examples he uses) have "minimal and maximal meanings," he suggests. Not that we distinguish these two meanings or that we consciously build our thick morality on our thin morality. We can respond to the cry for "justice" in another culture because we can understand that cry across cultures by virtue of the term's thin, or shared meaning—which includes at least a rejection of tyranny and oppression of the poor.[14] If we go on to try to say what justice positively involves, then we will begin to draw upon our own thick morality. So for Walzer too, then, all people may agree on the basic—thin—value of justice and disagree about what it—thickly—requires as a secondary value. All may agree that justice requires the rejection of tyranny, but many may disagree about when a government becomes tyrannous, as when there is disagreement about whether it is tyranny to keep down a public expression of opposition against a government's policies. All may agree that justice requires that the poor not be oppressed, but many may disagree about what is and is not oppression.

Max L. Stackhouse has observed: "The apparent agreements among all peoples regarding certain 'universal' ethical norms suggest that there are such things as universal principles, but the disagreements as to their contents force us to carefully examine and judge between the basic beliefs by which they are understood and between the functioning of these norms in social practice." He also observes: "Murder is differently defined according to divergent definitions of membership in humanity and society." Whether abortion is regarded as murder will depend on how a group considers "membership in humanity." Stealing, like truth and justice, is another candidate for universal prohibition. However the content of this value can also change from place to place. "Is capitalist profit, the expropriation of private

---

12. Kekes, *The Morality of Pluralism*, 18 and 19.
13. Michael Walzer, *Thick and Thin* (Notre Dame: University of Notre Dame Press, 1994), 17.
14. Ibid., 2 and 3.

property during collectivization, or uncontrolled usury among peasants in India stealing?"[15]

Herskovits gets at the kind of point that we have seen when he says that there are no "Absolutes," although there are "Universals." In some form "morality is a universal, and so is the enjoyment of beauty, and having some standard for truth," Herskovits says. But these universals do not constitute absolutes, for they have a varying form "from culture to culture." The "many forms these concepts take are but products of the particular historical experience." It seems that just as we can agree that having a morality in some form is a universal value and still hold that no particular moral value is a universal, so we can allow that murder and stealing are universally prohibited and that telling the truth is universally approved of, but point out that there is far from universal agreement on what these values are in a practical application.[16]

The long and the short of it seems to be that, although we can in a sense find a core of universal or shared moral values, in their particularized application they may turn out to be very different. Frank J. Hoffman, in a rather different context but in a way relevant to our present concern, has commented on the idea of a shared core of moral values. His comment is on a claim that Bimal Krishna Matilal made that "each (great) religion starts from a common focal point, accepting a basic core of morality necessary for the survival and co-existence of the human species in this globe." Hoffman comments: "Here the burden of proof is on the one who asserts this [basic core of morality]. . . . It is not that one wants to deny human commonality, but on matters of giving a philosophical account rather than practical allegiance one would not want to rest content without probing for the contents of this 'basic core.' It might turn out to be an onion."[17]

III. The Principle of Ascent

In the light of what we have seen about the shifting content of values thought to be universal and the difficulty of identifying universal values in the first place, a certain principle is suggested. It is this: "Ascending values tend toward universal-

---

15. Max L. Stackhouse, *Creeds, Society, and Human Rights* (Grand Rapids, Mich.: Eerdmans, 1984), 269.

16. Herskovits, "Cultural Relativism and Cultural Values," 74.

17. Frank J. Hoffman, "The Concept of Focal Point in Models for Inter-Religious Understanding," in *Inter-Religious Models and Criteria*, 173. Hoffman's quotation of Bimal Krishna Matilal is from his *Logical and Ethical Issues of Religious Belief* (Calcutta: University of Calcutta, 1982), xii.

ity: as the level of abstraction of a moral value increases, the breadth of its application and acceptability increases." Call this "the Principle of Ascent."

I want to discuss several cases that bear upon this principle. First, consider a report on an Eskimo practice given by Vilhjálmur Stefánsson, a scientist and explorer who lived with the Eskimos of Alaska and northern Canada from 1908 to 1912. He tells us that an Eskimo (or Inuit, as Native Americans of the Arctic region call themselves) man named Kirkpuk agreed to accompany him to Banks Island—and then changed his mind. Stefánsson takes the occasion to observe that, for Eskimos, a promise "means merely that a man tells you what he feels like doing at that particular moment," and if he changes his mind, the agreement is dissolved.[18] This makes it sound as though Eskimos lightly make promises and constantly break them without a qualm. It makes it seem as though for Eskimos making a promise creates no binding moral obligation. It does not occur to this author that what an Eskimo is doing in saying, "Yes, I'll do it," is not promising, but rather saying, "Yes, I'll do it, unless I change my mind." In the author's society, most often saying that one will do something implies a promise, but these words or their counterpart in another language, in Eskimo society, may well not be used to do so. If what the Eskimo is doing in saying "Yes, I'll do it" is more fully described, then it can be seen that there may well be a shared value: it is all right not to do what one said one only might do, without promising, explicitly or implicitly, to do it.

Here is another case from Eskimo society that again bears on the Principle of Ascent. It is reported that in Eskimo societies husbands offer to male guests the sexual favors of their wives, and this is approved by custom. Here, it seems, we find an instance of an action that is counted as morally allowable in Eskimo societies and is not regarded as morally allowable in our own society, the society of North and South America or of Europe, let us say. But this is not quite right. Let me supply a bit of background. In traditional Eskimo societies, married couples form an economic unit: the man hunts; the woman dries her husband's clothes, mends his boots, and sews any tears in his clothing (life-and-death matters in the polar region). She also prepares the skins and dries the meat of any animals that he kills, thus giving him more time to hunt. Sometimes, if a man's wife is sick or has a baby to care for, and he is going on a hunting trip where a woman is needed to warm the igloo that is built, to dry his clothes, scrape skins, and so on, he will take another woman, with the husband's permission and her understanding. And on these occasions, it is understood that there will be sexual relations. Does this mean that the Eskimos approve of "wife-trading"? I think not. Peter Freuchen, who has reported

---

18. Vihjálmur Stefánsson, *My Life with the Eskimo* (New York: Collier Books, 1962), 267, 270–71.

on this practice among the Eskimos, observes that Eskimo married people generally remain devoted to each other throughout their lives.[19]

The difference between Eskimo societies and, say, the predominant societies of North or South America or Europe is *not* that a lack of devotion, consideration, and fidelity are considered permissible in the former and not considered permissible in the latter, or that "being true" is counted morally right in the latter and not in the former. Rather, the difference is over the role of sex in devotion. In some societies, for better or worse, devotion assumes an expression that is essentially, though not exclusively, sexual. In these societies a husband's sharing his wife's sexual favors or vice versa hits at the devotion required by the marital relationship. In other societies, like that of the Eskimo, it does not. In each of these societies it may be the *same thing* that is counted right, namely, respecting and honoring one's spouse. But the way this is done, or can be done, may vary from one society to the other, depending on cultural beliefs, perhaps unspoken beliefs, about the significance of sex.

In this connection let me present one more example. I draw it from the reflections of John Kekes on relativism understood as conventionalism (one of the forms of relativism that Kekes identifies, as we noted in Chapter 1). Kekes directs our attention to a practice of the Dinka tribe in the southern Sudan, the practice of live burial.[20] Let me quote Kekes's description of the Dinka's practice of live burial of the spear-master:

> The custom is the burial alive of the most important and respected religious and political leaders the Dinka have, the spear-masters. At the appropriate time, the Dinka dig a deep hole in the ground and, in the midst of various religious ceremonies, place the living spear-master into it. Then the assembled people throw cattle dung on the spear-master until it cov-

---

19. Peter Freuchen, *Book of the Eskimo* (New York: World Publishing Company, 1961), 79–84. Freuchen allows that "wife trading" is approved of in traditional Eskimo society; however, his use of this term is misleading, for what he is referring to in Eskimo society does not violate either their marital relationship as originally entered and understood by married partners or the cultural understanding of the marital relationship; while what is referred to as "wife trading" in the predominant societies of North or South America or Europe does both. Here too the level and fullness of the description of the action labeled "wife trading" can make a moral difference.

20. The Dinka's practice of live burial has been outlawed by the Sudanese government; however, with Kekes, we may still reflect on its moral status when it was a practice. The traditional way of life and the livelihood of the Dinka in southern Sudan have been disrupted by the continuing civil war between the north and the south in Sudan.

ers the hole in which he lies, except for a very narrow opening, and the spear-master slowly suffocates in the excrement piled on him.[21]

As Kekes appreciates, this practice will strike many as morally repugnant. However, this is because of the way we initially understand what is being done. Kekes draws to our attention several morally relevant features of this Dinka practice. First, "the appropriate time for the live burial is when the spear-master is quite old and feels the proximity of death." Second, usually the time for the live burial is announced by the spear-master himself. Third, it is understood by the spear-masters that once they become spear-masters this is to be the manner of their death. And, fourth, for the Dinka, cattle dung is not repulsive, but in their cattle-dependent economy it is a source of "curative and restorative powers" (125–26).

The "significance of the ceremony," as Kekes reports it, has to do with the survival of the Dinka community. If the spear-master dies in an ordinary way, then, it is believed, his "breath," which is the life of the people, is lost. If he dies in the ceremony of live burial, then his breath passes through the narrow opening left in the cattle dung to the community, and the life of the community is conserved (126). Kekes is clear that, as he puts it, "The Dinka think as we do about the value of life. It is precisely because they value life as highly as we do," he observes, "that they celebrate the spear-master for sacrificing his life in order to sustain the life of the tribe" (129).

Kekes compares the sacrifice made by the spear-master in Dinka society to the donation of blood or the donation of a kidney in our society. In each case, we may say, there is an altruistic sacrifice or giving that is voluntary and intentional, made for the benefit of others. For the Dinka, Kekes observes, live burial "is morally justified because it is necessary for the transmission of life from the spear-master to his people." As with blood and kidney donations, there is believed to be "good reasons for violating the deep convention protecting life" (126–27)—that is, for Kekes, a convention that is deeper than a societal convention.

In reflecting on what such a case as this implies for ethical relativism, Kekes recommends that we keep in mind the distinction between the moral status of *agents* and the moral status of *actions*. Say the beliefs of the Dinka about the importance of the breath of the spear-master for the continuation of the life of the community

---

21. Kekes, *The Morality of Pluralism*, 125. In-text citations in the following paragraphs are from this work. Kekes's source here and for other cultural details he reports is Godfrey Lienhardt's *Divinity and Experience: The Religion of the Dinka*.

are false. Still, they may be reasonably held by the Dinka, given all that is available to the Dinka. "The position of the Dinka," Kekes says, "is analogous to what our position would be if future medical research were to reveal that blood transfusion and kidney transplants were harmful to the recipients. Since we have no reason to think that now, and we have good reason to think the opposite, we, as agents, like the Dinka, as agents, should not be blamed if future developments force a shift in the present weight of reasons" (127–28). So for Kekes, the Dinka *as agents* may not be blameworthy. Their actions are another matter, however. He allows that "we can subject various actions to a context-independent moral evaluation by asking how they affect the possibility of living good lives" (128).

Kekes's distinction is important, and his point is well taken. It allows us not to hold the Dinka blameworthy, just as we do not hold blameworthy sixteenth-century physicians who practiced "bleeding," while at the same time not encouraging live burial or "bleeding" as a good practice that ought to be followed. Still, although Kekes does not quite say so, he seems to leave it open that although the Dinka themselves are not blameworthy, their *action* is morally wrong. I say he *seems* to, for he says at one point that "the live burial of the spear-master should be seen . . . as a morally commendable sacrifice made by good people" (127). And he is speaking of the tribe's sacrifice of the spear-master, not the spear-master's sacrifice of himself. Yet there remains the suggestion that this "morally commendable sacrifice," by virtue of its effect on the possibility of living a good life, may be a wrong action by the Dinka. Here we may want to demur. But just what is it that the Dinka are doing? As we stand and watch, they are burying an old man with cattle dung. This, of course, is accurate, as far as it goes. And we can say, once we understand more of the setting, they are sacrificing the spear-master. Moreover, we can correctly say, at another level of description, they are *trying to conserve the life of their community*. One might want to reply that this is not what they are *doing*, this is what they are *trying* to do. However, one answer to the question "What are they doing?" is that they are trying to conserve their community. That is, at one level this *is* what the Dinka are doing.

And if this is what they are doing, and if we too regard it as morally right to try to conserve the life of the community—of our community—then once again, as in the other cases I presented, what they are doing and count as morally right, and what we are doing and count as morally right, is the same thing.

What we see in these three cases is that if our descriptions of what was done become fuller, then the actions can be seen to be in accord with a more widely shared value. In the last case, at one level of description the action is "sacrificing the spear-master"; and although the Dinka may see this as a moral value, many will not see this action, thus described, as morally valuable. However, the same action may be described as "trying to conserve the life of the community," and many will agree with this more abstract moral value. As our characterization of the action becomes fuller, we ascend, or our description ascends, toward a more abstract value that is more widely acceptable—hence, the Principle of Ascent.

A similar point can be made regarding the examples drawn from Eskimo culture. Take the Eskimo hunting-trip case. On these hunting trips the man and woman, though they are married to others, may have sexual relations. At one level of description they are having sex with one not their spouse, and though the Eskimo society may see this as in accord with moral value and so morally permissible, many will not see this action as morally permissible. Again, however, what they are doing can be differently described as acting in a way that does not violate marital trust. This description connects their action with the more abstract value of marital trust, and under this description the Eskimo practice is more widely acceptable in accord with the Principle of Ascent.

In the foregoing, I have tried to show how if we look at some cases where apparently one society morally approves of a particular practice or action and another society does not, we may well find that different actions are involved or that, at bottom, the two societies regard as morally right the same thing.

Important for my approach has been the notion that we can describe actions at different levels. Consider a person standing on a street corner. What is he doing? He is standing there on the corner, we may say. But also, we may say, he is standing on the corner waiting for his wife. Both descriptions may be accurate, at two different levels of description. Following out this notion, we may say that at one level of description two people are doing the same thing, and at another level of description they are doing different things. Consider two people standing on the corner of a busy intersection. They are both doing the same thing at one level. But now say that one is waiting for his wife and the other is waiting for the optimum time to detonate the bomb he has planted in a building down the street. At this level of description they are doing very different things.[22]

In my thinking about the Eskimo and Dinka cases, I assumed that when we describe actions at "higher" or fuller levels, incorporating into our description,

---

22. The idea that an action can be differently described has been recognized by a number of philosophers. See, for example, J. L. Austin, "A Plea for Excuses," reprinted in his *Philosophical Papers*, ed. J. O. Urmson and C. J. Warnock (Oxford: Clarendon Press, 1961), 148; and Eric D'Arcy, *Human Acts: An Essay in their Moral Evaluation* (Oxford: Clarendon Press, 1963), 10ff. Austin observes: "It is in principle always open to us, along various lines, to describe or refer to 'what I did' in so many different ways" (148).

for instance, background beliefs and the goal of action, we get closer to the moral significance of actions. In the light of such "higher," fuller levels of description, we can see that actions that initially appear to be the same are different and that actions that initially appear to be different are the same. And we can invite a wider agreement on the morality of what is done by ascending toward a more abstract moral value.

But now we come to another kind of problem. Why should we think that the "higher" or fuller level of description of an action is the right description? And what is it to get the description of an action right? It cannot be because the "higher" description comes closer to capturing the *essence* of an action. When the Dinka practice live burial, they may be described as sacrificing the spear-master, or they may be described as putting an old man in a hole and covering him with cattle dung. The first description, but not the second, requires a reference to the rituals or ways of the Dinka tribe. But it is too simple to think that the first description is closer to the essence of action.

In a different connection, with a different concern about action, Frank Ebersole suggests that it is too simple to think that we can identify actions—what someone did—simply and always in terms of the rules of a game or rituals or ways of a tribe. It is not that moving a pawn in a chess game is an action by virtue of the rules, whereas a child's shoving a chess piece around is not an action—both are actions.[23] In the same way, it is not that the description of what the Dinka did as sacrificing the spear-master (which refers to tribal ways) is closer to the essence of their action than the description of what they did as putting an old man in a hole and covering him with cattle dung. Both descriptions are descriptions of something they did. Each designates an action, we may say, in fact, the same action. Of course one is *fuller* than the other. Maybe that is the point to notice. Maybe a fuller description has a better claim to being the right description of an action. And maybe it is only when we have fuller descriptions that we should judge two actions in different societies to be the same or different. Maybe. But some would not agree. (John Ladd would not. I shall take up his concerns in a later chapter, when I return to a discussion of the Principle of Ascent and offer an account of it.)

In many cases, it seems to me, we display a moral insensitivity when we regard the actions of those in other societies—or the actions of others in our own society —at "lower" or less full levels of description. We are more sensitive in our moral understanding of what the Eskimos are doing and what the Dinka are doing when

---

23. Frank Ebersole, "Where the Action Is," in *Things We Know* (Eugene: University of Oregon Books, 1967), 285 and 300.

we regard their actions in the light of a fuller description that includes the setting of the action or explains what they are trying to do.

At the same time, I am not quite happy with where this idea would seem to lead. It seems to imply that, say, stealing—taking without permission what does not belong to one—is in itself neither right nor wrong; rather, it depends on what one is trying to do in stealing whether the action is right or wrong. I do not want to have to say that the judgment "Stealing is wrong" is mistaken. It seems to me that such a judgment, *tout court,* may well be correct. And this seems to me to be so *whether or not* moral relativism is a correct view. If moral relativism is correct, then "Stealing is wrong," *tout court,* could be correct relative to some group; and if moral relativism is not correct, this judgment could be correct nonrelativistically. To be sure, I do not want to deny that our prima facie obligation not to steal may be overridden (more or less in accord with W. D. Ross's thinking); however, what is wrong is stealing, *tout court.* At least I do not want to be in the position of saying that this has to be a wrong judgment.

So I seem to find a kind of tension in the moral understanding I want to bring forward. On the one hand, I want to say that the more sensitive moral description of actions is at the "higher" or fuller level, a level at which moral differences between societies tend to disappear. On the other hand, I want to say that there are actions that are right or wrong at a lower level of description. Perhaps it is not an unhealthy tension, and perhaps I find it because it is there to be found. I believe that a version of this tension can be found in the reflections on ethical theory and certain moral cases cited by Richard Brandt, to which we have already referred.

Brandt raises the question whether there are what he calls "ultimate disagreements of principle." What he means by such a disagreement is a disagreement about the rightness of an action that persists between two persons when they agree on the "kind" of action covered, when they agree on all the morally relevant properties of the action. Sometimes, and perhaps very often, Brandt allows, there is no *ultimate* disagreement between societies about the rightness of actions. He considers the apparent difference between the Roman moral attitude toward "the killing of one's father or mother" and the moral attitude in "some of the Eskimo groups." For the Romans it is "the most heinous of all crimes," whereas Eskimos think it right.[24] "But," proposes Brandt, "may it not be that the Eskimos and the Romans in some sense have different acts in mind?" And he continues: "Suppose that Eskimos, through their experience with the hardships of living, think of parricide as being normally the merciful cutting short of a miserable, worthless, painful

---

24. Brandt, *Ethical Theory,* 94–95 and 100.

old age. And suppose the Romans think of parricide as being normally the getting rid of a burden, or a getting one's hands on the parent's money—an ungrateful, selfishly motivated aggression against one whose care and sacrifices years ago have made the child's life a rich experience."[25] In short, Brandt proposes that, in my language, when the actions morally approved of by the Eskimos and morally condemned by the Romans are described at a "higher" or fuller level of description, they can be seen to be different actions.

But also, for Brandt, there may be some ultimate ethical disagreements. In fact, he says that he is "incline[d] to think . . . it is well established" that there are. He considers two instances: the plucking alive of chickens and the "chicken pull," both of which we discussed briefly in the last chapter. Let us consider them again more fully. Brandt cites reports that "in Latin America a chicken is *plucked alive,* with the thought it will be more succulent on the table," and he invites the reader "to ask himself whether he would consider it justified to pluck a chicken alive, for this purpose." The second instance involves the "game" played by the Hopi Indians of the Southwest, called the "chicken pull," in which a chicken is buried in the sand up to its neck. Riders on horseback try to grab the chicken by the neck and yank it from the sand. When one of the riders succeeds in pulling the chicken, the other riders try to take it away from him, the "winner" being the one who ends up with the most chicken. Brandt invites "the reader" to consider whether he or she approves of this practice.[26]

In the first case—that of chicken plucking—we should note that Brandt includes in his description of the practice the purpose of plucking the chicken while it is alive, namely, to make it taste better. In the second case, Brandt does not mention the purpose of the practice, although he does describe it as a "game"—in quotes. Both cases, however, are presented as instances of ultimate disagreement between either Latin American or Hopi society and "the reader's" society, that is, "our" society. And maybe he is right—even if we do consider some of the chicken-raising practices we condone in our society. Moreover, considering the cruelty to the animals involved, perhaps we should say that the Latin Americans who pluck chickens alive and the Hopi who play the game of chicken pulling are doing what is wrong—just as we should say the Romans were wrong to pit gladiators against one another in deadly combat and we Americans are wrong to condone boxing.

Or is it that if we seek a "high" enough level of description of the actions involved, we will find that there is no ultimate ethical disagreement between what the Latin American and Hopi societies accept and what we accept in our society—

---

25. Ibid., 100.
26. Ibid., 102 (Brandt's emphasis).

as Brandt argued that there is no ultimate disagreement between Roman and Eskimo societies over parricide? In my earlier Eskimo example relating to marital fidelity, it emerged that at the level of description where the faithfulness and devotion of Eskimo married couples is kept in place, there is no ultimate ethical disagreement between our society and Eskimo society. The same kind of point emerged in our discussion of the Dinka practice of live burial. Can we similarly argue for the cases of live chicken plucking and chicken pulling?

Can we say that chicken pulling, like watching American boxing, is a means of attaining a needed and replenishing relief from the burdens of life, that it is a means of releasing an aggressive energy that would otherwise be unbearable? Chicken pulling and watching American boxing, then, would be ways of *trying to* maintain a stability in one's life. At this level of description, chicken pulling seems to be the same thing we do in our society in various ways, and even to be morally permissible.

But now we have a pair of ethical judgments that are in tension with one another. On the one hand, we have "Chicken pulling is wrong"; and on the other hand, we have "Trying to maintain a stability in one's life (which the Hopi do through playing the game of chicken pulling) is morally permissible." This appears to show us that there can be moral disagreement *and* moral agreement at the same time regarding the same action.

The Principle of Ascent, despite some paradoxical implications, is essentially correct, I submit. Moreover, it has more to say about shared moral values and the possibility of moral universals and their significance. We shall return later to this principle and a discussion of what accounts for it.

IV. Conclusion

The existence of universally accepted moral values would not show moral relativism to be false, just as different moral beliefs from society to society do not entail that moral absolutism is wrong. Both moral relativism and moral absolutism are compatible with either shared values or the acceptance of different values.

Whether there *are* shared moral values is another question. It may be that two cultures both prohibit killing, but the *content* of the shared value is different. Whether there is a "core of morality" remains an open question.

The Principle of Ascent introduced in this chapter indicates on our first reading that as our descriptions of actions ascend in generality, they name values open to wider application and acceptance. But this principle gives rise to a question about *descriptions of actions* and also a tension or paradox involving such moral rules as "Stealing is wrong."

In later chapters I shall return to the issues left open in this chapter. In Chapters 6 and 7 a way of understanding morality will be developed that will address the "core of morality" concern. In Chapter 8 I shall return to the Principle of Ascent, its issues, and a discussion of what accounts for the principle.

FOUR

Some Proposed Root Bases of Morality

Whatever moral universals there are, however constant their content may be, they do not disprove moral relativism. Also thought to have severe implications for moral relativism is the *basis* of morality, its foundation, that without which it would not be—the "underlying objective causal factor," to use Harbour's phrase, which she believes shared moral values suggest.[1] Whether the basis of morality does have strong positive or negative implications for moral relativism

---

1. Harbour, "Basic Moral Values: A Shared Core," 157. Quoted above in Chapter 3.

will depend on just what the basis of morality turns out to be, if it should have one. Several root bases of morality have been proposed, and whereas some of them are thought to support absolutism over relativism, at least one has been marshaled in support of relativism. In this chapter we shall examine four proposed bases.

Each of these four is a proposed basis for the entirety of morality. Sometimes it is suggested that one category of morality is more fundamental than the others, which are secondary to it and rest upon it or emerge from it. In this way it may be thought that right action, or obligation, is fundamental and that the virtues are to be understood as tendencies to perform right actions. Or the good may be seen as the fundamental category underlying and explaining both right action and virtue. Yet again, moral rights may be seen as the fundamental category, in some sense prior to moral goods as well as to right action and virtue. In each of these variations, it is one part or department of the complex of morality that is put forward as being the basis for the rest of morality. The sort of basis that is of concern to us in this chapter is a basis for the entirety of morality—for *all* its recognizable categories, including right action, virtue, rights, and goods—whatever interior dependencies should exist between these elements of morality.

This is not to say, of course, that such a proposed basis cannot have moral import. Arguably, it will have to have moral import if it is to be fundamental to morality. This kind of root basis for morality may or may not be "natural" in the sense of "naturalistic": it may or may not be something open to "scientific" enquiry. But in itself it will not be a basis for morality in the sense of a prudential reason for persons to be moral. Such prudential reasons provide a self-interested reason for being moral and in this way make it "rational" to practice morality. Candidates for such prudential reasons are fear of punishment or of ostracism, or hope for mutual cooperation among persons. Though some prudential reasons may be associated with a proposed basis of the kind that is of concern to us, prudential reasons do not in themselves provide such a basis for morality. Thus, one may accept it that avoiding punishment is an excellent reason for keeping one's obligations or respecting the rights of others or endeavoring to be virtuous, without so far having any notion of what basis for obligation explains why these obligations exist or what the basis for moral rights is or on what basis virtue rests.

In short, we want to examine proposed bases for morality itself that will ground and thus justify or at least explain morality *and* why morality has the relativistic or absolute character it does. Our concern will be to address the following two questions: To what extent do the bases proposed for morality support absolutism? To what extent do they tell against absolutism and support relativism? The four proposed root bases that we shall consider are natural law, human nature, needs, and agreements between persons.

I. Natural Law

In one formulation, the natural law view is that "there is a pattern of general behavior, a code of things to do and not to do, which derives necessarily from nature itself, from the simple fact that man is man. It is what is called natural law."[2] This is the formulation of Robert C. Mortimer, an Anglican bishop. The natural law tradition is well established in Christianity, reaching back through St. Thomas Aquinas to Paul.

Thus, Aquinas argues that suicide is unlawful for three reasons, and the first he gives is that "everything naturally loves itself, the result being that everything naturally keeps itself in being, and resists corruption so far as it can. Wherefore suicide is contrary to the inclination of nature and to charity, whereby every man should love himself. Hence suicide is always a moral sin, as being contrary to the natural law and to charity."[3]

As Mortimer sees it, we may infer that there is a natural law "once the presupposition is granted that the universe is the work of an intelligent Creator."[4] At the same time, for Mortimer an appreciation of the moral demands of natural law does not require a belief in God, for "knowledge of [natural law] is not peculiar to Christians: it is common to man"; indeed, the natural law is "perceptible by reason."[5] Natural law is in accord with the nature God has created in all men, and the "precepts of natural law, therefore, are immutable and admit of no exceptions."[6] Mortimer affirms that "the first and most general principles of . . . natural law are immediately known, being self-evident, [a]s for example, 'good must be done and evil avoided.'"[7] At a more particular level, in many cases "nature makes it abundantly clear" what human beings ought to do: for instance, nature makes it clear that "human offspring require a long and close union of the two parents."[8] Mortimer admits, however, that it may be difficult to know just how to apply a precept in all instances (just what "do as you would be done by" demands may be unclear at times), and he allows that it may be difficult even to understand the general requirement of some precepts (such as "Thou shalt not kill," which he allows is not understood to include all instances of killing).[9]

---

2. Robert C. Mortimer, *Christian Ethics* (London: Hutchinson's University Library, 1950), 11.
3. *Summa Theologica* II–II, q. 64, a. 5.
4. Robert C. Mortimer, *The Elements of Moral Theology* (New York: Harper & Brothers, n.d.), 8.
5. Mortimer, *Christian Ethics*, 11–12; Mortimer, *Elements of Moral Theology*, 9.
6. Mortimer, *Elements of Moral Theology*, 12.
7. Ibid., 10.
8. Mortimer, *Christian Ethics*, 12.
9. Mortimer, *Elements of Moral Theology*, 13.

The natural law view need not be Christian. The idea that the basis of morality is inscribed in natural laws is found in other religious traditions as well. Harold Schulweis observes that "Jewish ethics is traditionally believed to be derived from God's revealed will," but he sees no contradiction between this traditional view and the natural law view. He goes on to say, "Natural law is congenial to divinity because 'the earth is the Lord's.' Chastity could be learned from the dove, modesty from the cat, not to rob from the ant, propriety from the cock, and 'if they had not been written [in Scripture] they should have been written.'"[10] Elliot Dorff also acknowledges a strain of natural law thinking in the Judaic tradition: "While Jewish law is specifically the law of the Jewish people, it is not only that: the classical Jewish texts picture it as rooted in nature. Psalm 19, for example, describes God's ordering of nature and then easily shifts to God's ordering of human life through the Torah in order to make the point that the two acts of God are parallel."[11]

"From the Buddhist perspective," says Bhikkhu Chao Chu, the Buddhist monk and commentator we quoted in Chapter 2, the reason "why people tend to believe in [certain basic values] is not far to seek." For Buddhism, "knowledge of moral values is considered to be like knowledge of other natural laws. Relations of cause and effect observed throughout the natural world are understood to extend into the realm of human volition and action." In the Buddhist ethical system, Bhikku Chao Chu observes, "no commandments are made." In Judaism and Christianity, as well as in Islam, there of course are the commandments of God. Rather, in Buddhism, "suggestions are offered, based on the knowledge of the natural laws of moral cause and effect that lead away from suffering to the greatest possible happiness for all beings [and] all perceive, however dimly, the same universal laws inherent in the world itself [against such actions as killing, stealing, and lying]."[12]

Several comments are in order at this point. Although Mortimer connects the natural law view with the idea that what is right is right because God commands it (that is, the Divine Command Theory), the two are distinct and separable.[13] Even if natural law is seen as expressive of God's will, as Schulweis and Dorff suggest it is, natural law can be seen as the basis of morality without its being accepted that what is right is right *because* God commands it. Moreover, it is possible to hold that

---

10. Harold M. Schulweis, "Judaism: From Either/Or to Both/And," in *Contemporary Jewish Ethics and Morality*, ed. Elliot N. Dorff and Louis E. Newman (New York: Oxford University Press, 1995), 30. Schulweis cites the Talmud: *Yoma* 67b, where there is a reference to "commandments which, if they were not written [in Scripture] they should have been written." The examples of learning chastity from a dove, etc. are from Euvin 100b.

11. Elliot N. Dorff, "The Covenant: The Transcendent Thrust in Jewish Law," in *Contemporary Jewish Ethics and Morality*, 64.

12. Bhikkhu Chao Chu, "Buddhism and Dialogue Among the World Religions," 168.

13. Mortimer, *Christian Ethics*, 8.

there are natural moral laws without believing that there is a God who established them. This should be clear if only because there is a Buddhist form of the natural law view. For that matter, while the natural law view may be found as a strain of the ethical thinking of various religious traditions, it need not be religious at all. One may, more or less in accord with an Enlightenment theme, think of natural law as *nature's* law—although this would not necessarily make it "natural" in the naturalist's "scientific" sense.

Bearing on our concern with the relevance of proposed bases for moral relativism, a signal element common to various expressions of the natural law view is that it holds for all human beings, perhaps by virtue of shared human nature, and that the moral demands of natural law are in principle discoverable by all, through "reason." Given this element of the view, those holding that natural law is the basis of morality would be inclined toward a form of moral absolutism.

But there are some problems associated with the natural law view. For one thing, there is the question of what *is* natural? What is and what is not in accord with nature and natural law? Are wearing clothes, traveling by air, using "artificial" sweeteners natural? Is a man's wearing long hair, and a woman's wearing short hair, natural? Paul asks rhetorically, "Does not nature itself teach you that for a man to wear long hair is degrading to him, but if a woman has long hair, it is her pride?" (1 Cor. 11:14–15). Here, it has been observed, it seems that Paul's thinking is fashioned by custom, not "nature."[14] Dorff, after noting that "since human beings are all part of nature, natural law theories could presumably have an equally expansive scope and detail," goes on to say, "In practice, however, they vary widely when it comes to specifying exactly what natural law demands."[15] Mortimer too, as we have seen, concedes that there is often unclarity regarding the natural law; for him, even if the law can be clearly stated ("Thou shalt not kill"), the precise requirements of the law may remain unclear.

A related problem has to do with the deliverances of "reason." Reason is supposed to tell us what the natural laws are. It seems, though, that rational people can disagree about what the natural law is or ought to be, about whether birth control methods are "artificial," and about much more besides.[16]

Furthermore, as a final difficulty, natural laws—or the "principles" they express—in the thinking of natural law theorists themselves may not be "exceptionless" or "universal." Here is Aquinas: "The common principles of the natural law cannot be applied to all men in the same way because of the great variety of human affairs;

---

14. J. Philip Wogaman, *Christian Moral Judgment* (Louisville: Westminster John Knox, 1989), 43.
15. Dorff, "The Covenant," 65.
16. Cf. James M. Gustafson, *Theology and Christian Ethics* (Philadelphia: United Church Press, 1974), 282.

and hence arises the diversity of positive laws among various people."[17] What is of interest is not Aquinas's conclusion, but his premise. It seems to allow a cultural application or determination of meaning of the natural law. If "natural law" works this way, then its force against relativism is negligible.[18]

II. Human Nature

Another possible basis for morality is human nature. Here the idea is not that there are precepts or moral laws that are detectable in the natural world; it is that human beings share a nature that provides a basis for morality. Of course, the two ideas can be held together, as they are by Mortimer, who sees both the natural law and the nature shared by human beings as created by God and reinforcing one another. Nevertheless, we can separate the two, as we should in order to recognize that ethical tradition that goes back to Aristotle in which human nature importantly determines what is valuable to human beings.

In this ethical tradition, reaching back from W. D. Ross and Hastings Rashdall, virtue is a prominent value. The underlying idea that human nature is the basis for what is morally valuable is found in several religious traditions as well. In Chapter 2 we noted how for Muzammil H. Siddiqi the *Qur'ān* recognizes a "general and common standard of virtue [*Ma'rūf*] and evil [*Munkar*]." Siddiqi goes on to quote the Muslim theologian A. A. Maudūdī: "The *ma'rūfāt* [plural of *ma'rūf*] are in harmony with human nature and its requirements in general and the *munkarāt* [plural of *munkar*] are just the opposite."[19] Damien Keown says that Buddhism "steers a middle course" between relativism and absolutism. For the Buddha, "forms of life may vary to some degree" and "the basic goods may be participated in in a variety of ways," so Buddhism's absolutism is "attenuated and qualified." However, the moral place Buddhism gives to human nature rules out a "position of extreme relativism" in that, for Buddhism, "the good for man is not arbitrary—it is governed by the facts of human nature and the inalienable characteristics of the world we inhabit, such as impermanence and change."[20] And of course this idea of the

---

17. *Summa Theologica*, I–II, q. 95, a. 2.
18. Cf. Ladd, "The Issue of Relativism," p. 122.
19. Siddiqi, "Global Ethics and Dialogue Among World Religions," 181. Siddiqi cites A. A. Maudūdī, *Islamic Way of Life* (Lahore: Islamic Publications, 1950), 19.
20. Keown, *The Nature of Buddhist Ethics*, 231.

moral role of human nature can be found in other religious traditions, including Christianity, as in the theological thinking of Mortimer, and of others too.[21]

There are two main problems with this view of the basis of morality. First, *is* there a human nature in the needed sense? For those following Aristotle or Plato there is, but after Sartre, questions may be raised. John Kekes suggests that our human nature is "partly open and partly closed"; no "ideals are imprinted on human nature." Instead our human nature allows a range of ideals of a good life.[22] For Keown, Buddhism allows that "the good for man," which is determined by human nature, may "be participated in in a variety of ways." Is human nature, then, at most a negative test for value? And what does it rule out? For Buddhists it allows, as a valuable moral life, pursuing Buddhist enlightenment; and for Christians it allows living in a Christian faith relationship to God. Does it also allow striving to maintain the epistemic standards of W. K. Clifford or following the ideal of Johannes the Seducer?

The second problem is related. Say that there is a human nature and that it does provide a basis for morality. For what form of morality does it provide a basis? Does it provide a basis for the one true morality (absolutism)? Or does it provide bases for several equally valid moralities (relativism)? We humans do share quite a few physiological and psychological capacities. About this there is no controversy. Cobble together a human nature out of these, and it is not at all clear whether it will support absolutism or relativism.

III. Needs

Undeniably human beings have certain very basic needs: air to breathe, food, water, shelter. These are needs of what Matilal calls "the naked man": men and women stripped of "all cultural underpinnings."[23] Can these needs provide the basis for morality? Not those bodily needs just named by themselves, it seems. Ethical thinkers who believe that human needs may provide the basis for morality recognize that other more distinctively human needs must be a part of any adequate

---

21. See, for instance, Hick, *An Interpretation of Religion*, 312.
22. John Kekes, *The Examined Life* (Lewisburg: Bucknell University Press, 1988), 183–86.
23. Matilal, "Ethical Relativism and Confrontation of Cultures," 357. Matilal cites Stuart Hampshire, from whom he borrows the term "naked man." Hamshire, *Morality and Conflict* (Oxford: Blackwell, 1983), 142.

basis for morality. Shia Moser, who is one such ethical thinker, makes this point. However, he concedes, as soon as we go beyond "bodily needs" into "the realm of those [needs] usually described as psychological, social or cultural, it becomes difficult to draw the line between what is determined by the human situation and what is mere cultural accident." "It would seem," he allows, "that the time has not come yet for the sciences to set up a list of basic needs, or to determine the relationships between such needs and some less elementary ones to which the former give rise."[24] Nevertheless, he does present sympathetically just such a theory, that of Abraham Maslow. For Maslow there is a hierarchy of basic needs. As the lower needs are met, the higher needs become dominant, the lower needs being bodily or physiological and the higher needs being those, for instance, for love, affection, and belongingness.[25] Although Moser would wish for a scientific theory of needs, and his reservations notwithstanding, he suggests that our ordinary pretheoretical knowledge teaches us that all people need proper food, shelter, sanitation, and even safety and self-esteem.[26]

Matilal makes a similar suggestion about human needs. The concept of "the naked man," for Matilal, consists of "numerous simple facts about needs, wants, and desires, for example, removal of suffering, love of justice, courage in the face of injustice, pride, shame, love of children, delight, laughter, happiness."[27] It is true that perhaps not all of these are needs; perhaps some are desires. However, if these are needs, they are beyond merely bodily needs.

To the extent that they are needs, Matilal suggests tentatively that they carry an implication for relativism and "nonrelativism" (absolutism): "The claim of the nonrelativist is minimum: certain basic moral principles are neither agent-relative nor contingent upon any specific type of social order. These principles are sometimes claimed to flow from the 'nature' of human needs."[28] Moser makes a more confident assertion. He endeavors to show "by means of an example" (the example being Maslow's theory of needs) "how a theory of needs, should it be found to be scientifically well grounded, could provide a very sound foundation for a nonrelativistic ethics."[29]

---

24. Shia Moser, *Absolutism and Relativism in Ethics* (Springfield, Ill.: Charles C. Thomas, 1968), 211.

25. Ibid., 212. Moser cites Abraham Maslow's *Motivation and Personality* (New York: Harper, 1954), 89, 102, 125, 339ff.; and a book Maslow edited, *New Knowledge in Human Values* (New York: Harper, 1959), 126.

26. Ibid., 212–13.

27. Matilal, "Ethical Relativism and Confrontation of Cultures," 357.

28. Ibid., 358.

29. Moser, *Absolutism and Relativism in Ethics*, 211.

Beyond the general view that needs provide the basis of morality, there are two secondary ideas here. One is that "higher" needs than bodily needs are required to fill out a sufficient basis for all of human morality, and there are such higher needs. The other idea is that universal needs account for universal moral principles. Moser apparently thinks this, for he says, "From the viewpoint of our ordinary knowledge of facts, one is led to the opinion that needs are sufficiently universal to lend support to the validity of various universal ethical principles."[30] The anthropologist Ralph Linton also thinks this. In the last chapter we noted that Linton held that "basic values" are "usually associated with the satisfaction of the basic needs of individuals, both physical and psychological." He furthermore believed that "If universal values exist, they must be sought for at the level of the deepest and most generalized conceptual values, those which stand in the closest relation to the individual needs and social imperatives shared by the whole of mankind."[31]

As I remarked, it seems beyond question that we human beings have certain basic needs. Not a few who have discussed needs—more than Matilal, Moser and Linton—have thought that "higher" needs are among such basic needs. John Kekes, we will recall, allowed that what he called "primary values" are "universally human." Kekes is clear that the benefits associated with physiological primary values "satisfy our basic physiological needs" (such as the need for food), and he leaves it open that the benefits associated with psychological and social primary values satisfy other basic needs (such as for love and respect, to use his examples).[32] Philippa Foot, in reflecting on moral relativism, observes that "all need affection, the cooperation of others, a place in a community, and help in trouble."[33]

Foot, like Matilal and Moser, believes that shared human needs tell against moral relativism. But is this true? Some problems attach to our thinking that it is true—even allowing that humans share basic needs, some of which are "higher" needs.

Let us accept it that needs *in some manner* give rise to values and moral principles. One problem is whether universal needs for such things as food or self-esteem give rise to universal moral principles. Might it not be that although there is a universal need for food, this need gives rise to a variety of moral principles, none of which is accepted universally?

But let us say that universal needs do in some manner give rise to universally accepted values and principles. We should not forget the point made by Taylor,

30. Ibid., 212.
31. Ralph Linton, "The Problem of Universal Values," in *Method and Perspective in Anthropology*, ed. R. F. Spencer (Minneapolis: University of Minnesota Press, 1954), 152; quoted by Brandt, *Ethical Theory*, 287.
32. Kekes, *The Morality of Pluralism*, 18.
33. Foot, "Moral Relativism," 164.

among others, noted in the last chapter, that universal values do not establish absolute norms; and it is absolute moral norms, not universal agreement on a norm, that relativism denies and absolutism affirms. Thus, it could be that a certain moral norm associated with a basic need is found in all societies—for example, "It is right to feed the hungry"—and nevertheless, what establishes it as a norm in each society are the conventions of the individual society in question, in accord with moral relativism in one of its constructions.

There is a another perhaps less serious problem that applies to the general view that needs are the basis of morality. It relates to Moser's concern that there be a scientific theory of needs. Max L. Stackhouse gets at it this way: "The problem in this approach [appealing to "the real, basic needs of humanity"] is the definition of what is 'real' and 'basic.' Which metaphysical-moral vision shall we adopt in order to identify what is real and basic?"[34] Different "religious world-views," he appreciates, postulate different ideal societal arrangements and different ideals of human fulfillment, and hence different basic needs. Granting that this is so, it of course still might be that very many basic needs—bodily and "higher"—could be identified irrespective of one's religious tradition. But even if a wide range of shared human needs could be identified and could be used to provide a basis for morality, it seems in the light of the first two problems that such a basis would do little to decide the issue between relativism and absolutism in morality.

IV. Agreements Made Between Persons

The agreement view of the basis of morality has it that morality arises from an agreement or contract that people enter either explicitly or implicitly. On this view—which in the modern era goes back to Hobbes's *Leviathan,* and in the present is found in the thinking of John Rawls—morality is a matter of give-and-take in accord with this agreement, and what is to be expected and given in return is a matter of this agreement between persons. On this view, in one expression, there is "a contractarian rationale for distinguishing what one may and may not do. Moral principles are introduced as the objects of fully voluntary *ex ante* agreement among rational persons."[35]

---

34. Max L. Stackhouse, *Creeds, Society, and Human Rights,* 269.
35. David Gauthier, *Morals By Agreement* (Oxford: Clarendon Press, 1986), 9.

The idea here is more than that there are agreements with moral force. Many recognize that there are moral agreements without regarding such an agreement as the basis of morality. Again, there may be many who accept it that certain agreements between persons, especially in society or in a political arrangement, generate obligations and rights, but who do not see such an agreement as *the* basis of morality.

There are several variants of this view, but at least one contemporary moral thinker, Gilbert Harman, sees it as giving support to a form of moral relativism. Harman's variant of the agreement view deserves our attention. Morality, Harman affirms, "arises when a group of people reach an implicit agreement or come to a tacit understanding about their relations with one another."[36] Relativism derives from Harman's agreement view in that it allows that different groups of people may have different agreements, and "an action may be wrong in relation to one agreement but not in relation to another." However, Harman wants us to appreciate, his relativism is asserted only regarding what he calls "inner judgments." Examples of inner judgments are "that someone ought not to have acted in a certain way or the judgment that it was right or wrong of him to have done so" (190). They are to be distinguished from the moral "judgment that someone is evil or the judgment that a given institution is unjust" and, as Harman allows at one point, they are even different from the judgment that an action is wrong (190, 192). These last judgments are not inner judgments because they are not made "in relation to an agreement"—or, more accurately, Harman says they are not what he has in mind as inner judgments, and he does not extend his argument to them. On the other hand, he allows that perhaps "all moral judgments are made in relation to an agreement," but he is not arguing that this is the case. Furthermore, Harman says that he is not denying, nor is he asserting, "that some moralities are 'objectively' better than others or that there are objective standards for assessing moralities." Harman's moral ground, then, is limited and carefully chosen. However, he is affirming a form of relativism in that, if he is right, an inner judgment may be correct in relation to one agreement and incorrect in relation to another.

Beyond making sense only in relation to some agreement, inner judgments have two further important characteristics for Harman: first, "they imply that the agent has reasons to do something," and, second, "the speaker in some sense endorses those reasons and supposes that the audience also endorses them" (193). These background moral agreements, in relation to which inner judgments make sense, are more than formal or ritualistic; when made, such agreements, whether explicit

---

36. Gilbert Harman, "Moral Relativism Defended," in *Relativism: Cognitive and Moral*, 189. In-text citations in the next few paragraphs are from this source.

or implicit, are made with the intention, or a strong disposition, to keep the agreement (196, 198). They importantly *are* agreements in intentions. So it is that the kind of reason appealed to by an inner judgment is a reason capable of motivating a hearer who is a participant in the relevant agreement. Those in the agreement recognize such reasons as reasons. And what counts as such a reason is a function of a specific agreement. Harman uses the illustrative example of "a contented employee of Murder, Incorporated." He was "raised as a child to honor and respect members of the 'family' but to have nothing but contempt for the rest of society." Now he is given the assignment to kill a bank manager. Harman observes that we would "merely amuse him" if we tried to convince him that it was wrong to kill the bank manager. Our reasons—perhaps something like "It is wrong to harm others"—are not reasons for him, because they do not operate within his agreement. In Chapter 2 I cited Harman as one who suggested that "there is no prohibition on harm to outsiders in the criminals' morality": here is the rest of his story. To be sure, Harman allows that we can judge the member of Murder, Incorporated to be a criminal and that he ought to be stopped. But we cannot make the inner judgment that "it is wrong *for him* to kill the bank manager" (although we can judge *his action* to be wrong) (191–92).

Harman says more about how we might understand such agreements: they might be with a group of friends or with society; they may be made for self-interested reasons, so that in society we make an implicit agreement to tell the truth in order to depend on information we get from others; while it may be difficult to "opt out" of such an agreement, sometimes it can be done, as when we change our circle of friends; and such agreements are open to "bargaining" and adjustment.[37]

What shall we say about the agreement view of the basis of morality and about Harman's version specifically? I think it can be maintained that Harman's version, as an account of the logic of "inner judgments," is unassailable. Harman himself says that his thesis is a "logical thesis about logical form" and presents the "logical form of inner judgments." That is, he defines the concept and traces its implications. Given how he understands "inner judgments," their correctness and what will count as a reason for one's being right or wrong in doing something (but not the rightness or wrongness of what one did), will be relative to some agreement. However, there are two problems here.

First, as Harman acknowledges, his view does not address large parts of morality. On Harman's own account, it does not address moral justice, the moral character of individuals, or even, when push comes to shove, the rightness and wrongness of actions.

37. Ibid., 195ff., and "Moral Relativism," 23.

Second, while Harman can spell out the logic of his concept of "inner judgment," it is another thing for the concept to apply significantly to morality and our moral lives. It may be in part this point that Matilal is making when he says of Harman's view and the relativism he defends that "the argument is sound, but is this plausible?"[38] It is a part of the logic of "inner judgments" that no reasons unsanctioned by the agreement tell for or against them. But why should we think this is so? One way for Harman to reply is to say that this is entailed by the concept of inner judgment. Then the question becomes, Why should we think any moral judgment is an inner judgment? At issue here is whether we can offer a reason that supports a judgment like "You were wrong in doing that" when that reason is not recognized as a reason by the hearer. Later, in Chapter 7, I shall return to this question.

Now let us go to the broader question of the validity or force of the general view that agreement is the basis of morality. As Harman appreciates, there are several traditional objections to agreement theories of morality. He addresses several and tries to show that his special form of the agreement view escapes their fire.[39] I shall at this point mention only one. Is every agreement entered into a binding moral agreement? For example, the criticism runs, agreements made under compulsion do not seem to be binding, and the validity of this moral principle indicates that there are "moral principles prior to those that derive from an implicit agreement." Harman does not deny the validity of this principle about compelled agreements, but he thinks that his version of the agreement view escapes this objection because his thesis is that morality derives from an implicit "agreement in intentions," and agreements in intention contain or imply the principle about compelled agreements.[40] But it would seem that the objection, with a slight redirection, relates to his version as well; for compulsion is only one example of what might make any agreement not morally binding. Let us allow that agreements of intention are always freely entered into. Is every agreement of intention to act certain ways a morally binding agreement?

There is another problem for the general view, to the extent that it is taken to provide support for relativism over absolutism. Although Harman's version may be enlisted to support a form of relativism, other agreement theories may be enlisted on the side of absolutism. Two examples will do. In the *Crito*, the primary reason the laws of Athens give Socrates as to why it would be wrong for him to escape from prison is that, if he were to do so, he would violate his agreement with them, with the state. Socrates' thinking embodies the idea of a social contract, according

---

38. Matilal, "Ethical Relativism and Confrontation of Cultures," 347.
39. Harman, "Moral Relativism Defended," 198ff.
40. Ibid., 199.

to which residents in a state implicitly agree with "the laws" to obey the law in return for the protection of the law. As Socrates makes clear, the resultant obligation holds absolutely, irrespective of the opinion of the majority of men. Similarly, the social contract thinking of Hobbes is absolutist. Once the social contract is entered, the sovereign has absolute authority, and, in contradistinction to Harman's relativistic thinking, individuals have no right to withdraw from the agreement and form a new arrangement.

V. Conclusion

Some proposed bases—natural law, human nature, and needs—can be and have been marshaled in support of absolutism, while at least one—agreement between persons—has been used in support of relativism. However, it does not seem that any of the first three proposed bases actually entail absolutism; nor is it the case that the agreement view entails relativism. Moreover, there are questions about the credentials of all of these proposed bases as a true basis of morality—which, of course, is not to say that any of them is morally irrelevant. Later, in Chapter 6, we shall return to the question of the basis of morality.[41]

41. Christine Korsgaard has pursued the "enterprise of founding ethics on practical reason," as she puts it, and this makes it sound as though she were pursuing the basis of morality. In fact, she is seeking to show that "the standards that govern the realm of the practical [choice and action] are standards of reason . . . the same reason that governs our quest for understanding and explanation in the realm of theory" (*The Standpoint of Practical Reason* [New York: Garland, 1990], 18). Her focus is on Kant's ethics, and she undertakes to "present and explain the arguments by which Kant establishes that the categorical imperative is a principle of reason" (23). To the extent that her effort is to show that the same "standards" that apply to reason in general apply to practical reason, we should note that it does not address the root basis of morality in the sense we have discussed in this chapter. One may agree that moral reasoning is or should be governed by the general "standards" of reason without commitment to a view on morality's root basis.
In fact, we may agree that practical reason should be rigorous and disagree about what considerations it should appeal to—whether or not such considerations are candidates for morality's root basis. Onora O'Neill is aware that different conceptions of practical reasoning are abroad. She points out that it can be conceived of as "end-oriented reasoning" or "act-oriented reasoning," with subdivisions in each category. Her concern is with justice and virtue and their perceived tension, and she argues for a "rigorous conception of reasoning about action" that will allow "substantive accounts" of both justice and virtue, and heed the obligations of both (*Towards Justice and Virtue: A Constructive Account of Practical Reasoning* [Cambridge: Cambridge University Press, 1996], 6, 50, 64–65). Charles Taylor also recognizes different conceptions of practical reason with appeals to different considerations. He identifies two "models" of practical reason: the apodeictic and the *ad hominem;* and he argues for an *ad hominem* model ("Explanations and Practical Reason" in *The Quality of Life,* 210ff.).

FIVE

Pluralism, Monism, and Relativism

At the end of the last chapter, I suggested that there is more to be said about the basis of morality. So there is. This topic is of no little importance for the main concern of this book, and I shall return to it in the chapter that follows this one. In the present chapter, however, I need to address a matter that amounts to a preliminary issue. We have, to this point, spoken of moral relativism in contrast with moral absolutism. The distinction is impeccable once we have it in place that moral relativism is the view that there is no single true morality.

Moral absolutism, then, is the view that there is *but one* true morality. Before we proceed further, however, we should observe that, for some, there are other competing moral views contending with relativism in its explanatory or metaethical space. One view that particularly deserves our attention is moral pluralism. Another view that deserves our attention and that pluralists oppose is moral monism.

I. Moral Pluralism

Moral pluralism recognizes that there is a plurality of moral points of view and affirms that, among many moral points of view, no one is clearly superior to another. Strictly speaking, under our working definition taken from Wong, moral pluralism may qualify as a form of moral relativism; but pluralists tend to reject relativism because, as they see it, relativism allows no limit on the range of moralities or denies that there are "objective" moral judgments. Moral pluralism is analogous to John Hick's religious pluralism (discussed in Chapter 1); as Hick tries to address and accommodate the religious plurality of the world, so many moral pluralists try to address and accommodate the moral plurality of the world.

Moral pluralists are struck by moral diversity, although how they regard that diversity can vary. They may perceive that there are a number of moral *systems* or *theories*, like Mill's and Kant's theories, none of which seems to be clearly and exclusively correct. When the focus is on the diversity of moral theories, the resultant form of moral pluralism is the view that in morality and moral decision making one may appeal to one or another moral theory in different moral settings. "The Moral Pluralist," says Christopher Stone, "holds that a public representative, a senator, for example, might rightly embrace utilitarianism when it comes to legislating a rule for social conduct (say, in deciding what sort of toxic waste program to establish). Yet, this same representative need not be principally utilitarian, nor even a consequentialist of any style, in arranging his personal affairs among kin or friends."[1] J. Baird Callicott, who is critical of moral pluralism, says of Stone's pluralism that it "invites us to adopt one theory to steer a course in our relations with friends and neighbors, another to define our obligation to fellow citizens, a third to clarify our duties to more distantly related people," and so on, Callicott sug-

---

1. Christopher D. Stone, *Earth and Other Ethics: The Case for Moral Pluralism* (New York: Harper & Row, 1987), 118. Quoted by J. Baird Callicott, "The Case Against Moral Pluralism," *Environmental Ethics* 12 (Summer 1990): 104.

gests, up through six further theories to treat our moral concerns relating to future generations, nonhuman animals, plants, the elemental environment, ecosystems and other environmental collectives, and, finally, the planet as a whole.²

Stone and Callicott consider pluralism in the context of environmental ethics, although this is not to say that either sees it as a moral view that applies only to the issues of environmental ethics. Many have discussed moral pluralism from the standpoint of a central focus other than environmental ethics, and many have seen moral pluralism as addressing a less theoretical moral diversity. Some, for instance, have characterized moral diversity as a plurality of equally valid *moral outlooks* or *perspectives*. Elizabeth Wolgast considers moral pluralism not so much as an ethical view relating to competing ethical theories as a view relating to the current state of human affairs in which we are all confronted by a "pluralism of perspectives" and challenged "to imaginatively see inside another's moral universe, as we determine which moral differences are tolerable and which not."³ For her, moral pluralism is a *perspectival* pluralism.

Yet others see moral pluralism as a view embracing a range of competing and sometimes incommensurable goods or values. These strains can be interwoven to create a composite pluralistic view, as Donald Crosby has done. For him, moral pluralism involves not only the recognition of a plurality of useful moral theories, but also the acknowledgment of a plurality of different moral perspectives and a plurality of sometimes irreconcilably conflicting goods.⁴

In some manner, moral pluralism recognizes and seeks to accommodate moral diversity. But of course so do both moral relativism and absolutism in their respective ways. Moral pluralism, however, emphasizes moral plurality and looks to it as a favorable phenomenon; in doing so, it is closer to moral relativism than to absolutism. It is close enough to moral relativism that it is sometimes considered to be a kind of moral relativism; for example, Ralph Ellis speaks of "the benign pluralisms of discourse ethics and communitarianism" as "kinds" of ethical or moral relativism.⁵ Usually, though, moral pluralism is distinguished from moral relativism.

The form of moral pluralism that I want to concentrate on in this chapter is that elaborated by John Kekes in his book *The Morality of Pluralism*. Kekes has explicitly thought out, in a detailed way, the relation of moral pluralism to moral

---

2. J. Baird Callicott, "The Case Against Moral Pluralism," 104.
3. Elizabeth Wolgast, "Moral Pluralism," *Journal of Social Philosophy* 21 (1990): 111 and 114.
4. Donald A. Crosby, "Civilization and Its Dissents: Moral Pluralism and Political Order," *Journal of Social Philosophy* 23 (Fall 1992): 112–14.
5. Ellis, "Moral Pluralism Reconsidered: Is There an Intrinsic-Extrinsic Value Distinction?" *Philosophical Papers* 21 (1992): 46.

relativism as well as its relation to the other competitor to relativism that we want to discuss in this chapter, moral monism. In Chapter 1 I drew upon Kekes's thinking about the character of moral relativism for help in formulating a working definition of it. In the next section we shall remind ourselves of the distinctions Kekes draws between kinds of moral relativism, and we shall see how for him these kinds of moral relativism relate differently to moral pluralism. In this section we shall examine Kekes's own moral pluralism and its contrast with moral monism.

Kekes's form of moral pluralism is not stated in terms of a diversity of theories, principles, or perspectives, but in terms of a diversity of "values." Kekes distinguishes between "primary" and "secondary" values, as we have seen in Chapter 1. Primary values are rooted in human nature, for Kekes, and bid fair to be universal. They may be physiological, psychological, or social; thus—to remind ourselves of Kekes's examples—food is a primary physiological value, love a primary psychological value, and respect a primary social value. Secondary values owe something to, for instance, our social roles and individual aspirations. Those with whom we eat, and what we eat are secondary values. Kekes also distinguishes between "moral" and "nonmoral" values. Love and justice are moral values; knowledge and a choice of a suitable career are nonmoral values. Moral values, for Kekes, are those that "affect others." Moral and nonmoral values are related and interdependent in various ways. For instance, the moral value of generosity requires one to have the nonmoral value of the needed resources. For Kekes, "the distinction between moral and nonmoral values cuts across the distinction between primary and secondary values," so that there can be primary values that are either moral or nonmoral, and there can be secondary values that are either moral or nonmoral. Both primary moral values and primary nonmoral values are "universal" in that both types address the "universal requirements of all good lives." So for Kekes, the plurality of values, upon scrutiny, contains the four types of values that constitute his schema, and none of these types "is dispensable for living a good life."[6]

For Kekes, there is a plurality of values, and there is "a plurality of equally reasonable conceptions of a good life" with its different values. For his pluralism, values can be ranked, but rankings are only reasonable in relation to a particular conception of a good life. Accordingly, there can be a plurality of equally reasonable rankings of values.[7] Thus, although two individual conceptions of a good life may both embody the values of political activism and scholarly reflection, the first good life may rank political activism higher, and the second good life may equally

---

6. Kekes, *The Morality of Pluralism*, 44–45.
7. Ibid., 22–23.

reasonably rank scholarly reflection higher. This is to say, in Kekes's language, that values are "conditional": for pluralists "the plurality of values implies the conditionality of values."[8] For pluralism, then, no value is "overriding," where an overriding value is one that *always* takes precedence over any other with which it conflicts; and the only justification for violating it in one instance is that in doing so we more greatly realize that value generally (as when in taking one life we preserve many).

For W. D. Ross, prima facie obligations can be "overridden" by superior prima facie obligations, so that in a particular situation the obligation to do good might override the obligation to keep a promise; but Ross did not think that the obligation to do good would therefore always be superior to and override the obligation to keep a promise.[9] In Kekes's definition, an overriding value would *always* be overriding, regardless of the conception of a good life; and there is no such "highest value," given the correctness of his pluralism.[10] The issue of the existence of an overriding, highest value is a nodal issue between moral pluralism and moral monism for Kekes. But before we pursue the contrast between moral pluralism and moral monism, let me fill out Kekes's conception of pluralism.[11]

To begin with, Kekes's moral pluralism recognizes what many who are not moral pluralists find it hard to deny: there is a plurality of values among human beings in the world—not only concerning life, love, justice, and honor, but also leisure, competition, and spelunking (to use Kekes's own examples). Associated with this plurality is the further claim that values are moral or nonmoral, and primary or secondary. Moreover, for Kekes, values are "conditional" in the sense we have discussed: there is no "overriding" value. Often values conflict: for pluralists, Kekes observes, values are often related, so that the realization of one excludes the realization of another. Value conflicts are often internal to a single conception of a good life, where *incompatible* and *incommensurable* values come into conflict. Incommensurable values (values that "exclude any reasonable comparison"), like patriotism and spelunking, may be compatible; and incompatible values, like going camping to be alone and flying to a strange city to be alone, may be commensurable. But often values are both incompatible and incommensurable, and within a good life we may want to realize values that are both incompatible and incommensurable.[12]

---

    8. Ibid., 19.
    9. W. D. Ross, *The Right and the Good* (Indianapolis, Ind.: Hackett, 1930), chap. 2.
    10. Kekes, *The Morality of Pluralism*, 19–21.
    11. Kekes refers to "the six theses of pluralism" (17) and devotes a chapter to each thesis. Here we shall discuss the defining themes of Kekes's pluralism, drawing upon these six theses.
    12. Kekes, *The Morality of Pluralism*, 21–23 and 53ff. I have used Kekes's examples.

(The idea of incommensurability is in high relief in more than one formulation of pluralism; for Crosby, for whom moral pluralism is importantly perspectival, there is "some significant degree of incommensurability among perspectives."[13])

For Kekes, as we observed, values can be ranked. Normally, in every reasonable ranking of values, primary values, which address the "minimum requirements of all good lives," will have a greater importance than secondary values.[14] However, beyond this, primary values and secondary values that are found in a tradition or that are incorporated in a conception of a good life can be further ranked, although they have no absolute ranking. In this further ranking, several different rankings of values may be equally reasonable. This is not to say that for Kekes such rankings are not "objective." For Kekes's moral pluralism, such a ranking can be objective in that judgments as to the importance of one value in relation to another "can by justified on context-independent grounds."[15] For moral relativists, on the other hand, there is no such context-independent justification of the judgment that one value is more important than another. This, for Kekes, is the nodal issue between moral pluralism and moral relativism. (Other moral pluralists also see objectivity of judgment as a dividing difference between pluralism and relativism, although the conception of "objectivity" may vary.[16])

Kekes introduces a distinction between "deep and variable conventions." Deep conventions do not vary with societies but connect to "basic human needs shared by all normal members of our species"; they "protect the minimum requirements of all good lives" however they are conceived; they have a context-independent justification and importantly relate to primary values, but also to certain secondary values.[17] It is a deep convention that heeds the primary value of social stability, for instance, which (like food and other values related to our shared human nature) is a primary value. Moreover, the *form* of social stability can vary from tradition to tradition; thus, it becomes a secondary value in different traditions: "Primary values are the content, while secondary values give form to them," Kekes observes (32–33). Thus, *this* secondary value gives expression, or "form," to the primary value of social stability, so it takes an objective context-independent justification as a part of the minimum requirements of good lives as well. This is not to say that such a secondary value and the deep convention protecting it are "beyond reasonable challenge." They can be challenged "on the grounds that some other interpretation of the primary value would provide better protection of [the] particular

---

13. Crosby, "Civilization and Its Dissents," 114.
14. Kekes, *The Morality of Pluralism*, 77.
15. Ibid., 31–32.
16. Cf. Crosby, " Civilization and Its Dissents," 117–19.
17. Kekes, *The Morality of Pluralism*, 31–32. Parenthetical page numbers in the text refer to this work.

requirement of good lives." Similar comments clearly apply to the objective status of other secondary values relating to and giving form to other primary values Kekes identifies, such as food, respect, and life (81–82).

Finally, in setting out Kekes's pluralism, we should note the theme or idea of moral progress in his thinking. Kekes allows that both monism and relativism can accommodate the possibility of moral progress if it is understood in the respective terms of these moral positions. Similarly, his moral pluralism can accommodate the possibility of moral progress if it is understood in distinctly pluralistic terms. For pluralism, moral progress occurs with "a closer approximation of valued possibilities not just from one particular point of view but for humanity as a whole." Moral progress is to be understood as movement toward the realization of a particular *ideal,* which finds expression "both on the level of traditions and on the level of individual lives." For traditions, the ideal is a tradition "that is as receptive to a plurality of conceptions of a good life as is consistent with the limits [as embodied in primary values] needed to maintain the tradition" (35). For individual lives, the ideal is to construct "a reasonable hierarchy of the possibilities we value." In each case, "the ideal is of a form of life in which the widest possible range of specific values may be pursued," as opposed to drawing "closer to a preestablished pattern [of values]," for "there is no such pattern" (36, 141).

II. Pluralism versus Monism

Now let us compare Kekes's moral pluralism with moral monism. Pluralism denies that there is any overriding value; monism does not. For pluralism, there is no supreme value or preestablished hierarchy, whereas monism insists on a highest value. In broad terms, pluralism and monism agree on the following: (1) there is a plurality of values, (2) it is possible to rank values, (3) conflicts over values can be decided with objectivity, and (4) moral progress is possible. Still, when we descend to the details of *how* these points are understood, pluralism and monism are seen to be in essential disagreement.

Though both monism and pluralism recognize a plurality of values—including life, knowledge, friendship, leisure, and perhaps many more—for monism there is but "one true system of values" (14). (Thus, strictly speaking, monism may qualify as a form of moral absolutism; however, if so, it is a special form.) For pluralism there can be a number of reasonable systems of values reasonably determined by any of several conceptions of a good life. For monism, but not for pluralism, there is an overriding value, a single value that is highest in every case. Perhaps a supreme example of a moral monist is John Stuart Mill, the author of *Utilitarianism;* Kekes himself regards Mill as one of the exemplars of monism (67). As Kekes sees it, Mill regards different values as "fungible" in that they can be expressed in terms of the "medium" of a supreme value and thereby compared or ranked. That value, for Mill and Bentham, of course, is pleasure (67–68).[18] Without putting too fine a point on it, we may say that for Mill the highest value—indeed, the only "good as an end"—is pleasure; and although knowledge, for instance, has value, it does so by virtue of its contribution to the presence of pleasure. In this way, for Mill and other hedonistic utilitarians, the highest value can be used to rank other values in various contexts of comparison. Not so for pluralism. Pleasure may be a value, but it may well not rank highest in many conceptions of a good life; and it is not commensurable with many values.

For monism, values can be ranked, but the ranking is by virtue of an overriding value. Thus, there is one and only one true ranking. For pluralism, there is a plurality of reasonable rankings in the light of different equally reasonable conceptions of a good life. Judgments about which conflicting value is more important are objective for monism because for monism the ranking of values is context-independent and is a matter of the natures of the values being compared: whatever value is overriding is always overriding. For pluralism, such judgments are objective because they are context-independent; but they are so not by virtue of an overriding value: their objectivity derives in part from the status of primary values and those secondary values that give "form" to primary values.

The idea of moral progress, says Kekes, is "most at home" in moral monism. This is because, for monists, moral progress is understood straightforwardly and simply as progress "toward the realization of whatever the overriding value [is]" (139, 140). So for Mill, as more and more the pleasure of humanity (or of "sentient creation," as he allows at one point)[19] is attained, moral progress occurs. For Kant the overriding value would be different—something like acting out of respect for the moral law—but his ethics too would straightforwardly accommodate the idea of moral progress. As Kekes observes, this does not mean that monists must be optimistic about the occurrence of moral progress: Mill was, but Kant was not, he says.[20] For pluralism, moral progress does not occur as more and more some particular value is realized. In fact, for pluralism, moral progress would be thwarted by the maximization of any one value. Moral progress, for Kekes's pluralism is, as

---

18. But cf. p. 12, where Mill, in *On Liberty,* is among those "whose approach was receptive to pluralism."

19. John Stuart Mill, *Utilitarianism,* ed. George Sher (Indianapolis: Hackett, 1979), 12.

20. Kekes, *The Morality of Pluralism,* 139.

we have seen, progress toward the ideal "in which the widest possible range of specific values may be pursued" (36).

Pluralism is inconsistent with those forms of monism that explain value conflicts in terms of human imperfection and ignorance (Kekes cites Plato as such a monist), and with those forms that see all values as expressible in terms of one supreme value or "medium" (Kekes cites Bentham and Mill), and with those forms that posit a canonical principle based exclusively on "the nature of values." These forms of monism deny that conflicting values are incompatible and incommensurable. Nevertheless, Kekes maintains, there is one form of moral monism that is consistent with pluralism. This form of monism allows that the ranking of values may be based partly on intrinsic characteristics and partly on "our attitude toward them" (63–75). It allows that conflicting values are incompatible and incommensurable but that they can be ranked, as pluralism maintains, according to our judgment of "their relative importance," based on both the intrinsic nature of values and our attitude toward them. Thus, this form of monism can allow what pluralism claims: first, that although the ranking of primary values in relation to each other remains "an open question," the intrinsic nature of, say, the value of life will justify the judgment that this primary value is more important than all secondary values (which presuppose this and other primary values); and, second, that judgments of the respective importance of various secondary values "will vary with the tradition and the conceptions of a good life from whose point of view they are made" (77).

In sum, although pluralism and monism importantly agree on a number of points, *mutatis mutandis,* including the objectivity of judgments about conflicting values and the possibility of the ranking of values, and although one form of monism agrees with pluralism on the incompatibility and incommensurability of values, pluralism and monism irrevocably disagree about the value of a plurality of values.

III. Pluralism versus Relativism

Many who hold moral pluralism in some form see pluralism as being in opposition to moral relativism. Pluralism opposes relativism, for Wolgast, in that relativism, unlike pluralism, allows that "all perspectives are equally worthy."[21] For Stone, moral pluralism allows that in moral decision making a plurality of moral theories

---

21. Wolgast, "Moral Pluralism," 113.

may be appealed to, but this pluralistic position is not to be confused with moral relativism, which, for him, is the position "that each moral claim must be related to a particular place, its validity turning upon whether it correctly identifies the prevailing moral sentiment of the relevant community."[22] For Crosby, relativism, unlike pluralism, denies "the possibility of making objective moral judgments."[23]

Kekes also sees an opposition between pluralism and relativism even though pluralists and relativists agree, against monism, that no value always overrides all other values.[24] For one thing, relativism cannot compare traditions and conceptions of a good life, because relativism "admits of no context-independent grounds for making such comparisons." Relativism, unlike pluralism, does not recognize context-independent primary values. And although moral relativism can allow a species of moral progress, it does not allow moral progress across traditions or from one conception of a good life to another (35). Take a societal or cultural form of moral relativism according to which cultural mores or moral beliefs determine what is morally right or virtuous within a culture: moral relativism could consistently regard it as moral progress if more members of a culture came to adhere to and follow the moral beliefs of their culture. But it could not allow for a context-independent judgment that one tradition or a particular conception of a good life might be better or worse than another tradition or conception of a good life. Thus, Kekes observes, relativism cannot answer such a question as "whether the contemporary Western tradition is morally better or worse than China under Mao" (35).

As Kekes sees it, relativism, unlike pluralism, does not recognize a "need for limits." This is because it does not give proper attention to deep conventions and the primary values they protect. Kekes is not accusing relativism of failing to give absolute status to primary values. Kekes's pluralism and relativism agree that all values are conditional. The problem here for relativism, as Kekes sees it, is that it fails to appreciate that there are context-independent reasons for allowing primary values and for justifying violating a primary value. Earlier, in Chapter 3, I used Kekes's discussion of the Dinka and their practice of live burial to illustrate the Principle of Ascent. Kekes uses the example in his discussion of the "need for limits" and how the form of moral relativism that he calls "conventionalism," unlike pluralism, fails to appreciate this requirement. As we have seen, Kekes observes that the Dinka "think as we do about the value of life." In Kekes's terms, the Dinka, as much as others, as much as we ourselves, have a deep convention that gives a

---

22. Stone, *Earth and Other Ethics*, 123.
23. Crosby, "Civilization and Its Dissents," 117.
24. Kekes, *The Morality of Pluralism*, 31.

high value to life: they treat life as a primary value. Kekes argues that what justifies the live burial of the spear-master—if it is justified—is not a context-dependent reason, as the conventionalist would have it, but a context-independent reason that we all can recognize, namely, sustaining the life of the tribe. True, the Dinka and others in "our tradition" would disagree about whether violating the deep convention of protecting life by sacrificing the spear-master is reasonable, about whether sacrificing the spear-master is justified on the grounds that it was required for the survival of the tribe. But this is not a disagreement over the primary value of life and a deep convention protecting it. It is a disagreement over the truth of the Dinka's belief about the effect on the tribe's life of sacrificing the spear-master. Kekes argues that conventionalism is wrong because it fails to see that this disagreement we have with the Dinka is not "closed to a reasoned resolution." Indeed, he points out, the fact that the tribe survived after the practice was outlawed provides a context-independent reason for such a resolution (129, 130).

A second reason that conventionalism is wrong, for Kekes, is that this disagreement is possible only because there is "a deeper agreement between them and us that the taking of a life is morally permissible if it is the best way of preventing the loss of even more lives" (129). Our disagreement presupposes that we agree on the primary value of life and on when the taking of life is permissible. "What moral conventionalists miss is that moral disagreements are possible only if there are moral agreements in the background" (133). Moral disagreements of this sort are possible only if we recognize that the "minimum requirements of good lives are the same" for human beings. This "layer of agreement, made possible and inevitable by our common humanity, . . . constitutes the context-independent basis for some moral judgments" (132)—which conventionalism denies and pluralism allows and even insists upon (129–32).[25]

Nevertheless, Kekes does not simply dismiss relativism. His view of the opposition between relativism and pluralism is more nuanced than that. We will recall

25. There is an interesting parallel between, on the one hand, Kekes's thinking about primary values existing by virtue of human nature and certain secondary values giving them "form," and, on the other hand, Damien Keown's reflections on Buddhist ethics. Keown says that for Buddhist ethics, "the good for man is not arbitrary—it is governed by the facts of human nature and the inalienable characteristics of the world we inhabit, such as impermanence and change. A position of extreme relativism is therefore ruled out. Yet within these confines forms of life may vary to some degree, a fact acknowledged by the Buddha, and the basic goods may be participated in in a variety of ways." In this way, Keown says, Buddhism "steers a middle course" between "Relativism and Absolutism." However, what he has just presented, he says, "does not mean that none of the [Buddhist] precepts are absolutes, only that not all of them are" (*The Nature of Buddhist Ethics*, 231). Since for Keown "absolute" means "applicable in all circumstances," and hence "overriding" in Kekes's sense, some differences may remain.

from our discussion in Chapter 1 that Kekes distinguishes three forms of moral relativism. First, there are *radical relativists,* who "think that all moral judgments are relative to the particular conception of morality that has emerged in a specific historically, culturally, and socially conditioned setting." Second, there are *conventionalists,* who "concede . . . that all reasonable conceptions of morality must recognize that some values are primary and that these values depend on human nature. . . . [They] claim that only secondary values are relative . . . to the conventions of particular traditions, [but say] some of these conventions prescribe the acceptable interpretations of primary values." And third, there is *perspectivism,* which accepts it "that human nature and traditions require the recognition of both primary and some secondary values, but it holds that what other values are regarded as secondary is relative to the conception of a good life of the agent" (48). Each form in its way wrongly holds that values are "context-dependent."

Radical relativism has to be wrong, for Kekes, if only because it does not recognize primary values that derive from human nature independently of social context. But what of the other two forms, which *do* allow such primary values? As we have seen, Kekes argues that conventionalism is wrong if it denies that there are context-independent reasons for resolving the issue of whether sacrificing a life is morally justified. What if these forms of relativism allow that conflicting evaluations "can be criticized by reasons whose force does not depend on the evaluations themselves"? That is, what if they allow an appeal to "objective," "context-independent" reasons? In that case, Kekes says, "there may be no substantive disagreement between pluralists, on the one hand, and conventionalists and perspectivists, on the other" (52).

IV. Conclusion

Allowing Kekes's three forms of moral relativism to stand intact in the forms he gave them originally so that they contrast with and deny pluralism, still Kekes's pluralism is in some ways like, and in some ways unlike, relativism. It is like moral relativism in that it leaves open a range of "values" and affirms that none is an overriding value in conflict situations, thus allowing, as relativism allows, that the value of life, for instance, may or may not take precedence over freedom or justice. In sympathy with moral relativism, or that form of it he calls conventionalism, he acknowledges its "strength [in] its insistence on the richness and variety of human possibilities and its reluctance to condemn moral possibilities from a point of view alien to them. These are useful and needed correctives of moral dogmatism" (131). But Kekes's pluralism is also unlike moral relativism in that it insists on context-independent primary values and an "objectivity" in judging value conflicts that is not determined by a group's conventions or an individual's attitudes. In the terms of our working definition of moral relativism, adopted in Chapter 1—"There is no single true morality"—Kekes's considerations tend both in its favor and against it.

In recent years, not only Kekes but a number of pluralists have brought the diversity of values and moral diversity in general to a new critical attention. I have cited several, and Kekes names others, from Annette Baier to Bernard Williams, who have "been struggling in recent years with the more or less systematic development of pluralism" (12). Kekes in particular sees the value of a plurality of values. He makes it clear how there are many values in human experience and that they can be differently regarded in importance in the light of different conceptions of a good life, so that even when it is agreed that justice and life are values, it may be that there is reasonable disagreement about which is more important. He draws to our attention that there may be many ways to lead a good life in accord with one of many reasonable conceptions of a good life.

Kekes seeks to address relativism with both honesty and sympathy; he neither utterly dismisses it nor completely embraces it on ideological grounds that he brings to his examination. Rather, in the light of his pluralistic thinking, *inter alia* he tries to explain what is right and what is not right about moral relativism. His explanation, and his discussion of pluralism, can, I think, only be helpful to our own effort to discover what is right and wrong about moral relativism and to our effort to go further and give a structural explanation for the intuitions that recommend relativism and absolutism. A not insignificant way that Kekes's thinking about pluralism and relativism helps us is by raising a number of questions. I shall note five.

1. If moral progress is a movement toward an ideal tradition that is receptive to more conceptions of a good life, or a movement toward an ideal form of life that allows the widest range of values, then once all the primary values are recognized, along with those secondary values that give them "form," it seems that there will remain a vast range of secondary values that might be incorporated into some conception of a good life. (As Kekes says, "Primary values represent only a very thin layer of context-independent requirements for all good lives"; they, and the secondary values that give them form in a particular tradition, protect us from only "starvation, humiliation, exploitation, and the like" [32].) Will any of the remaining secondary values that might be chosen as a part of a particular good life be as

good as any of the others that were not chosen? Is gormandizing—not the connoisseurship of one with refined tastes in food, but overindulgence—as good? Is miserliness? Why not?

Kekes says, "The point they [pluralists like himself] insist on is that rankings [of values] are reasonable only in particular situations because they depend on the variable and individual conceptions of a good life held by the participating agents" (22–23). He goes on to say that those moral relativists who are perspectivists accept the objectivity of primary values and of some secondary values but regard "some secondary values as relative to the context of individual conceptions of a good life" (48). Why then are perspectivists not ipso facto pluralists? They are not, Kekes might say, because they do not make *objective* context-independent, *reasonable* value judgments. But if the pluralist's value ranking, which depends on one of many "variable and individual conceptions of a good life" is reasonable, why isn't the relativist's identification of certain secondary values, which is "relative to the context of [one of many] conceptions of a good life" also reasonable?

In short, once primary values are recognized along with the secondary values that give them "form," pluralism does not seem to give us a way to think about or to assess those many other values that we might choose or be tempted to choose as a part of our conception of a good life.

2. Values are ranked within the conception of a good life. Will *any* conception of a good life do? Is every *conception* of a good life a conception of a *good* life? Such conceptions often come out of a tradition, but they need not. Are all conceptions, if they recognize all primary values, equal or "equally reasonable"?

Kekes does allow that conceptions of a good life can be "defective." Some conceptions of a good life may be "unsuitable" for certain individuals due to their "character and circumstances," he observes. A conception of a good life can also be defective because it allows either "a too-narrow or a too-wide range of values." If too narrow a range of values is chosen, the life is "impoverished"; if too wide a range is chosen, the life is "too scattered." "Good lives," says Kekes, "should have some scope for the appreciation of beauty, playfulness, and nonutilitarian relationships, as well as tackling difficult projects that require hard work" (97). But why should all good lives have *these* values? Why couldn't one kind of good life be a focused and concentrated life—that of an artist, say, or of a writer? And why couldn't one kind of good life be diversified—that of someone interested in many things, although "master of none"? Pluralism has no answer for these questions.

3. Just what are the primary values? Primary values are universal because they address our basic needs and are derivable from universal human nature. But some would raise an issue about what is and is not such a basic need. For Kekes food

and love and respect and life are primary values, as we have noted, but so too are security and leisure (40). Is artistic expression a primary value? Communion with God? Religion is a secondary value, says Kekes (50). But it is only on a certain assumption about human nature.

4. Living in a civilized state, as opposed to "a state of nature," also seems to be a primary value for Kekes: "We all prefer the civilized state to a primitive one," for in a civilized state "we have leisure, choices, and the security to go beyond necessity" (39–40). Do all of us have this preference? And is it preference that makes it a primary value? Or is it need? Is there such a need acknowledged by all, as a need for food is? There *is* a value to being civilized, we may allow, but can pluralism account for it?

Similarly, there may be a value to "the appreciation of beauty, playfulness, and nonutilitarian relationships, as well as tackling difficult projects that require hard work," all of which Kekes sees as essential to good lives (although he does not label them "primary values"). But if these are essential values, it is far from clear how pluralism can account for this being so.

5. Granting there is no "highest value"—like life, justice, love, friendship—might there nevertheless be a different kind of morally significant factor that could have relevance in value-conflict situations, irrespective of the conception of a good life?

If we are to make progress in our effort to grasp what is significantly right and significantly wrong about relativism, we shall have to address these questions in some manner—as we shall do in Chapter 7. Meanwhile, it is to our profit to note how pluralists like Kekes and others have recognized a plurality of values, or a plurality of moral perspectives. It is time to acknowledge that we live in the midst of moral diversity, across and within cultural settings. Just what this diversity means for the issue of moral relativism remains to be seen.

SIX

Moral Diversity and Relationships

Undeniably, there is moral diversity in the world: a diversity of values, of moral perspectives, of acknowledged obligations, of ways of understanding obligations, and more. This moral diversity in itself, of course, does not entail moral relativism or moral pluralism. We raise another kind of concern, or another dimension of the concern with diversity, if we ask whether diverse moralities (in the form of different values, different moral perspectives, different acknowledged obligations, or different ways of understanding obligations) are equally valid or true. An affirmative reply here would seem to entail pluralism or relativism.

In this chapter I want to explore and begin to argue for a way of understanding how diverse moral perspectives, diverse ways of understanding obligations, and diversity in other areas of morality—in short, diverse moralities—can be equally true, and at the same time there can be a "single true morality." My effort will be to present an analysis of the structural basis of morality that will explain how both points can be correct. The structural basis I propose consists of human relationships.[1]

The idea that relationships are in some manner morally fundamental is found here and there in the thinking of various moral philosophers and others who have thought about the nature of ethics. It is, of course, recognizable in much of feminist ethical thinking, going right back to Carol Gilligan's seminal work *In A Different Voice*.[2] But it is also found in other quarters of ethical thought. J. Baird Callicott, near the end of an article to which I referred earlier, allows that "the root moral concept" is "the community concept," and elaborating this community concept, he goes on to suggest that "we have before us . . . the bare bones of a *univocal* ethical theory . . . that provides . . . for a *multiplicity* of hierarchically ordered and variously textured moral *relationships* . . . each corresponding to and supporting our multiple, varied, and hierarchically ordered social *relationships*."[3] It is not accidental, I suggest, that Callicott finds himself offering this formulation in terms of *relationships*—relationships between human persons and between human persons and other entities of the environment. Again, Christine Korsgaard, writing from a strongly Kantian perspective, says that "[values] supervene on the structure of personal relations" and observes that "to say that you have a [moral] reason is to say something *relational*, which implies the existence of another, at least another

---

1. The structural basis of morality to be examined, consisting of human relationships, is the structural element that will enable us to understand moral diversity. I am not claiming that the only relationships with structural importance for morality are relationships *between human persons*. There are, in addition, relationships that human persons have to themselves, relationships they have to nonhuman beings and to the environment, possible relationships to nonhuman persons, and possible relationships to God or the Absolute. But it is human relationships between persons that will most help us to understand moral diversity, as we know it, and the issue of moral relativism.

2. Carol Gilligan, *In a Different Voice: Psychological Theory and Women's Development* (Cambridge: Harvard University Press, 1982). Much has been written on Gilligan's ideas about relationships and a feminine ethic of care. See, for instance, Mary Jeanne Larrabee, ed., *An Ethic of Care: Feminist and Interdisciplinary Perspectives* (New York: Routledge, 1993), which includes Gilligan's "Reply to Critics."

3. J. Baird Callicott, "The Case Against Moral Pluralism," 121 and 123 (my emphasis on "relationships"). Drawing upon the thought of David Hume, Charles Darwin, and Aldo Leopold, Callicott also suggests that the "proto-moral sentiments of affection and sympathy [Hume]" were "naturally selected in mammals as a device to ensure reproductive success [Darwin]" and then enlarged to embrace other beings that make up ecological communities [Leopold] (121–23). However, this etiological

self." She goes on to say that "the acknowledgment that another is a person is not exactly a reason to treat him in a certain way, but rather something that stands behind the very possibility of reasons." Korsgaard, unlike Callicott, is thinking exclusively of relationships between human persons, and her comments signal the moral importance of such "personal relations."[4]

I. Human Relationships and Morality

Personal relationships typically are between human persons and, in our accessible moral experience, involve at least one human person.[5] Though a person may have a relationship important in his or her life to a being other than a human being—a pet, say—paradigmatic personal relationships are between human persons. In this range there are a great variety of human relationships: marital, friend to friend, parent to child, worker to fellow worker or workers, worker to employer, student to teacher, individuals to other individuals in their society or in their cultural group or in their nationality, citizens to other citizens or to the authorities of the state, and so on. Many of these relationships are close personal relationship, but some are not, though they are yet relationships between human persons.

We speak of relationships being *violated*—as when a man is unfaithful to his wife or a friend betrays a confidence. When a relationship is violated, when a friend betrays a confidence, she has done what she should not have done. Several points deserve our notice:

1. Relationships between persons carry with them obligations: we speak of marital duty and of what friends owe friends. However, these obligations arise from, and are explained by, the relationships, not the other way around.

2. This basic rubric—obligations have their source in, and are explained by, relationships—holds for many obligations to which we might not initially think to apply it. For instance, it holds for the obligation we take up when we make a promise and for the obligation to tell the truth. We incur the obligation to do what we

---

4. Christine M. Korsgaard, "The Reasons We Can Share: An Attack on the Distinction Between Agent-Relative and Agent-Neutral Values," reprinted in *Creating the Kingdom of Ends* (Cambridge: Cambridge University Press, 1996), 276 and 301 (Korsgaard's emphasis). Korsgaard does not mean to deny that a person can have duties to herself or to himself, although she thinks that duties to oneself and "questions of value . . . for the self" are to be understood in terms of "relations between stages of a self" (302 n. 3). In Chapter 7 we shall have occasion to reflect on duties to oneself and one's relationship to oneself.

5. Karen J. Warren makes a similar point in "The Power and Promise of Ecological Feminism," *Environmental Ethics* 12 (Summer, 1990): 135 n. 15.

promise by entering into a relationship with another person, a relationship we enter precisely by making a promise to that person. W. D. Ross appreciated that we make an implicit promise to tell the truth by entering into a conversation.[6] However, though Ross did not say so, making such an implicit promise again marks entering into a relationship. If we undertake to answer a question that asks for information, it is understood that we will tell the truth. In giving information to our hearers, we enter into a relationship with our hearers that entitles them to expect us to tell the truth.

Similar comments hold for the other prima facie duties Ross identified, even the general ones, such as the duties of beneficence (to do good for others) and the duties of nonmaleficence (not to do harm to others), under the latter of which Ross would place our general duty not to steal. They all come under the rubric I have given. Thus, in the case of stealing, when one individual takes the property of another without explicit or implicit permission, he violates the relationship that obtains between himself and the owner, a relationship that requires a respect for the owner's use of his property. Similarly, when an individual does good for another, as in helping someone in need, she respects the relationship that obtains between herself and the other person who is in need.[7]

3. Different *types* of relationships create different *types* of obligations. What violates one type may not violate the other. True, many types of relationships may require honesty and even loyalty of a kind. But the kind of deep and personal commitment that the marital relationship requires one spouse to give to the other is not required of an employee toward his or her employer in the employment relationship. Again, although one's employer may be one's friend, the relationship between employee and employer is different from that between friend and friend: the loyalty one owes to one's employer is different in scope and depth from that which one friend owes to another. In this way we may say that *types* of relationships create different *types* of obligations. It is as Aristotle said, "How man and wife and in general friend and friend ought mutually to behave seems to be the same question as how it is just for them to behave; for a man does not seem to have the same duties to a friend, a stranger, a comrade, and a schoolfellow."[8]

4. We should not think that once we see how relationships give rise to obliga-

---

6. W. D. Ross, *The Right and the Good*, 21.
7. To observe that this rubric—this order of provenance and explanation—holds for obligation is not to deny that it holds for other areas of morality, e.g., moral rights and virtues, although I cannot argue for the full scope of the rubric here. See my *Relationship Morality*, Chapters 8 and 9. Later, in Sec. VI of the next chapter, I shall try to show that a fundamental relationship between persons, the person/person relationship, along with other relationships, accounts for human rights.
8. *Nicomachean Ethics* 1162a30, trans. W. D. Ross, in *Introduction to Aristotle*, ed. Richard McKeon (New York: Modern Library), 490–91.

tions it will always be clear just what meets those obligations. Of course, sometimes it may be. If I promise to meet someone at a certain hour, then it is clear what meets my obligation. In the case of other relationships, as with friendships, for instance, it may often be much less clear. We may be clear that our friendship relationship requires loyalty to our friend (and that that loyalty is different in *type* from the loyalty we owe to our employer), but there can still be a question about just what *form* of loyalty to our friend is required. In such cases, it is again relationships that clarify the *form* that obligations take, what they specifically require of us.

Aristotle recognized that there are different types of friendships.[9] Going beyond Aristotle and his basic types, we can recognize how friendships within his types can vary and create different forms of obligations. Consider two men who are friends. Let us say that they are colleagues at work and that outside of work they often go on outings together. These connections provide the provenance and occasion of their friendship. The two men enjoy each other's company. One, however, has an abiding interest in motorcycles that the other thinks is a little silly, although he does not announce this thought to his friend. In the setting of their particular relationship there are certain moral requirements, and one is that the one who is not a motorcycle enthusiast not ridicule his friend's fascination with motorcycles behind his back. Even secretly harboring, and so not resisting, negative thoughts about his friend's fascination with motorcycles can violate the friendship. Their relationship may require the one friend to now and then listen patiently to the other's rhapsodic accounts of the glories of the Harley-Davidson. So it may be in some friendships along these lines. In other cases—where, say, the one's abiding interest in motorcycles is impinging on other values they both hold dear—the friendship may require the one friend to try to show the other that such a consuming interest is unworthy.

In this way friendships carry obligations, and the form of these obligations can vary from friendship to friendship depending on the particular relationship formed by the particular individuals who are friends. When we violate such an obligation, we violate the relationship, and we violate such a particular obligation of friendship by virtue of violating the particular friendship relationship. I will assume it is clear that this point could be illustrated and supported by examples from a range of relationships, such as marital relationships, parent-child relationships, and so on.

Summing up, we may say that obligations arise from and are explained by relationships between persons, that the type of obligation is explained by the type of relationship, and that the form of the obligation is explained by the particular relationship.

9. *Nicomachean Ethics* 1155b16–1157b4.

II. What Human Relationships Explain: Relationships and Different Societies

Relationships between persons explain two elements of moral phenomena across societies. First, relationships explain why the same *types* of values/obligations (such as loyalty, family commitment, and marital duties) recur in different societies and cultures. Second, relationships explain why such values/obligations take different *forms* in different societies and cultures.

The same *types* of values/obligations recur in societies because the same types of relationships recur across societies. The marriage relationship is found in virtually all societies. In many if not all societies, there are friendship relationships as well as family membership relationships. In all or many societies, then, marital fidelity will be a moral value and an obligation arising from the marriage relationship. Similarly, the loyalty of friendship is a value in various societies, and in these societies not being loyal to a friend counts as a moral failure by virtue of violating the friendship relationship.[10] A parallel comment can be made about family membership relationships giving rise to a loyalty-to-family obligation. Many other relationships are to be found across virtually all societies, such as the parent-child relationship and the relationship between the individual and the social group. Other kinds of relationships, such as that between an employee and his or her employer, will be found only in societies with the requisite economic arrangement, but still within a wide range of societies. All of these relationships create types of obligations determined by the type of relationship.

However, although the same types of relationships—friendship, the marital relationship, and more—are found in many, if not virtually all societies, the character of these relationships can vary greatly form one society to another. In many societies, notably those with roots in the Judaic and Christian traditions, the marital relationship is monogamous. In societies formed by the Islamic tradition, the marital relationship may not be monogamous for men: a husband may have up to four wives (when certain conditions are met). In each case, the marital relationship carries with it the commitment of fidelity. However the *form* of marital fidelity will

---

10. Martha Nussbaum observes: "Friends in England will have different customs, where regular social visiting is concerned, from friends in ancient Athens. Yet both sets of customs can count as further specifications of a general account of friendship that mentions, for example, the Aristotelian criteria of mutual benefit and well-wishing, mutual enjoyments, mutual awareness, a shared conception of the good, and some form of 'living together'" ("Non-Relative Virtues: An Aristotelian Approach," in *Quality of Life*, 256). I would add that the forms of the mutual benefit, well-wishing, etc. can themselves vary from friendship to friendship both intraculturally and interculturally.

vary from the monogamous relationship to the nonmonogamous relationship in the Islamic society. The specific character of these different marriage relationships differently shapes the form of the required fidelity.

In Chapter 3 I discussed Eskimo marriage and fidelity in connection with the "Principle of Ascent." Let me return to the example of Eskimo practice, since it bears directly on the present concern with how different types of relationships can take different forms in different societies and hence give different forms to basic obligations. In traditional Eskimo societies, we will recall, if a man's wife is sick or has a baby to care for, and he is going on a hunting trip where a woman is needed to warm the igloo that is built, to dry his clothes, scrape skins, and so on, he may take another woman, with the husband's permission and her understanding. On these occasions it is understood that there will be sexual relations. In many societies, like the main societies of Europe and North and South America, marital devotion requires sexual exclusivity. In these societies for a married couple to share their sexuality is counter to the devotion required by the marital relationship and violates that relationship. In other societies, like that of the Eskimo, it does not. In each of these societies there are forms of respecting and honoring one's spouse. But the way this is done, or can be done, varies in form from one society to the other by virtue of the specific character of the marital relationship in these different societies.

In the light of these reflections, I think that we can now better understand why some thinkers have distinguished between primary, or basic moral values, and values that are not primary. Harbour, we will recall, suggests that there is a "shared core" of "primary moral values." Among the primary core values she lists are justice, good faith, veracity, and courage.[11] But also, for her, there are secondary and tertiary values. If justice is a primary value, the cultural specification of justice is a secondary value, and principles of justice in specific codes are tertiary values. Tertiary values, then, are finer grained versions of secondary values.

For Kekes also there are primary and secondary values. Primary values are "universally human" in that they derive from a shared human nature. For Kekes, we will recall, primary values may be physiological, psychological, or social. In this way they are, as he says at one point, primary values "of the self, intimacy, and social order."[12] Moreover, as we have seen, Kekes allows that primary values can be given one "form" or another by different "traditions," in which case a tradition-created secondary value gives form to a primary value. For instance, although social stability is a primary value, the form it takes in a particular social setting is a function of a tradition.

---

11. Harbour, "Basic Moral Values: A Shared Core," 156 and 163.
12. Kekes, *The Morality of Pluralism*, 58.

Kekes's pluralism is developed in terms of "values," and not in terms of obligations; but his discussion at points has clear implications for obligations, as when he speaks of "rules" and "restrictions on what we can do" generated by a particular form of "social life."[13] Ultimately, traditions provide the "set of secondary values" that render primary values "concrete and specific." It is a tradition that addresses the primary value of life and speaks to the "status of suicide, capital punishment, war, euthanasia, family quarrels, infanticide, and the like."[14] So for Kekes, a tradition's secondary values give form to primary values and create "restrictions" or "rules" that pertain to life and to the other primary values he recognizes. To be sure, traditions are open to a reasonable evaluation for Kekes, but for him they are nevertheless the source of those secondary values that express concrete obligations, whereas needs associated with human nature are the source of primary values.

I think that the essential validity of the kind of distinction that Harbour and Kekes offer between primary and secondary values can hardly be denied. What is to be noted, in accord with the theme of this section, is that the explanation of the distinction between many if not all *culturally shared primary values* and *culturally specified or tradition-created secondary values* is to be made in terms of human relationships. Consider Harbour's example of good faith and Kekes's example of love (one of his primary values of intimacy). Good faith and love are primary values by virtue of the *types of relationships* that require them. There can, of course, be *various* types of relationships that require good faith and love—the good faith required between friends as distinguished from that between employee and employer, and similarly for love in different types of relationships. If the type of relationship is friendship, the type of good faith it requires is that of friendship. At the same time, the specific expression or *forms* of these values—the secondary values—will vary with different instantiations of these types of relationships, so that the *form* of good faith in a friendship in one culture may be different from its form in a friendship in another culture. In this way, recurring relationship *types* across cultures explain the shared (primary) content across cultures, and the different *forms* of these relationships in different cultures explain the different (secondary) content from culture to culture.

Another thinker we mentioned earlier, Samuel Huntington, also speaks of "basic values"; however, he does not contrast them with secondary values. Rather, alluding to Michael Walzer and using his term, he speaks of a "'thin' minimal morality." Walzer, as we have seen, distinguishes between "thin" and "thick" morality. For him, thin morality consists in "principles and rules" that are shared across cul-

---

13. Ibid., 40.
14. Ibid., 81.

tures, whereas thick morality requires a particular moral culture. *Justice* has both a minimal and a maximal meaning. Across cultures, by virtue of the term's thin, or shared meaning, we can understand justice to require a rejection of tyranny and oppression of the poor. If we go on to try to say what justice positively involves, then we will begin to draw upon our own thick morality. So for Walzer, all people may agree on the basic—thin—value of justice and disagree about what it—thickly—requires in a particular setting. Justice is one of Harbour's primary moral values, and the same kind of point I made above about human relationships providing an underlying explanation for primary and secondary values applies here as well. We can agree that people owe it to one another to treat one another with justice; this is a requirement of the general relationship people have to one another in the world (for now I will leave aside the question of whether this requirement extends to everyone, or, as some may think, to only some significant population, since this question is neutral regarding the present point). This requirement flows from the relationship type. But in a particular setting, it is the particular relationship that determines what will count as just treatment (or what will count as equal treatment). Particular relationships that occur in some social setting, and their requirements regarding justice, will determine whether it is just treatment to give equal pay for equal hours worked or to practice Affirmative Action—which is not to say that it is always clear to all, or clearly determined, what particular relationships require in specific settings.

As we noted, Harbour speculates that shared moral values across cultures are "suggestive of some underlying objective causal factor." The factor that accounts for shared "primary" values, and for "thin" morality, is relationships, *types* of relationships. And it is relationships again, particular *forms* of relationships, that account for variations in (secondary) values and for "thick" morality.

III. Human Relationships Also Explain Intracultural Moral Differences, Including Differences in Perspective

In Section I I brought out how relationships clarify and explain the particular form that obligations take in particular instances of, for instance, friendship. A corollary of this point is that different friendships might involve different requirements. To return to my earlier example: in one instance, friendship may require a friend to listen patiently to his friend's exuberance about a fascination; in another instance, friendship may require a friend to argue against such a fascination. Though I did not multiply illustrative examples, the same point, I suggested, is to be seen in respect to particular instances of marriage, parent-child relationships, and a range of other relationships. The friendship example I used and its corollary, like other examples that might be adduced and their corollaries, are, of course, intracultural.

In a similar way, it is different relationships *within* a culture that explain how different individuals may have different responsibilities and obligations toward some person or group of persons within a culture. Herman Melville's short novel *Billy Budd, Foretopman* will allow us to illustrate this point with a particularly graphic example. Two philosophers who have reflected on *Billy Budd* and the crucial episode that will be of concern to us are Peter Winch and, more recently, Elizabeth Wolgast. As Winch recounts the critical action, "Billy Budd, a foretopman of angelic character, is impressed into service on the *Indomitable*. . . . He is persecuted by the satanic master-at-arms . . . Claggart, in a campaign which culminates in Claggart's falsely accusing Billy before Vere [the captain of the *Indomitable*], of inciting the crew to mutiny. In the stress of the situation, Budd is afflicted with a speech-impediment which prevents him from answering the charge. Frustrated, he strikes Claggart, who falls, strikes his head and dies."[15] In Wolgast's account of what comes next, Captain Vere acknowledges "the purity of Billy's character," but "nevertheless argues for his execution under the British naval laws, and persuades the court-martial to his side. His decision turns on the weight of his responsibilities as captain and the dangers of any lapse of discipline in those uncertain times."[16] The "uncertain time" is the end of the eighteenth century, following mutinous uprisings on other British naval ships. Billy Budd is found guilty and executed by Captain Vere under naval law.

Winch uses Melville's story to reflect on moral judgments and their universalizability. There are instances, he suggests, when, without any change in the situation or circumstances, an action might be right for one person and not be right for another—and the action of Captain Vere in *Billy Budd* is just such a case. Vere, in arguing for Billy Budd's conviction of a capital offence, did what was right for him, Winch allows. But he himself would find it "morally impossible" to condemn Billy Budd, although he would not "appeal to any considerations over and above those to which Vere himself appeals."[17]

---

15. Peter Winch, "The Universalizability of Moral Judgments," in *Ethics and Action* (London: Routledge and Kegan Paul, 1972), 155.
16. Wolgast, "Moral Pluralism," 111.
17. Winch, "Universalizability of Moral Judgments," 163–65.

One thing that strikes Winch as important is that Vere, when he lies dying later in the story, has no remorse: his moral judgment to condemn Billy Budd was sincere and serious. However, for Winch it is not Vere's lack of remorse alone that is morally significant, but his lack of remorse "alongside his whole course of conduct during and after the trial and with the moral ideas in terms of which he was shown to be thinking during the trial." These elements together, for Winch, indicate that Vere's action was right for him. Vere, as Winch presents him, came "to an understanding of what he must do," morally, even though another person, like Winch himself, might come to a different understanding of what was morally possible for himself.[18]

Wolgast, who is a moral pluralist, is concerned about a "relativism of a kind where what is 'right for A' need not be right for anyone else." She suggests that we should speak of different moral *perspectives,* but do so in a way "less individualistic" than Winch's discussion allows. Winch's perspective "is more humanitarian than Vere's," and it is "less respectful of British naval laws" than is Vere's perspective. "Many readers," she says, "join in Winch's view of Budd's conviction." Our thinking of the difference between Winch and Vere as a difference in such nonindividualistic, shared moral perspectives will not lead us to say Vere was mistaken or incorrect, she says; and she agrees with Winch that Vere was not mistaken or incorrect. But for Wolgast, this is "because a moral perspective which shapes our judgments does not need to be described as true or false."[19]

So Winch and Wolgast are in a way in agreement: neither wants simply to denounce as wrong Vere's course of action, and yet both, I think, are themselves inclined morally to embrace the more merciful course of action (as Winch does explicitly). At the same time, they disagree about the most revealing way to characterize the moral situation. Wolgast stresses different moral perspectives; Winch stresses finding out what is morally possible for oneself.

But there is more to the moral story: a deeper level of explanation. The explanation of Vere's and Winch's different moral perspectives, and of why Vere has no remorse and finds that it is morally impossible to grant mercy to Billy Budd, while Winch finds it morally impossible to condemn him, has to do with the relationships that Vere and Winch have to Billy, as well as to others. Vere and Winch have very different relationships to Billy Budd—a point that both Winch and Wolgast fail to examine. Captain Vere is related to Billy Budd as a British naval captain is related to a sailor serving on a ship under his command. Winch has no such relationship

18. Ibid., 168–69.
19. Wolgast, "Moral Pluralism," 112. Wolgast is clear, however, that she is not saying that "we must hold all perspectives as equally worthy" (113).

to Billy Budd. As the captain of the *Indomitable*, furthermore, Vere has relationships to his ship's crew and to his naval superiors and to the Crown that Winch does not have. What accounts for the different moral judgments made by Vere and Winch, at bottom, is the different relationships in which they stand, with their different moral requirements.

Wolgast notes that Winch's more humanitarian perspective is one many might share. This is true, for many are related to Billy Budd as Winch is. I would add that many might share Vere's perspective too. For many British naval officers, contemporary with Vere or not, and other military officers, would have the same or the same kinds of relationships to men and women under their command and to superior officers and to the Crown or supreme commander.

Our putting in place this deeper level of explanation does not necessitate our saying that what Vere did *was* right, only that it *could be* right for him in his relationship or relationships, but wrong for another in different relationships. Nor are these points affected by Melville's story being a work of fiction or by Captain Vere's being a late-eighteenth-century British naval captain, while Winch is a twentieth-century philosopher, for they would hold if even if Melville's story were not fiction and if Winch were Vere's contemporary.

This intracultural point—that within a culture different relationships can explain why an action is right for one person and not right for another (or morally required of one person and not morally required of another)—can be seen as well in many everyday cases: the relationship of promisor is different from one who did not promise, and accordingly, it is the promisor who has the obligation to do the thing promised and *ceteris paribus* would do what is wrong if he did not keep his promise; while the person who did not make such a promise would do no wrong in not doing that thing. True, in the case of promising one might say that the morally relevant circumstances are different, for one made a promise and the other did not. This point is, of course, right, although it does not deny that different relationships obtain precisely by virtue of a promise having been made or not. Moreover, in other illustrative cases, as in the Billy Budd case, there do not seem to be such differing circumstances. A father has obligations to his young son that a stranger does not have, such as the obligation to provide needed food and clothing, even though the father and stranger may have equal resources and understand equally well the boy's needs. Here the relevant difference is that the relationship the father has to *his* son is different from the relationship to him that a stranger has. And in a friendship relationship, by virtue of the relationship, it may be that one friend ought to listen patiently to his friend's rhapsodic musings about motorcycles, while others not in that friendship relationship do not have this duty.

IV. Human Relationships and Social Practice

At this point let me briefly consider a counterview. Some would say that different societal practices account for different relational requirements as well as, or better than, different relationships account for the different moral requirements of those relationships. The moral requirements of Christian monogamous relationships and the moral requirements of Islamic nonmonogamous relationships are accounted for by societal practices, they will say. I would not want to deny that social expectations (along with religious roots and the heritage of ethnic and national traditions) can influence the character of relationships. Nevertheless, different relationships explain moral differences better than do different societal practices. There are at least four reasons why this is so.

First, societal practices do not address or explain different moral expectations between, for instance, different marriage relationships *within* a society. Consider a society in which all marriages are monogamous, such as the dominant or mainstream American society. Still there can be a large range of particular monogamous marital relationships. Though none of these marriage relationships may be disapproved of by the society, they may be different in their respective demands or expectations in ways not addressed by the customs of the society. For example, in one marriage relationship a husband and wife may share the activity of shopping for antiques, which they do with an enjoyment that is enhanced by their doing it together; it would violate this marriage relationship for the husband, with no mention of it to his wife, to plan a trip to the antique stores of London for himself alone on a business trip to England. In another, rather different relationship, a wife may have her own study area and valued time by herself to prepare research or to do her legal homework or to pursue her reading; here it may violate the relationship for the husband to put even mild pressure on his wife to give up her needed and cherished time alone to accompany him to London in pursuit of his hobby.

Second, societal practices do not explain the moral expectations of idiosyncratic relationships that go counter to societal models. There have been and are societies, or subsocieties, in which there are customary gender roles of a rigid sort, such that the husband is the wage earner and the wife is the maintainer of the house. In such a societal setting there nevertheless could be a marital relationship in which these roles are reversed: the wife is the wage earner, and the husband maintains the house. Such a relationship could have coherent moral expectations, understood by the husband and wife—but counter to, and inexplicable in terms of, the customs of their society.

Third, societal practices themselves do not explain the possibility of judgments on evil or morally wrong societal practices. We can without contradiction imagine societies that countenance evil practices by allowing relationships between persons that ought not to exist. In fact, historical examples are readily available. The social approval of slavery in the American South is a classic example. Other examples might be cited. John Cook provides two contemporary examples. In some rural Arab societies, custom approves what are called "honor killings": the societal practice requires that when a woman becomes pregnant without being married, she is to be killed by her relatives for the sake of family honor. In Sicily there is a social practice, going back to the Middle Ages, that allows a rejected suitor to kidnap and rape the woman who has rejected him, which presents the woman with the choice of either marrying him or being "dishonored" in a way that makes it impossible to marry another.[20] Less dramatically, and nearer to home, it is arguable that in the United States societal approval still exists for various forms of racial and gender discrimination. Cook presents his examples in the context of a critical discussion of moral relativism, specifically its social form; and Kekes, we will recall, criticizes "conventionalism" for recognizing no "context-independent" reasons that limit societal practices. The present point, however, is that societal practices do not explain the moral requirements of relationships, since societal practices can also give approval to relationships that ought not to exist. (Later, in Sec. I of Chapter 7, we shall see why there is no analogous problem relating to possible "evil relationships"—why, that is, reflection on *all* the relationships of moral importance that we have provides a basis for explaining why some relationships, like abusive or domineering relationships, are in themselves wrong and should not be participated in.)

Fourth, societal practices do not adequately account for recurring moral expectations in relationships across cultures. Social practices themselves—which of course are practices *within* some society—do not explain the broad similarities in the moral expectations of, for instance, marriage relationships (marital fidelity) or friendship relationships (the loyalty of friendship) *across* cultures.

---

20. John W. Cook, *Morality and Cultural Differences* (New York: Oxford University Press, 1999), 35 and 39. Two other examples are provided by Elizabeth M. Zechenter: a 1987 instance of the practice of *sati* (or sutee) in India, and a 1996 instance of the actions of the "holy warriors" in Algeria ("In the Name of Culture: Cultural Relativism and the Abuse of the Individual," *Journal of Anthropological Research* 53 [Fall 1997]: 328 and 330).

V. Human Relationships and Agreements

We earlier addressed the question of whether agreements between persons will do as the "basis" of morality (Chap. 4). I argued that the agreement, or contractarian view could not very well be marshaled as a basis for either moral relativism or moral absolutism, since variants of the agreement view may be presented on each side of the issue between relativism and absolutism. But I did not undertake a general assessment of the agreement view, given the earlier concern. Now such an assessment should be taken up, for in this chapter I am proposing that human relationships provide the structural basis of morality that will enable us to understand moral diversity and the issue of moral relativism. And if this is correct, the agreement view of the basis of morality cannot be correct as it stands.

Peter Singer has succinctly presented a number of reasons against the agreement view, and I shall draw upon his presentation to help show why the general agreement view cannot account for morality. Then we will see how reasons against the agreement view, including Singer's, are quite in accord with relationships providing the basis for morality. Singer finds "echoes" of the contractarian, or agreement view of morality in the thinking of several contemporary moral philosophers, and he names John Rawls and Gilbert Harman. Harman's variant of the view has the special feature that it relies on the concept of "inner judgment," and I shall return to it and to its use of this feature later (in Sec. VIII of the next chapter). Here are Singer's several reasons against the general contract view of ethics:

First, on the agreement view, animals would be excluded from moral consideration, for animals are incapable of entering into an agreement, implicit or explicit, to curtail their behavior in exchange for beneficial conduct toward them (though clearly, as Singer would insist and most would agree, we have at the very least a moral obligation not to make animals suffer). Second, the same point can be made about young children and the mentally impaired: they, too, are not capable of entering into such an agreement. Third, on the agreement view, slave traders had no reason not to capture Africans and sell them as slaves, for they had nothing to fear from them and hence no agreement was in force: the moral community of their agreement, and so their obligations, did not extend to Africans. Fourth, powerful nations, like the United States, would have no moral obligations to countries from which they have nothing to fear, like the nation of Chad. Fifth, since future generations—or those past 2100—can do nothing for us, we would have no obligations toward them.[21]

---

21. Peter Singer, *Practical Ethics* (Cambridge: Cambridge University Press, 1979), 69–71. Harman

These reasons seem to me to be telling. However, there is one other that deserves mention here: Is every agreement entered into a binding moral agreement, as the agreement view requires? It would seem not. It is counterintuitive to think that if two men freely agree to murder one another's enemy, they are thereby morally bound to do so. (This is the criticism of the general agreement view, raised by Harman, that we noted in Chapter 4, and in the form I have given it, it holds as well against Harman's version of the view, which sees an agreement of intention as the basis of morality.)

All of Singer's reasons and examples are understandable in terms of relationships. We have moral obligations toward young children and the mentally impaired precisely because we have relationships to them as *persons,* either special relationships, such as the parent-child relationship, or the general relationship we have to persons in need. We have obligations toward those we might make slaves not to inflict harm on them by virtue of another general relationship we have to people at large, a relationship that is violated when we inflict harm on them. And a nation like the United States has some obligations toward less-well-off nations because of the relationship between the two nations or between their populations. The obligations that humans have toward animals are accounted for by the relationships between human persons and nonhuman animals, and the obligations living people have toward yet unborn generations, their own offspring and others, regarding, say, the resources of the earth (like the rights of future generations) are a function of the various relationships between living people and future generations.[22] Furthermore, relationships explain why not all agreements are morally binding. Relationships are a limiting factor on entered agreements: we cannot enter a morally binding agreement to do what grossly violates other relationships.

In the same way, relationships can account for what is right about the agreement view, for there is something right about it. Agreements can create obligations. They do so just as making a promise creates an obligation. Socrates argued in the *Crito* that the adult residents of a *polis,* or state, have an implicit agreement with the state whereby obedience to the laws is a moral obligation. But in these instances, entering an agreement is entering a kind of relationship. When the agreement is broken, the relationship is thereby violated.

---

endeavors to answer some of these criticisms, or very similar ones, as they relate to his variant of the agreement view, in "Moral Relativism Defended," 198–204.

22. Obligations toward animals and animal rights are discussed in chapter 15 of my *Relationship Morality,* and obligations toward future generations and the rights of future generations are discussed in chapter 9, passim.

VI. Human Relationships and Needs

Needs are no more basic to morality than are agreements. Earlier (Chap. 4) we critically discussed the idea that needs provide the basis of morality in a way that would decide between relativism and absolutism. Now, as we did with the agreement view, we should provide more in the way of a general assessment of the needs view as the underlying basis of morality. Earlier I did not deny that needs *in some way* give rise to values and obligations. Let us grant that this is so. In this section I will try to show how, nevertheless, needs cannot wholly and consistently account for all values and obligations.

The needs view of the basis of morality may be held in one of several forms. Kekes, we will remember, sees primary values as deriving from universal needs. For him primary values are grounded in a shared human nature and are "context-independent." He would allow that universal needs do not provide a complete basis for morality or for all values, for he allows that there are also secondary values deriving from social arrangements and tradition. However, on Kekes's view, the universal needs of humanity do create a layer of agreement in reasonable moral judgments across traditions regarding primary values.

But universal needs, even basic needs, do not always create values in the way Kekes supposes. For one thing, in some cases values and moral obligations go counter to basic needs, such as the need for food. Walzer, who does not concede that there "is a single set of primary or basic goods conceivable across all moral and material worlds," in a passage quoted by Kekes says, "If the religious uses of bread were to conflict with its nutritional uses . . . it is by no means clear which should be primary."[23] Kekes, who calls Walzer "another relativist" for not recognizing food as a primary (non-context-dependent universal) value, is aware that food can have religious value; however, he accuses Walzer of confusing the primary value of food with the secondary value of religion.

For Kekes food, but not religion, is a primary value because we have a basic need for food that is grounded in our common human nature, while there is no such basic need for religion. This makes food, but not religion, a "minimum requirement of all conceptions of a good life" for Kekes. Here Kekes relies on a certain understanding of our human nature, according to which human beings do not by their nature have a need for religion. But also he relies upon his needs thesis.

---

23. Michael Walzer, *Spheres of Justice*, 8; Kekes, *The Morality of Pluralism*, 49–50. Kekes's quotation is from *Spheres of Justice*, 8.

Now undeniably we all have a physiological need for food. But does this make it a value? Consider the ascetic desert fathers—for them the value is *abstinence* from food. Nor need we cite religious ascetics. In starvation situations, parents who give what food they have to their children count as the value *giving food to their children*. It would be a failure on the parent's part to value the food for themselves, although it would undeniably meet their need for food. What makes the value is not the need per se, but the role of food in respecting the demands of relationships. Normally I hurt myself if I gratuitously deprive myself of food (as in extreme dieting inspired by vanity or a misplaced regard for a fashionable body weight); however, the ascetic's relation to God or the parents' relation to their children may make, not food and its consumption, but abstinence from eating food, the value.[24]

Again, where food is a value, that fact may not in itself indicate where one's moral obligation lies. Although there is a general obligation to help those who are hungry, parents have a special obligation to provide sustenance for their own children. Food may be just as much a value to strangers as to the parents' children; however, the overriding obligation of parents is first to provide food for their own offspring. What accounts for this being the parents' obligation is, of course, the special relationship that parents have to their own offspring and not the fact that food is a need for all concerned.

VII. Human Relationships and Incommensurability

As I remarked in Chapter 5, incommensurability in morality is often noted by moral pluralists, as it is for instance by Kekes and Crosby. Kekes observes that often values are both incommensurable and incompatible. One of Kekes's examples of incommensurable values is that of patriotism and spelunking. It is true that these values (and they are activities that may be valued) may "exclude any reasonable comparison," as Kekes says, if we try to compare the two activities as activities. Yet, as Kekes also says, a person could rank these values for her or his life. For, he allows, we can judge the "respective importance" of different values. "Some of these judg-

---

24. Kekes allows that "there may be occasions on which the claim of some particular form of nutrition, like bread, is defeated by the claim of some particular form of religious observance, like fasting." But, he says, "the second could defeat the first only in a context where the minimum requirements of the prevailing conceptions of a good life are generally met" (50). This assumes that religion cannot be a minimum requirement of a conception of a good life—something the religious would deny. Second, and more important for our present concern, it concedes that what is valued—fasting—is not grounded in, and goes counter to, a basic need.

ments [those based on secondary values] will be relative to traditions and conceptions of a good life, but some [those based on primary values] will not be."[25]

What is to be noted here is that the incommensurability of values like patriotism and spelunking does allow them to be compared as to their relative importance. It is at this point that *relationships* shed light on the comparison and moral ranking of values. Kekes sees that such a ranking may be relative (my word), but he does not identify the role of relationships in explaining that relativity. Consider patriotism and spelunking. There may be times when we can compare them in importance—moral importance—because we can judge how serious not fulfilling one relationship is, compared to not fulfilling other relationships. Say that one is a member of an extended family that values a show of patriotism on national holidays, but that in one's immediate family relations are strained. Spelunking, a newly discovered family activity, has come to provide an opportunity for members of the immediate family to share something and to renew their understanding and appreciation of one another. Things are such that attending the extended family's patriotic celebration rules out spelunking. In this scenario, the more important value may well be spelunking. In another setting—where spelunking is done for one's private enjoyment and not putting in an appearance at the family celebration would be deeply offensive to some family members—it may be more important to attend the patriotic family gathering.

The same would hold for those more basic values Kekes calls primary values, such as food, love, and respect. If a single man who has had little affection in his adult life meets a woman and they become friends with the evident possibility of a more affectionate relationship developing, his effort to nurture that relationship may properly cause the value of food to pale in significance. If, on the other hand, a man provides food for his several children by his labor, the value of food may take precedence over the pursuit of what, for him in this case, would be but a "love affair." Despite the sketchiness of these presentations, I think it is clear enough that the particulars of the relationships in them have a determining moral significance.

For Crosby, human beings have moral perspectives that are "shaped by the various cultures and historical epochs within which they find themselves"; and for Crosby's form of pluralism, these moral perspectives are incommensurable. So it is, he says, that what may seem "obvious and eminently reasonable from one perspective may appear quirkish and wrong-headed from another."[26] Crosby's

---

25. Kekes, *The Morality of Pluralism*, 77.
26. Crosby, "Civilization and Its Dissents," 114. Crosby holds that there is "some significant degree of incommensurability among perspectives," but he also says that they are frequently "com-

claim has both an intercultural and an intracultural application. I will consider both in connection with the importance of relationships. Although there may be a number of perspectives within a culture, still, as Crosby is aware, the moral perspectives of persons within a culture are partly shaped by their cultural setting. That this is so hardly seems deniable. But even if we allowed that each of us has a moral perspective that has been wholly formed by her or his culture, this in itself would not mean that we can only look at other cultures in terms of our own culture. With some attention and sensitivity to ways other than those with which we have grown up, we can, at least to some extent, assume a cultural perspective not our own. Nevertheless, many of us may fail to do so or may deliberately resist doing so.

Recall again, if you will, our discussion of Eskimo marital devotion: in traditional Eskimo society, marital devotion and fidelity do not require sexual exclusivity. Some in the predominant societies of North or South America or Europe may experience difficulty in appreciating the form of marital devotion in Eskimo marriages. They may also have difficulty appreciating the role of marital fidelity in households in Islamic cultures where a man may have four wives. Relationships, or a particular focus on marital—and sexual—relationships in our culture, explain why this may be so. If we judge marital relationships in other cultures in the light of those marital relationships and their requirements that we are familiar with in our culture or surroundings, then we will fail to appreciate the different ways marital fidelity can be expressed. Or if we allow there can be different expressions but judge them in terms of the relationships we know, we will feel other expressions of marital devotion to be deficient.[27]

Crosby's point in its intracultural application is illustrated by his example of the impasse in the abortion debate. One side regards abortion as the "murder of an innocent person, whereas the other has little difficulty in denying personhood to the fetus." Given such different moral perspectives, Crosby observes, appeals to such principles as "right to life" or "freedom of choice" simply beg the question and fail to address either perspective in a significant way.[28] Although there can

---

plementary," so that one perspective highlights goods that another tends to ignore (115), and that different perspectives "overlap" in areas of agreement (116–17).

27. Judging or understanding the marital relationships of other cultures in terms of the relationships of one's own culture is an instance of (or closely related to) what John W. Cook calls "the Projection Error" (*Morality and Cultural Differences*, 66). We will come back to this idea and the particular kind of ethnocentrism it represents in Chapter 8.

28. Crosby, "Civilization and its Dissents," 114 and 115. On this point Crosby cites Wolgast's discussion of abortion in her "Moral Pluralism."

be an issue about the moral status of abortion *after* it is allowed that a fetus is a person in a way Crosby does not mention, still one can agree with Crosby that the "abortion debate" at times comes down to the impasse he identifies.[29] When it does, there is a difference over the moral status of the fetus. But this is to say that there is a difference over the understanding of our *relationship* to the fetus—the relationship between the mother and the fetus, and the relationship between other persons and the fetus.

To sum up this section, the incommensurability of values like patriotism and spelunking, as presented by Kekes, is in accord with relationships contributing to, or wholly accounting for, the ranking(s) in the importance of such values, which Kekes rightly insists can be made. Where incommensurability applies to moral perspectives, as it does for Crosby, it may be a lack of understanding of the *forms* of relationships outside one's culture that accounts for instances of the incommensurability of moral perspectives across cultures. Within a culture, the incommensurability of perspectives may be due to different understandings of relationships, or even of their existence. For example, in the issue of abortion, at or near the bottom is the question of the possibility or impossibility of a morally significant relationship to a fetus as a person.

VIII. Conclusion

In this chapter I have begun to show how relationships between persons can address the moral diversity we experience in our multicultural world. The relationships to which I have appealed include the many common and familiar relationships that we all readily identify, such as the relationships we have to our friends, marital relationships, the relationship between parents and their children, and so on. I have also drawn attention to other relationships between persons, less personal but still palpable, such as the relationship we have to others in our community and the relationship we have to others in our society.

The moral diversity addressed and explained by relationships is, at one level, the diversity of moral *beliefs* that may be encountered in the world. More significantly,

---

29. Two philosophers who have argued that abortion in permissible even if a fetus is a person are Judith Jarvis Thompson in her often-cited paper "A Defense of Abortion," *Philosophy and Public Affairs* 1 (1971): 47–66; and Jane English, "Wrongs and Rights," *Canadian Journal of Philosophy* 5 (1975): 233–43.

the moral diversity that relationships explain is the diversity of actual *moralities* in the world. Relationships explain how there can be different moralities— different ways of honoring marital commitment, for instance—from one culture or society to another. And relationships can explain how there can be different moralities within a culture as well. As relationships explain both intercultural and intracultural diversity, they also explain the primary/secondary value distinction used by moral pluralists and the distinction between "thick" and "thin" morality.

Relationships, better than needs, I have argued, account for the source of various values; and relationships shed light on the ranking of values and on the incommensurability of values and moral perspectives.

In much of this chapter I have focused on *obligations,* and I have tried to show that a basic rubric applies to them: obligations have their source in, and are explained by, relationships. However, I have stressed that this rubric is not limited to obligations. In the next chapter I shall try to show how this basic rubric has a wider application, and I shall introduce a relationship between persons that further contributes to our understanding of moral diversity.

SEVEN

Moral Diversity and the Person/Person Relationship

In the last chapter I drew mostly on familiar relationships that we have no trouble identifying as "personal" relationships, such as marriage relationships and child-parent relationships. Such relationships are close, personal relationships in which the persons involved are well acquainted. However, many relationships between persons, such as our relationship to others in our larger urban community (if we live in a city), in our nation, and in our ethnic group, are not of this close personal character. We may not think about these relationships very often, but that does not mean they do not obtain. Another relationship that we may not think about much is the relationship we have to all persons—not by virtue of marriage, parenthood, friendship, citizenship, or ethnic identity—but simply by virtue of being persons. I shall call it the *person/person relationship*.

I. The Person/Person Relationship

As a relationship involving all persons, and one that each person has to each person by virtue of nothing more than being a person, this relationship extends to persons unseen by us and that we will never meet. It is also a relationship that each of us has to himself or herself. (That there are relationships we have to ourselves is indicated, for instance, by self-love and self-loathing.) In the last chapter I considered relationships as the basis for ranking the values of patriotism and spelunking. Which is the more important value, I argued, depends on how various *relationships* are affected, and I considered relationships one might have with one's extended family and with one's immediate family. We should now acknowledge that the relationship one has to oneself may also be relevant to the ranking—especially if what is involved is not merely one's own private enjoyment but something necessary for one's self-respect or self-esteem.

Relationships between persons, like the marital relationship and relationships of friendship, can be lived up to or violated. In the case of the familiar relationships that I have used for illustrations of various points, their requirements present themselves as recognizable obligations; thus, the requirement of marital fidelity is recognizable as a marital duty. The person/person relationship can also be violated when its requirements are not met. It also gives rise to obligations. The central requirement of the person/person relationship is that we treat persons *as persons*. We violate this relationship, as it exists between us and some other persons, when we fail to treat them with the kind of respect that persons deserve as persons.[1]

Not treating persons as they deserve can, of course, take many forms. We vio-

---

1. This is not to say that the person/person relationship requires us to treat other persons with *every* kind of respect; for instance, it does not require us to treat every person with that respect for mathematical expertise that we reserve for those who are expert in mathematics. Nor does it require us to approve of the actions of all persons. It does require us to treat persons as persons, which involves respecting them as persons or having some attitude like respect toward them. While I cannot here explore the *range* of attitudes that might meet this requirement, I have done so elsewhere (*Relationship Morality*, Chap. 5).

late the person/person relationship when we fail to keep the general obligation not to harm others and when we fail to observe the general obligation to be just in our dealings with others. Earlier I referred to the commonly agreed upon point that people owe it to one another to treat one another with justice. This, I observed, is a requirement of the general relationship people have to one another in the world, but I left it open whether this requirement extends to everyone or to only some significant population, such as one's own "people." Now we can say that to the extent that treating others with justice is a requirement of the person/person relationship, it extends to all persons—and so too for the other general obligations we have mentioned, such as the obligation not to harm others.

The person/person relationship is an underlying moral relationship: other specific and limited moral relationships presuppose it, at least as a test for what is allowable. Thus, whatever the requirements of a parent's relationship to her child may be in her specific and perhaps unique parent-child relationship, they will not allow her to fail to respect her child as a person. The person/person relationship explains why some personal relationships are themselves morally forbidden: rape, assault, abuse, domination, cruelty, and various "power relationships" are by their nature a violation of this basic relationship, for by entering such relationships, one treats another in a way that is incompatible with treating another as a person and hence violates the person/person relationship.

In this way the person/person relationship is the root explanation of why some agreements and the relationships they establish—such as an agreement between two men to murder one another's enemy—ought not to be entered and are not morally binding. In the last chapter I said that "relationships are a limiting factor on entered agreements; we cannot enter a morally binding agreement to do what grossly violates other relationships." Although this is true, we can now say that when our other relationships are grossly violated, we are not treating persons as they deserve to be treated as persons and are thus violating our person/person relationship to them.

II. The Person/Person Relationship and Recurring Basic Values

Though I think we would do well to recognize the person/person relationship as I have presented it, I will in Section VIII take up in a more critical way the question of whether there *is* the person/person relationship between persons. For the present, however, let us allow that there is this relationship. Under the scope of this assumption, we can appeal to the person/person relationship to explain why loyalty, fidelity, and other values recur in different cultures and within cultures. Being loyal to a friend in any of the various ways such loyalty is expressed in different cultures is an instance of respecting the requirement of this basic relationship between persons in one of the many ways that can be done. *Mutatis mutandis*, the same applies to marital relationships in their various cultural manifestations and to a range of other close personal relationships.

Again, if we are disloyal to our friend, or severely disloyal to her so that we discount her worth as a person, we violate both our friendship and the person/person relationship we have to our friend. *Mutatis mutandis*, the same holds for other close personal relationships, such as the marriage relationship. In respecting and living up to such personal relationships in their variegated forms across cultures, human beings begin to live up to the person/person relationship by treating others with the respect they deserve as persons. Similarly, when any in any culture have a concern that those discriminated against receive justice or that those who suffer in a natural disaster be given relief, they act in accord with the requirements of the person/person relationship.

My suggestion is that whenever we respect the requirements of a relationship we have to persons, we must be acting in accord with the person/person relationship, and whenever we grossly violate the requirements of some relationship, we ipso facto violate the person/person relationship as well. The person/person relationship, with its requirement that persons be treated as persons, is a kind of broad test for the range of forms of friendship relationships, marital relationships, and other types of personal relationships. However, it must be conceded that being clear on this much does not show us with any specificity what constitutes loyalty or disloyalty in friendship, or fidelity or infidelity in marriage, or what constitutes just treatment of others—in the same way that being clear that an abusive relationship violates the person/person relationship does not, in itself, tell us what constitutes abuse.

Nevertheless, we can be clear that (1) it is the underlying person/person relationship that explains the recurrence of, for instance, loyalty and fidelity relationships in their various forms across and within cultures, and that (2) whatever form such a relationship—say, a marital relationship with its requirement of fidelity—takes, it must not violate the person/person relationships and its requirement that persons, the persons in that marital relationship, be treated as persons.

Adultery

But what *specific* forms might marital fidelity take? Richard Wasserstrom has explored the role of sexual exclusivity in marriage and its connection to marital fidelity. He asks the question "Is adultery immoral?"—meaning, by *adultery*, "any case of extramarital sex."[2] In effect, he pursues the question of whether there can be a marital relationship that is not violated by extramarital sex. He considers two arguments against extramarital sex that are, he allows, "moral" arguments because they turn on what are clearly moral categories. One is that extramarital sex is immoral because it breaks a promise, namely, the marriage vow, which is a promise of much greater importance than other promises, and the breaking of which is more hurtful than the breaking of other promises. The second argument is that adultery is wrong because it involves deception. The deception may be active, as in the case of an overt lie, or passive, if no mention of the adultery is made (94–95). But there is a deeper and subtler form of deception, Wasserstrom brings out, which involves feelings of love and affection. Wasserstrom observes that "there is a connection in our culture between sexual intimacy and certain feelings of love and affection" (96), so that these feelings are associated with sexual intimacy. Related to this connection is the understanding, in our culture, "that sexual intercourse ought to be restricted to those who are married to each other, as a means by which to confirm the very special feelings that the spouses have for each other" (98). Revising and redirecting slightly the deception argument Wasserstrom offers, when adultery is committed under these conditions of understanding, deception about these feelings of affection seems unavoidable, for by committing adultery the adulterous spouse (let us make it the husband) will deceive his wife about his special feelings toward her.[3] Although Wasserstrom does not emphasize the point, both of the arguments he considers relate to the violation of relationships: the relationship we establish when we make a promise, the general relationship we have to others that requires us to be honest, and the marriage relationship itself.

    2. Richard Wasserstrom, "Is Adultery Immoral?" reprinted in *Philosophy and Sex*, ed. Robert Baker and Frederick Elliston (Buffalo, N.Y.: Prometheus Books, 1984), 93–106. Parenthetical page numbers in the following paragraphs refer to this work.
    3. Wasserstrom's argument regarding deception is more complex. It is in part that deception of someone seems unavoidable. "If the adulterous spouse does not in fact have the appropriate feelings of affection for the extramarital partner, then the adulterous spouse is deceiving that person about the presence of such feelings. If, on the other hand, the adulterous spouse does have the corresponding feelings for the extramarital partner but not toward the nonparticipating spouse, the adulterous spouse is very probably deceiving the nonparticipating spouse about the presence of such feelings toward that spouse" (98).

However, Wasserstrom raises these arguments in order to reply to them. He proceeds to imagine "what is sometimes characterized as an 'open marriage.'" It is a marriage in which a husband and wife have agreed that extramarital sex is acceptable and that there will be no deception, even regarding feelings of affection (101). Wasserstrom is not imagining a marital relationship in which the partners have agreed that *cheating* is allowable. He is imagining a marital relationship in which extramarital sex is not cheating, but openly agreed to. For such a marriage as this, sexual exclusivity is not required, Wasserstrom suggests—"at a minimum," he says, adultery cannot be morally condemned on the grounds that it breaks a promise or involves deception (101). If he is right, then *some* marital relationships would not be violated by extramarital sexual intimacy. Is Wasserstrom right? Is his imagined "open marriage" a real possibility for a marital relationship?

Wasserstrom's reasoning is that there *could be* marriage relationships in other cultures besides what he calls "our culture" (101) or "the dominant culture" (105) in which marriage and marital fidelity do not require sexual exclusivity. In fact, the example of Eskimo marriage and fidelity that we have discussed illustrates that there does indeed seem to be such a culture, as does the existence of marriages in Islamic cultures that need not be monogamous for men (although they must be for women).

Laurie Shrage has reflected on Wasserstrom's discussion of adultery. Without quite denying that Wasserstrom's suggestion is correct, she criticizes Wasserstrom on procedural grounds. Wasserstrom, she observes, "sees the distinctive peculiarities of the dominant culture's marital practices—e.g., their tendency to link sex and romantic love," but, she says, "he fails to see the distinctive peculiarities of the counterculture's practices—e.g., their tendency to promote sexual interactions outside of ongoing social relationships."[4] Her comment on the counterculture's practices draws attention to relationships and how for the counterculture there could be much sexual intimacy but no lasting personal relationship (as for one form of Aristotle's friendship between "young people"[5]). Eskimo marriages are different: in Eskimo culture, although extramarital sex is allowed, there is a lasting marital relationship.

Wasserstrom proceeds by presenting the best arguments he can devise for the immorality of adultery—and then refuting them. Shrage urges using an "interpretive" approach whereby we would both look at the marital ideal of the dominant culture from the standpoint of the counterculture and vice versa, working

---

4. Laurie Shrage, *Moral Dilemmas of Feminism* (New York: Routledge, 1994), 9, and see 9–10 and 40.

5. *Nicomachean Ethics* 1156b1–5.

toward a "compromise."[6] At bottom, however, the question is whether the person/person relationship is honored in the different forms of marital relationship. It is the answer to this question that provides the test for Wasserstrom's reasoning about the possibility of "open marriages" and for the moral status of the different viewpoints important for Shrage and any "compromise" between them. If the person/person relationship itself does not tell us all the forms of marriage that there might be, it does give us a broad means of testing the possible forms we might find or imagine.

One thing Wasserstrom and Shrage do not bring out is that it may be possible for us—in the "dominant culture," or that predominant in the Americas or Europe—to appreciate that marital fidelity can take a form that is foreign to marital fidelity as we know it and yet that entering such a relationship may not be open to us. Not all relationships are open to us: for instance, the relationship of feudal allegiance is not open to us because the societal structure it presupposes no longer exists. Other relationships may be theoretically open to us but realistically impossible, such as the relationship of the President of the United States to the people of the United States. But also it may be wrong for us to try to enter some relationships that we can see do not violate the person/person relationship in the lives of others, such as the Eskimo marriage relationship. Why? Because if *we* were to enter such a relationship, we would violate existing relationships we have, including the person/person relationship, but also other relationships that we have to those in our society, which are in part informed by societal and personal expectations. Thus, in our society for a young man to suggest to a young woman an open marriage—even with full consent by both—would run the risk of ultimately subjecting each to the other's disrespect and to the social distancing from many to whom they have other valuable relationships.

Autonomy

The person/person relationship helps us to explain and understand both the importance and the relative unimportance of certain values that may be given an almost a priori importance in some cultural settings.

Let us take an example from medical ethics and the culture of medical practice: autonomy. It is now widely allowed in the background theorizing about medical ethics and in the culture of medical practice that there are four principles that apply to the giving of medical care by medical practitioners: the principles of autonomy,

---

6. Shrage, *Moral Dilemmas of Feminism,* xii and 43.

nonmaleficence, beneficence, and justice. Since 1979, with the publication of Beauchamp and Childress's *Principles of Biomedical Ethics,* these principles have been carefully formulated and discussed in their biomedical application.[7] These moral principles, of course, are not limited to medical practice: each has a history in general ethical thought and moral application. The principle of autonomy (or the principle of respect for autonomy) affirms that individuals should make their own decisions without constraint by others.[8] It reaches back to the Enlightenment and to the moral thought of Immanuel Kant, and, as a general moral principle, connects to the concept of a moral or human right of individuals to act and make their own decisions "autonomously." Especially in its medical or biomedical application, this principle connects to "informed consent." In order to decide for ourselves about a medical procedure, we need to be given all pertinent information. It is the use of the principle of autonomy in the culture of medical practice that I want to look at here.

As Robert Baker points out, these four principles are "sometimes conflicting and sometimes convergent."[9] However, it is not this dimension of the principle of autonomy in its potential competition with the other three principles that concerns us. What concerns us amounts to a cultural difference about the principle of autonomy itself. It may seem nearly self-evident that patients should be fully informed about the medical procedures open to them and about the prognosis they face. It comes as something of a surprise, then, that in some cultures this may not be so.

For instance, investigators have found that those Navajos who follow the ways of traditional Navajo culture—as opposed to those "more acculturated to mainstream American society"—do not see their being informed about the negative aspects of their medical condition or the risks of treatment as a value. Important in traditional Navajo culture is the concept of *hózhó,* which "combines the concepts of beauty, goodness, order, harmony, and everything that is positive of ideal." To act in accord with this concept is to "think in the Beauty way" and "talk in the Beauty way," that is, to think and talk in a positive way. Being presented with negative medical information causes discomfort and goes counter to *hózhó,* and traditional Navajos might request medical providers seeking to present the facts necessary for a patient to be fully informed to *Doo'djíniidah* ("Don't talk that way").

---

7. Tom L. Beauchamp and James F. Childress, *Principles of Biomedical Ethics,* 3rd ed. (New York: Oxford University Press, 1979); and see Robert Baker, "A Theory of International Bioethics: The Negotiable and the Non-Negotiable," *Kennedy Institute of Ethics Journal* 8 (1998): 258–59.

8. This is one formulation. Cf. Beauchamp and Childress, *Principles of Biomedical Ethics,* 72.

9. Baker, "A Theory of International Bioethics: The Negotiable and the Non-Negotiable," 258.

In the background is the cultural belief that the language we use does not mirror reality, but can shape reality.[10] To be sure, it can be argued that autonomy and full disclosure are respected when the medical practitioner acts in accord the patient's decision not to be given full information.[11] However, at a minimum, the way that autonomy is respected—the role of providing pertinent information for an informed decision—would be different. And would it be contrary to *Doo'djíniidah* merely to ask Navajo patients if they want to be fully informed?

Similar findings regarding autonomy hold for different ethnic strains within mainstream American culture. Other investigators found in a study that "Korean-American and Mexican-American subjects were more likely to hold a family-centered model of medical decision making rather than the patient-autonomy model favored by most of the African-American and European-American subjects." Although most in all these ethnic groups wanted the family to be informed, in the Korean-American and Mexican-American groups individuals were more likely to believe that the family, and not the patient, should be told the truth. On the basis of their investigations, the authors of this report conclude with the suggestion that we broaden "our view of autonomy so that respect for persons includes respect for the cultural values they bring with them to the decision-making process."[12] What these authors see is that at times respect for persons requires that they *not* be treated with autonomy if autonomy is understood as making one's own informed decision. They suggest that a commitment to autonomy be kept, but that autonomy be construed to include "respect for cultural values."

I think we can appreciate that one way to respect individuals as persons—and to honor the person/person relationship—is to respect their wish to have their family act for them in making a serious medical decision. It may be too inclusive, though, to insist that all "cultural values" be respected in this context. We can imagine cultures where on the basis of gender half the population is not allowed to participate in medical decisions on their medical treatment. And might there not be instances when patients should be given negative and upsetting information about their medical condition that they do not want to hear (when it demeans them not

---

10. Joseph A. Carrese and Lorna A. Rhodes, "Western Bioethics on the Navajo Reservation: Benefit or Harm?" *Journal of the American Medical Association* 274, no. 10 (Sept. 13, 1995): 826–29.

11. This point is made in an editorial article in the same issue of *JAMA:* Lawrence O. Gostin, "Informed Consent, Cultural Sensitivity, and Respect for Persons," *Journal of the American Medical Association* 274, no. 10 (13 September 1995): 844.

12. Leslie J. Blackhall, Sheila T. Murphy, Gelya Frank, Vicki Michel, and Stanley Arzen, "Ethnicity and Attitudes Toward Patient Autonomy," *Journal of the American Medical Association* 274, no. 10 (13 September 1995): 820, 822, and 825.

to tell them), as well as other instances when it is better not to tell them and instead keep silent or give the news only to their family (when it is merely harmful to tell them)? Once more, it is the person/person relationship and its requirement that we respect persons as persons that provides the broad test here.

Abortion

Earlier, in our discussion of relationships and incommensurability, we saw that, for Crosby, there are two opposed perspectives on abortion. For one perspective, abortion is the murder of an innocent person, and for the other a fetus is not a person. The one perspective appeals to the fetus's right to life, and the other appeals to the freedom of choice of the woman who is pregnant. Although, as I noted earlier, the abortion issue can persist even after it is agreed that the fetus is a person, still Crosby's version of the issue may strongly echo the popular issue in what we may call "American mainstream society."[13] In this version, or a variant of it, one side appeals to the rights of the unborn, and the other appeals to the rights of women.

Here I will not try to show that the person/person relationship clearly establishes that abortion is right or that it is wrong, but I will try to show that in the area of abortion there are recurring values in different cultural settings that are accounted for by the person/person relationship, and that reflection on this relationship helps us to understand what is valued in various cultures.

Starting with American mainstream society, there does seem to be a strong bifurcation of opinion relating to the status of the fetus. Is the fetus a person or not? As I said earlier, the issue of the personhood of the fetus is the issue of our relationship to the fetus: Do we have a person/person relationship to the fetus? Clearly, at a minimum, much depends on whether we do or do not have this relationship to the fetus. If the issue is understood as an issue over *rights*—the rights of the woman in opposition to the rights of the unborn fetus—it is again an issue over relationships. The issue over rights, as a moral issue, relates to moral rights, not legal rights. The primary moral right that persons have is to be treated as a person. So once again the question arises: Do we have a person/person relationship to the fetus—a relationship that requires us to treat the fetus as a person?

But beyond this primary right to be treated as a person, there are other moral rights and candidates for moral rights. One is the right of a woman to make choices regarding her own body, and another is the right of an unborn person not to be

---

13. This is the term used by the authors of "Ethnicity and Attitudes Toward Patient Autonomy," quoted above. It seems equally serviceable in a discussion of cultural attitudes toward abortion.

harmed. Let us assume that a fetus is an unborn person; there still will be this secondary issue over which right takes precedence. How should we think about this secondary issue? One way is to think of it as the issue: Which is the greater violation of the person/person relationship: not respecting the woman's right, or not respecting the fetus's right? Putting the issue this way, of course, does not settle it. As I said, it is not my intention to try to show that abortion is right or that it is not right. My intention is to show how the "abortion issue" in its various cultural manifestations, including its form in American mainstream society, can be understood in terms of relationships, and the person/person relationship in particular.

If the issue of abortion has been much discussed in a highly visible, or audible, way in the United States, elsewhere it has not been. In India, for instance, according to Julius Lipner, the issue has not entered into the arena of public debate, although this is not to say that there is no cultural attitude toward abortion in India. Drawing upon classical Hindu texts, Lipner has written on abortion and the moral status of the unborn in the traditional Hindu view. The Hindu tradition "has always accorded personal moral status to the embryo/foetus throughout pregnancy," he concludes; and in the traditional Hindu view, abortion "at any stage of pregnancy has been morally condemned as violating the personal integrity of the unborn, save when it was a question of preserving the mother's life."[14]

Lipner cites several classical sources for this view. For one thing, he observes that in the moral evaluation of *śruti* (Hindu scriptures), those who practice abortion are mentioned with thieves and other offenders of *dharma* (the moral order). Lipner also finds that abortion is referred to in at least four contexts in the *Mahābhārata*—a vast Sanskrit epic from the early period of Hinduism that touches on politics, morality, and religion—and in each case "abortion was reckoned a serious wrong." On the other hand, the *Mahābhārata* and other epics contain many stories of *apparent* abortions or miscarriages that come to term by some means, so that "in the end the sanctity of the embryo is upheld." Moreover, both belief in *karma* (meritorious and unmeritorious action) and rebirth, and in the principle of

---

14. Julius J. Lipner, "The Classical Hindu View on Abortion and the Moral Status of the Unborn," in Harold G. Coward, Julius J. Lipner, and Katherine K. Young, *Hindu Ethics: Purity, Abortion and Euthanasia* (Albany: State University of New York Press, 1989), 60. Lipner tells the following from his own experience: when he visited two well-known universities in India, he offered a range of topics for seminar discussion or public lecture, including the topic of abortion and the moral status of the unborn; this topic was politely declined by the Indian institutions "on 'cultural' grounds." Later he visited a university in Canada and one in the United States, and he offered the same range of topics; at these institutions this topic was the one preferred (61 n.1).

ahiṃsā (non-injury) in traditional Hinduism militated against performing abortions. The belief in *karma* and rebirth opposed abortion in that abortion would cut short the developing of the effects of past *karma* in a person's life and affect that person's destiny and progress toward liberation from rebirth; and *ahiṃsā*, though more ambiguous in its influence in the Hindu tradition than in the Jaina and Buddhist traditions, opposed abortion in that "since abortion entailed the inflicting of (mental and) physical violence to the point of death on the unborn person, it flew in the face of the ingrained reference for (the seed of) life."[15]

While Lipner's subject is the traditional Hindu view, as indicated in classical Sanskrit texts (ranging from 600 B.C.E. to 600 C.E.), and not a sociological study of contemporary Indian views on abortion, he observes that it "is typically Hindu to debate an important issue for life with reference to traditional religious and moral roots." Though in modern India abortion is permitted by law under certain circumstances, the issues relating to abortion have not been given a full public discussion. Yet Lipner cites a "modern debate that is already emerging," and in this respect the "Hindu stress on the wider social and moral obligations attaching to pregnancy (not excluding those to the child-to-be and the father), rather than the making of pregnancy a matter exclusively of individual rights (especially of the mother) must be noted."[16] Lipner's allusion to the debate in the West with its emphasis on rights is clear enough. He refers to an article by Veena Das on the abortion debate in which she says, "We have been tricked by modern philosophy into thinking that the morality of abortion involves strictly the relation of a WOMAN to the foetus. In fact this dyadic relationship is embedded into a number of relationships involving not only the responsibility of a genitor to the embryo/foetus, but also the relationship of adult men and women. Further this arrangement of relationships involves the rest of society."[17]

Lipner, and especially Das, make clear the connection of the abortion issue and relationships in the emerging Indian debate: not only the relationship between the woman and the fetus, but other relationships between persons in society, including but not limited to relationships involving the father, are recognized as morally relevant. Although neither Lipner nor Das draws explicitly upon the concept of a relationship that binds all persons as persons, that relationship—the person/person relationship—helps to explain how the "arrangement" of the various morally relevant relationships "involves the rest of society." Moreover, the traditional Hindu

15. Lipner, "The Classical Hindu View on Abortion," 43–44, 46–48, 57, and 59.
16. Ibid., 60 and 61.
17. Veena Das, "The Debate on Abortion," *Seminar* (Nov. 1983): 34. Cited by Lipner, "The Classical Hindu View on Abortion," 69 nn. 73 and 74.

view is a nearly verbatim embrace of the existence of the person/person relationship as far as the fetus is concerned.

Finally, in our discussion of abortion under the topic heading of recurring values, let us look at Buddhist tradition and culture. Earlier, in Chapter 2, on the question of whether there are universal moral values, I drew attention to the Five Precepts of Buddhism, the first of which is "to abstain from the taking of life." This precept is binding on all Buddhists, and we will recall that for some commentators on Buddhism, it is seen as binding on all "rational beings." Is it understood to cover abortion? Shundo Tachibana observes that of the 227 precepts that relate to the Buddhist monk or *bhikku,* the four most grave are the *Pārājikās,* the transgressing of which can result in a monk's expulsion from the monkhood. The third *Pārājikā* regards "killing a human being," and Tachibana says that according to Buddhist commentary "abortion or the destruction of life in the womb" are counted as transgressions of this rule.[18] Although Tachibana does not say so, it would seem that this implication would hold for the precept against the "taking of life," binding on all Buddhists.

P. D. Premasiri, in an essay on the ethics of the Theravada tradition, observes, "While contraceptive birth control would not be objectionable from the point of view of Buddhist morality, abortion is definitely condemned on moral grounds," and he refers to the *Pārājikā* discussed by Tachibana. However, he goes on to say that one could "question whether abortion is unconditionally a moral evil from the Buddhist point of view." Premasiri points out that "the reasons given in Buddhism for abstaining from the destruction of life are, the evil nature of the psychological source of such action, the resulting damage to one's character, and a need for sensitivity to the interests of other sentient beings who have similar psychological, physical, and emotional constitutions." But in "dilemmatic situations" there are no "hard and fast moral rules." He considers a case "in which it is medically determined that the child that the young mother is carrying is stricken with some complication that could result in its being born with serious abnormalities, and that the birth would be at the cost of the mother's life." Here, Premasiri says, "the physician . . . might hold the opinion that it is morally more worthwhile to save the mother, and that abortion is the best recourse in this difficult situation," whereas the "mother may . . . reckon this situation as an opportunity to cultivate her moral character by determining to sacrifice her life for the sake of her child." Both judgments are countenanced by the Buddhist point of view, the mother's judgment or decision relating most obviously to the Buddhist doctrines of *kamma*

---

18. Tachibana, *The Ethics of Buddhism,* 80–81.

(or *karma*) and rebirth, and the Buddhist understanding that each individual is on a *samsaric* journey (of rebirth) heading toward the ultimate goal of *Nibbāna*. Also countenanced would be the mother's possible judgment that she should have an abortion for the sake of her other children's well-being. "From the Buddhist point of view," says Premasiri, "what is of primary moral importance in situations of this sort is the goodness of the intention."[19] In the case of each judgment, from the Buddhist point of view, the proper basis is concern for the well-being of those making their way toward the goal of *nibbanic* perfection. This concern extends to all sentient beings, and particularly to human beings, since in the *samsaric* cycle of rebirth one must be a human to attain *Nibbāna*.

In effect, then, there is in Buddhist thought an implicit respect for the person/person relationship—even if the way persons and their well-being are understood is distinctly Buddhist. We see this implicit respect in the Buddhist respect for all human persons and for all sentient beings (which, for Buddhism, are potential human persons). We also see it in the thinking that there is no absolute moral rule about abortion, but rather, where the health of the mother is at risk or she has other children to care for, different judgments about having an abortion are countenanced by Buddhism. This is just the outcome we should expect if the moral requirements of different relationships are considered along with an effort to respect the well-being of all persons affected in accord with the person/person relationship.

However, Buddhism has interacted with different cultures, and these interactions can result in culture-specific manifestations of Buddhism. Such an interaction has occurred in Japan, with interesting ramifications for abortion. At present there is a high abortion rate in Japan, and Japanese Buddhism has responded to and accommodated the practice of abortion. William LaFleur, in his book on abortion and Japanese Buddhism, observes that there is currently no debate in Japan over abortion (there was a debate, but it took place more than a century ago). As things are, because the use of the contraceptive "pill" is resisted by Japan's doctors, abortion is widely practiced by Japanese couples as "the main contraceptive method" available to them.[20]

In Buddhist temples a service for aborted fetuses is available. This ritual, called *mizuko kuyō*, is a memorial rite for "miscarried, aborted or dead-born babies," but in today's Japan in by far the majority of cases it is offered for aborted babies or fetuses. A growing number of Buddhist temples in Japan offer such services, and

---

19. P. D. Premasiri, "Ethics of the Theravada Buddhist Tradition," in *World Religions and Global Ethics*, 56–57.

20. William R. LaFleur, *Liquid Life: Abortion and Buddhism in Japan* (Princeton: Princeton University Press, 1992), 103 and 136. Parenthetical page numbers in the next paragraphs refer to this work.

in fact, there is now a new kind of Buddhist temple "for which the mizuko kuyō is the original and only reason for the temple's existence" (4–5).

The Japanese term for an aborted fetus or a dead or stillborn infant is *mizuko,* which literally means "water-child." LaFleur brings out the connection to the *Kojiki,* an early Japanese myth in which the primal couple make "a ritual mistake" and give birth to a "leech-child." They place it in a reed boat and float it away back to the waters. In Japanese mythology, as in other mythological traditions, water symbolizes the source of life as well as death, LaFleur notes. This element from Japanese culture, we may say, complements the Buddhist contribution to Japanese thinking about abortion and amends the *early* Buddhist rejection of water as symbolic of life (22–23, 17).

For the Japanese, coming into life and dying are progressive. Each is a long process. Being born "is really taking progressive leave of the world of gods and Buddhas and entering that of humans." For this way of thinking, one is not fully human at the instant of birth. Rather, one goes through a series of stages in childhood, and only at age 21 (age 15 in the medieval period) does one become an adult or *ichinin* (literally "one human"). Dying is a continuation of the process during which one passes through adulthood and old age, finally taking leave of the human world and returning to the sacred realm, from which one may be reborn. Until modern times there were no funerals for children—because they had not entered the world as an *ichinin* (33–35, 39).

A water-child is very far from being fully a human, having only begun to take shape as a human-being-to-be. Returning to the waters and having become "liquid," it is dead (24), but also it has returned to a state from which it can be reborn. It is worth noting that a fetus in Japan is often referred to as a child—even by a couple with plans to abort it (11). Thus, the *mizuko kuyō* is for children or for babies who are miscarried, stillborn, or aborted. These children, though dead, are in some way still "alive"—in that they are capable of returning to the sacred realm, from which they can be reborn into the human world (9). In this way of thinking, for those who die as children or are not born, there is a return to the sacred realm of gods and Buddhas whence they have so recently come—not through completing the entire cycle of adulthood and old age, but through a brief reverse journey. It is only a small step to the perception that parents can intervene and take action to return the fetus to the sacred world—and this is what abortion accomplishes (37, 40). This understanding of abortion makes sense in terms of the Japanese and Buddhist conception of birth and dying.

A significant Buddhist contribution to the Japanese understanding of abortion is the Jizō figure. Jizō is a divine being in the Buddhist pantheon, a Bodhisattva (a Buddhist savior), and a figure of compassion especially for children. In contemporary Japan, little statues of Jizō are found in many places, including street corners, and there is a Jizō cult in popular Japanese Buddhism (44). In the temples where the *mizuko kuyō* is performed, in the cemeteries for children, there may be rows of Jizō images, small stone statues, all about the same size and with the same basic form (6). Each has been set up by parents for their dead child, most often their aborted child. The Jizō figure has a double aspect. On the one hand, the figure has the bald tonsure, half-closed eyes, attire, and tranquil, meditative expression of a monk; on the other hand, it is the size of a very small child, wears a bib of the sort infants wear, and has been given toys. In this way the Jizō figure represents at once the Buddhist savior in monk's robes and the parents' dead child—the first acting to save, and the second being saved (6, 8, 53).

LaFleur observes that the Japanese offer *kuyō* rites (rituals of memorialization) for dead relatives, and that doing so seems to be part of Buddhism in all the cultures into which Buddhism has penetrated. Moreover, he and others point out, the Japanese offer *kuyō* rites for many kinds of objects that have given service, including needles, dolls, chopsticks, and pairs of spectacles, offering thanks without any suggestion of guilt. There also is a yearly *kuyō* for eels, offered by restaurateurs and their customers, presided over by Buddhist priests, offering thanks and also, since eels have "life" in them, apology, LaFleur says. He further suggests that in *kuyō* rites there is a continuum of what these rites express, ranging from pure thanks (as for everyday objects like needles), to thanks with a modicum of apology (as for eels), to "almost exclusively guilt" (as "when fetuses are involved," in the *mizuko kuyō*) (144–46).

What emerges here is that the Japanese acknowledge guilt for abortion, and the widespread participation in the *mizuko kuyō* ritual reflects this. However, there is no sense of a great moral issue over the practice of abortion as there is in American society. LaFleur writes, "The problem as perceived by most Buddhists has not been over the morality of abortion per se [but] over the propriety and morality of tatari, the notion that the spirit of an aborted fetus is causing harm to its parents or siblings still in the world" (163). The concern is with how this sense leads to extortion and the manipulation of those parents who feel guilty.

The respect of Japanese for relationships makes understandable the practice of Japanese parents apologizing to their aborted fetuses, for we can understand their apology in terms of their honoring their relationship to their "child," as we can understand their guilt as arising from a violation of that relationship. That is, the act of apology makes it manifest that a relationship—a personal relationship—to the aborted child is acknowledged. Furthermore, in some sense, even though their water-child is far from being fully human (an *ichinin*), the status and worth of their "child" is implicitly acknowledged by their apology as well as by their hope, prayer, and expectation that their child is "saved" by Jizo and returned to the sacred realm. That such a status is acknowledged by Japanese parents is explainable in terms of a respect for what I am calling the person/person relationship as it includes the human-being-to-be that is their aborted "child."

Although the person/person relationship in itself does not tell us the many ways we can respect persons as persons in the many personal relationships open to us, it does provide us with a broad test for what is allowed in those relationships: we must not fail to treat others as persons in our relationships to them. And it gives us an explanation of recurring values in their different forms. Friendship and marital fidelity are able to take the different forms we observe because these different forms are all in accord with the person/person relationship. And the person/person relationship helps us to understand how other recurring values can take different cultural forms. It gives us an understanding of different forms of autonomy in contexts of medical treatment, and of how autonomy in its narrow or strict form may be wrong at certain times and in certain cultural settings. In regard to abortion, the person/person relationship provides, in some cases, a kind of broad test for conflicting claims (about rights); while in other cases, it provides a backdrop of understanding for the different ways that abortion and the relationship to the unborn fetus or aborted "child" is thought of in different cultures.

III. The Person/Person Relationship and Transcultural Values

Let us designate values that are understood to apply across cultures as *transcultural values*—values that can be applied by one society to another and can be applied to several societies at once. Such values allow us to ask of a given society how well or to what extent that society respects the transcultural value in question, and they make it possible for us to recognize, or judge, that a culture or society has practices that are "evil" or morally wrong. Many if not all of Kekes's and Harbour's primary values, and Walzer's thin values, are transcultural in this sense; whereas Kekes's and Harbour's secondary values, and Walzer's thick values, would not be. Transcultural values also allow us to say that there are duties or obligations that hold across societies and that one society may have toward the populations of other societies. Some candidates for transcultural values are justice, respect for human rights, and a concern for human welfare in the face of deprivation or suffering.

In Section II of the last chapter, I argued that human relationships account for primary values (as well as for their secondary expressions) and that the obligation people have to treat one another with justice (in its "thin" form, as Walzer would say) is a requirement of "the general relationship people have to one another in the world." In this chapter I have identified that "general relationship" as the person/person relationship. To this extent we have already seen how one transcultural value—justice—rests upon the person/person relationship. In Section IV of the last chapter, I argued that relational differences explain moral differences better than do different societal practices because societal practices can be evil in that they may allow social relationships that are morally wrong. I offered several historical examples—slavery as practiced in the American South and "honor killings"—although I did not *argue* that they are indeed evil practices. Other intuitively clear examples of evil social practices might include discrimination against those of one gender or ethnic type and gratuitous cruelty toward some members of the society. I submit that we are capable of recognizing at least aggravated examples of such evil practices.

Allow me to use a constructed example to underline the point in graphic terms (with apologies to Jonathan Swift). Imagine a society in which it was considered permissible for those who had wealth or social privilege to abduct, from the poorer sections of the society's cities, young boys for their own purposes. These boys would be Shanghaied, as it were, but they would not be pressed into any kind of work. Instead, they would be taken to some chamber; and there, for the amusement of the privileged, they would be sexually tortured for hours and finally killed in some gruesome way—after which a small cash payment might or might not be anonymously made to the boys' families, this not being mandatory.

How is it that we can recognize these practices and the social relationships they allow as wrong? The explanation that we may now offer is that we can because these practices grossly violate transcultural values such as justice and respect for human rights. And these values are transcultural because they exist by virtue of a transcultural relationship between persons, namely, the person/person relationship, which is a relationship that persons have to persons by virtue of being persons, across geographical and cultural boundaries. We can recognize "evil" societal practices because we can see, or judge, that they violate transcultural values and ultimately the person/person relationship, regarding at least some persons. *Mutatis mutandis,* the same point holds for evil personal values and evil agreements.

Transcultural values also allow us to recognize *duties* that are transcultural, that is, duties that extend beyond cultural limits, such as the obligation to provide famine relief for societies other than our own. Consider the obligation to provide famine relief.

It is true that there is an issue about what form the provided famine relief should take. In fact, there may be an issue about whether famine relief should be provided at all. But these issues can be addressed in the light of the requirements of the person/person relationship and other relationships that we or others might have. Regarding the first, the person/person relationship itself leaves open the form that famine relief might, or ought to, take. Other relationships that we have or that others are in, however, can resolve this issue. Let us say that it is a Muslim society that is in need of food. Our knowledge of Muslim practice (which is a part of the understanding Muslims have of their relationship to God and what it requires) and a respect for the relationship that we have with those in the Muslim society (which would require us not to offend their religious sensibilities) would indicate that our offered famine relief should not be in the form of tinned ham. The issue of whether famine relief ought to be provided at all, on the other hand, is an issue about conflicting obligations—that is, it is an issue about the conflicting requirements of different relationships we have. Thus, in one case, the issue might be about the conflict between obligations to provide relief (arising from the person/person relationship we have to those in need of relief) and the obligation to provide for family members (arising from our relationship to those in our family). Some think that famine relief ought not to be given to starving peoples because doing so will dangerously increase the world population and ultimately harm posterity.[21] This version of the issue also is understandable in terms of relationships: our relationship to those in need of famine relief, and our relationship to future generations.

It must be granted that utilitarian and deontological ethical theories can also begin to address these issues. However, they do not so much give us an understanding of the issues and the subtleties of the requirements of relationships, as they dictate a final moral judgment on the basis of a proffered "first principle." As a consequence of their setting up a rigid "criterion" or "standard," invariably utilitarian and deontological theories of obligation suffer counterexamples. On the other hand, the appeal to human relationships and the person/person relationship does not run afoul of counterexamples because it sets up no such rigid criterion.

I conclude that (1) transcultural values account for our ability to recognize or judge that there are evil societal practices (and evil personal values and evil agreements), and the person/person relationship accounts for these transcultural values, and (2)

---

21. Garrett Hardin, "Lifeboat Ethics: The Case Against Helping the Poor," *Psychology Today* magazine (1974); reprinted as "The Error of Famine Relief," in *Ethics for Modern Life*, ed. Raziel Abelson and Marie-Louise Friquegnon (New York: St. Martin's, 1995).

transcultural values account for our ability to recognize or judge that there are transcultural obligations that extend to other societies, and the person/person relationship accounts for such transcultural obligations. However, although it seems to me that such recognitions are in a number of cases unavoidable, and that the judgments that correlate with them are correct, I will put this section's conclusion more circumspectly: let it be that *if* there are such recognitions or judgments, they are to be explained in terms of transcultural values, which are in turn explained by the person/person relationship.

IV. The Person/Person Relationship, Other Relationships, and Indeterminacy

Moral decisions about what one should do can at times be clear—sometimes disconcertingly clear, requiring no deliberation. The requirements of a relationship may be this evident. At other times the right course of action may be difficult to discern; in fact, regarding some moral issues we may feel that there is an indeterminacy. Just as relationships can make understandable the obligations we recognize, so relationships can help us understand the indeterminacy that sometimes relates to moral decisions.

Perhaps one example of an indeterminate moral issue is the issue of abortion. (Earlier I tried to show how the issue of abortion was understandable in terms of relationships, not that considering relationships would lead forthrightly to a clear judgment about the rightness or wrongness of abortion.) Other issues that are indeterminate may be euthanasia and capital punishment. These issues are indeterminate in at least the sense that they persist well into the small hours of discussion, long after each side has had its say, and that they resist the most careful and sincere efforts at resolution. They may also be indeterminate in the stronger sense that in principle they can have no satisfactory resolution. In either case, as things stand, it is unclear what would settle them to the satisfaction of all or most people.

Another apparently indeterminate moral issue is whether torture is always wrong. It seems clear that torture is *often* wrong, but whether it is always wrong is another matter. Philip Quinn allows that "the shared morality of our society holds that torture is generally wrong," but he recognizes that there is a deep rift of opinion over some "hard cases" of torture. He presents this case:

Suppose the only way to find out where a bomb is located in an airplane, before it explodes and kills all on board, is to torture the terrorist who planted it. Does the prospect of saving many lives that would otherwise be lost render it morally permissible for security forces to torture the terrorist? Or suppose the terrorist would remain mute under torture but would crack if her child were tortured before her eyes. Would it be morally right for security forces to torture the terrorist's child? Respectable opinion divides on the answers to questions about such hard cases.[22]

Quinn himself, however, holds that torture is always wrong. He is, he says, an absolutist "of a sort" in that he thinks "that the moral prohibition of torture is binding on absolutely everyone and at all times." Appreciating that many will not agree, Quinn seeks an argument that will justify to everyone the conclusion that torture is always wrong. Such an argument he cannot find, but he expresses hope for the prospect that multiple arguments can lead to an "overlapping consensus" about torture always being wrong.[23] What I find interesting is that he does not return to his terrorist/airplane example and say that in this case, too, torture is wrong; rather, his last word about this example is that respectable opinion is divided.

It is a virtue of the idea that relationships are structurally basic to our obligations that it leaves unclear what is unclear and leaves indeterminate what is indeterminate in morality. If we give attention to relationships, especially the person/person relationship, we can explain the indeterminacy of Quinn's terrorist/airplane case. On the one hand, torture is wrong because it violates our person/person relationship to the one tortured (and perhaps to others, such as the terrorist mother, if her child is tortured), while, on the other hand, not preventing the bomb's exploding on the airplane is wrong because our not acting discounts the value of the persons on the airplane and violates our person/person relationship to them. The resolution of this conflict is indeterminate, if it is, because it is indeterminate which violation of the person/person relationship is the most serious.

But let us go beyond Quinn's discussion of the torture issue. Joseph Runzo, commenting on Quinn's discussion, maintains that from "the moral point of view" we can justify the principle that torture is always wrong. "The reason torture is always wrong," for Runzo, "is that torture inherently treats the person being tortured as an 'it'; torture is diametrically opposed to treating a person as a 'thou.'" Torture

---

22. Philip L. Quinn, "Relativism about Torture: Religious and Secular Responses," in *Religion and Morality*, ed. D. Z. Phillips (New York: St. Martin's, 1996), 151.
23. Ibid., 153 and 167.

"can never be used for treating persons as an end in themselves," and torture "violates the moral point of view itself."[24] But is Runzo right? Surely he is for cases of gratuitous torture. Still, might there not be times when torture is carried out for the sake of the person tortured? On some accounts, in the medieval period torture for heresy was administered (in part) out of a concern for the welfare of the heretic: those heretics who died without recanting were denied eternal salvation, it was believed.[25] Here it seems torture was administered with respect for the worth of the person, despite the infliction of terrible pain.

Though we may suspect the historical accuracy of such accounts of inquisitorial intention, our doing so is beside the present point. And if we persist in condemning such torture, isn't it because we cannot see *how* it can be for the good of the one tortured, how it could possibly be thought to be in accord with respect for persons (and with the person/person relationship and its requirement that persons be treated as persons)? Of course, in Quinn's terrorist/airplane case, in the first version where the terrorist is being tortured (and not her child), the terrorist is being tortured exclusively for the sake of others, those on the airplane. Or so it seems. Could it be that one intending an intensely evil act could be tortured to gain information to avert the completion of the intended act at least in part for his or her own sake, to prevent the soul-destroying burden of such a responsibility?

However, let us allow that the terrorist in Quinn's case is being tortured for the sake of others exclusively. Then, as Runzo suggests, the terrorist is treated as a means only and is not being treated as a person. The problem is, as many will say, if she is not tortured, the security forces, by their act of omission, do not treat those on the airplane as individuals with the value of persons. In either case, it seems, someone is not treated as a person, and that is to say that the person/person relationship is violated. In this case it is the apparently unavoidable violation of that relationship that accounts for the strong appearance of indeterminacy.

Let us consider one other example, an example in which relationships other than the person/person relationship explain indeterminacy. I have in mind the Clinton "scandal" involving his relationship with Monica Lewinsky. The description of the relationship itself is difficult enough. Who was the initiator? To what extent was it consensual? Was the relationship of president to intern such that,

---

24. Joseph Runzo, "Reply: Ethical Universality and Ethical Relativism," in *Religion and Morality*, 182 and 183.
25. See *Summa Theologica*, II–II, q. 11, a. 4 for Aquinas' treatment of the question of "Whether the Church should receive those who return from heresy?" The good of the heretic is not irrelevant to his consideration.

by taking the role he did in their sexual relationship, he was virtually bound to take advantage of her?

But let us focus on other relationships in order to bring out the indeterminacy of the precipitated moral question: Should the president be impeached? Our question is not the legal or constitutional question, but the moral question whether the president ought to be impeached. On the moral question of the president's impeachment, national opinion was unevenly divided. It is this division, and the question's resistance to resolution—its indeterminacy—that is explained by a recognition of the moral importance of relationships and of the underlying person/person relationship. Some thought that, although Clinton may have broken trust with his wife and daughter and with his associates, and although he may have lied to or misled many, including the American people, he still was an effective president. That is, they thought that though he had violated his relationships to his wife and his daughter, and to his associates, and even his relationship of trust to the American people, he had maintained the more important leadership relationship to the nation, his presidential relationship. Others thought that by doing all that he did, he showed he was unfit to continue as president. That is, they thought that in violating the relationships he did, he finally violated the presidential relationship itself. In this case too, then, relationships provide the key to understanding the issue's indeterminacy, although it is not the competing demands of different relationships that explain the indeterminacy but the different ways of understanding the demands of the relationships involved.

Similar comments hold for the other chief candidates for indeterminate moral issues: abortion, capital punishment, euthanasia, and others. That is, if they are indeterminate, the explanation for that indeterminacy is in terms of the irresolvable competing demands of relationships and the opposed understandings of the demands of relationships. True, one can begin to account for such moral indeterminacy in terms of conflicting principles or moral duties, but the deeper explanation is in terms of relationships. For relationships account for principles and moral duties, not the other way around.

V. The Person/Person Relationship and Duties to Oneself

The person/person relationship also explains duties to oneself. That one can have, and does have, moral duties to oneself has been acknowledged by many who have reflected on morality and is, I think, in accord with a widely shared moral intuition.[26] Not all, to be sure, have recognized duties to oneself. Mill apparently did not.[27] But Kant did.[28]

We readily think of some moral duties we have, such as the duty to stand up for what we believe in or to enhance our understanding, as duties to oneself. We may also speak of our *right* to stand up for what we believe in or to enhance our understanding. Both claims may be correct. Moreover, the duty that one has to oneself to stand up for what one believes in may also be a duty to others. Often this may be the case with duties to oneself, but this would not mean that such duties were not to oneself; it would mean that they are *also* duties to others. Further candidates for duties to oneself are, for instance, the duty not to let oneself go in some form of self-indulgence and the duty not to sell short one's capacities.

There is, as we may say, what "we owe to ourselves," what each owes to herself or himself. Kant, in his consideration of duties to oneself, said, "Man owes it to himself . . . not to let his natural predilections and capacities . . . remain unused, and not to leave them, as it were to rust."[29] I quote Kant here, not to appeal to his authority regarding a specific duty to oneself to develop one's capacities, but to show that he took seriously the idea that we could owe to ourselves something, which then has the status of a duty we have to ourselves.

Marcus Singer, on the other hand, understands "I owe it to myself to . . ." as at most an expression of a right, or of one's determination, or perhaps a nonmoral prudential judgment about what is in one's "interest."[30] It does seem to me that very often these days when we say "I owe it to myself to . . ." or "You owe it to yourself to . . ." something along these lines is being said. Thus, to use a variant of Singer's example, when one says, for instance, "I owe it to myself to take a vacation" this may mean something like "I would be foolish not to take a vacation" or perhaps only "I'd like a vacation and I fully intend to take one!" But this being so does not show that there are no duties we have to ourselves or that we never

---

26. Two contemporary moral philosophers who recognize or seriously consider duties to oneself are Thomas E. Hill Jr., in "Servility and Self-Respect" and "Self-Respect Reconsidered," both reprinted in his *Autonomy and Self-Respect* (Cambridge: Cambridge University Press, 1991), 17 and 24; and Christine M. Korsgaard, in "The Reasons We Can Share: An Attack on the Distinction Between Agent-Relative and Agent-Neutral Values," 302, n. 3; and "Personal Identity and the Unity of Agency: A Kantian Response to Parfit," reprinted in *Creating the Kingdom of Ends*, 381–82.

27. John Stuart Mill, *On Liberty*, ed. Elizabeth Rapaport (Indianapolis, Ind.: Hackett, 1978), 76–77.

28. Immanuel Kant, *Metaphysical Principles of Virtue*, "First Part of the Elements of Ethics: Concerning Duties to Oneself," *Akademie* edition (Ak.), 417–47.

29. Ibid., Ak. 444.

30. Marcus George Singer, *Generalization in Ethics* (New York: Alfred A. Knopf, 1961), 314.

appeal to them. Singer believes that we may have come to think that there are duties to oneself because of a confusion about "self-regarding duties." There can be self-regarding duties in the sense of duties that primarily affect oneself, Singer allows, but such duties *regarding* oneself are not ipso facto duties *to* oneself.[31] If the latter is Singer's point, then here too he may be correct. But, again, this does not rule out there being genuine duties to oneself.

Singer argues against the idea of duty to oneself on the grounds that if one had an obligation to oneself, then one could release oneself from the obligation simply by not wishing to perform the action. He argues that one can always release *another* from an obligation because one can give up his or her right, but if one could release oneself from an obligation, this would make a mockery of the concept of obligation. In connection with this point, Singer considers promises. The one to whom a promise was made can release the promisor by giving up his or her right to have the promise kept, but although the promisor could, of course, break the promise, the promisor cannot release herself or himself from its obligation.[32] Singer's point holds well enough for promises and for certain other rights, such as property rights. In these cases one can give up one's right and so release others from their obligation. But this point does not hold across the board. Parents have duties toward their children from which their children, at least while they are young children, cannot release them. Here rights cannot be given up. The explanation for this difference is that the relationship entered by making a promise is quite different from the relationship existing between parents and their children. The relationship that is created when another makes one a promise is dissolved when one releases the promisor. The parent-child relationship cannot be similarly dissolved. In the case of duties to oneself, it is the person/person relationship that is their source; and this relationship operates more like the parent-child relationship than like the relationship entered by making a promise. Just as the child cannot give up his or her right and so release the parents from their duty because the child cannot dissolve the parent-child relationship, so one cannot release oneself from a duty to oneself because one cannot dissolve the person/person relationship one has to oneself.

Given the person/person relationship, we can understand that there are duties *to* oneself, not just *regarding* oneself. For one is related to oneself in this relationship

---

31. Ibid., 316. Kant uses this same distinction to argue that those who think we have moral obligations toward "other beings" such as nonhuman animals confuse "duty *regarding* other beings with a duty *toward* these beings." "Metaphysical Principles of Virtue," Ak. 442, in Immanuel Kant, *Ethical Philosophy*, trans. James W. Ellington (Indianapolis, Ind.: Hackett, 1983), 105 (emphasis in the text).

32. Singer, *Generalization in Ethics*, 313.

just as much as one is related to any other person; and just as one can violate the person/person relationship to other persons by not treating one of them as a person, so one can violate the person/person relationship to oneself by not treating oneself as a person. The person/person relationship is the source of the *primary* duty to treat oneself as a person. What is involved in treating oneself as a person may be open to question. But surely it involves respect for one's "dignity" as a person,[33] that is, the inherent worth one has as a person. So it is that self-abasement, or degrading oneself with over-indulgence, or not realizing one's clear potential may be violations of this relationship. The connection to self-respect that our earlier examples had—those relating to self-indulgence and developing our capacities—is not accidental.

However, the range of duties to oneself may be much broader than our earlier examples might suggest. One can have a duty to, say, one's child and at the same time a duty to oneself relating to one's child. So if I fail to provide affection for my child, I fail to respect the requirements of the parent-child relationship I have to my child, but also I fail myself in that I fail to live up to the demands of the person/person relationship to myself. For I fail to act in accord with that respect for myself that I deserve—in this case in the domain of my behavior as a father. Though similar comments could be made about other obligations arising from other relationships, let us pursue the point with the example of a father's obligations to his child.

A possible illustration that attracted my attention is in an account given by Lynne Mastnak, a psychiatrist working in Gorazde in Bosnia in 1997. She tells of a middle-aged patient whose twelve-year-old daughter was killed by a grenade while she was playing.[34] For the three years since her death he has not cried and feels it would "be wrong to do so." Parents "crying over children fill the grave with tears, and prevent the child [from] being happy in paradise." The belief that tears are detrimental to the dead is common among Muslims in the Balkans, and Mastnak has been told that for this reason women are not encouraged to attend funerals.[35] Clearly, the patient feels an obligation to his child. But also there may be an obligation he feels to himself, in fulfilling his role as a father. The patient is a Muslim, and we are

---

33. One may use the Kantian term "dignity" (*Würde*) in this connection without tying it to rationality, as Kant did.
34. Lynne Mastnak, "Diary," *London Review of Books*, 21 August 1997, 29.
35. Mastnak, personal communication to the author. Tone Bringa cites a custom among Bosnian Muslims "which forbids women from attending the actual burial ceremony" because, as the accepted explanation has it, "women are generally prone to cry when emotional" (*Being Muslim the Bosnian Way: Identity and Community in a Central Bosnian Village* [Princeton: Princeton University Press, 1995], 186).

told he is a deeply religious man, although his religious commitment may not be essential to his moral feeling about the wrongness of crying over the death of his daughter.

Mastnak observes that she does "not necessarily think that the insistence on the expression of emotion, beloved by Western psychiatrists, will be healing if it goes against the grain of what he believes right." In addition to not being healing, it may not be right either, not if he has to violate his relationship to his dead child. "But the child is dead and so there is no more relationship," one might say. This is not necessarily so—the father may still be a relationship to his daughter. In some cultures, for example in Japanese and other Asian cultures, there is an acute awareness of what is owed to the ancestors and how the living can violate their relationship to their ancestors. In Bosnian Muslim culture there is the concern that crying, or thoughts of closeness by the spouse of the deceased, can "pollute the soul" of the deceased.[36] In other cultures there is a similar awareness of a relationship to the deceased, expressed in a sense of the appropriateness of honoring the dead. So the Bosnian father may still be in a relationship to his dead daughter that requires his respect. However, we shall set that relationship aside. Still, in going against his best, most sincere beliefs, he would violate his own sense of being a committed father, that is, his relationship to himself.

True—and this must be clearly said—in another cultural setting—in an Orthodox Christian setting within Bosnian society or in another setting in the Muslim world—a *failure* to express in tears one's grief might violate the relationship to oneself. As we have seen, the *form* that obligations flowing from a relationship can take may be subject to cultural, or intracultural, particulars.

VI. The Person/Person Relationship and Human Rights

I have referred to rights in this chapter, in Section II (regarding the abortion issue) and in the last section (regarding giving up a right). In each case the rights referred to are moral rights, not legal rights. If there are human rights, they are moral rights—indeed, universal moral rights.

"The notion of human rights builds on our shared humanity," says Amartya Sen. At the end of Chapter 2, where I quoted him earlier, I observed that if there

---

36. Bringa, *Being Muslim the Bosnian Way*, 185

are human rights, then they must be culture-neutral in that they exist by virtue of what is common to all human cultures. There are human rights, I believe we should acknowledge, and they are culture-neutral in the sense indicated—even though they are in another way culture-dependent.

The person/person relationship explains the existence of human rights transcending cultural restrictions, whereas the requirements of other relationships, themselves partially molded by societal factors, explain the culture-dependent aspect of human rights. So I will argue.

Given that there are culture-neutral human rights, there is a problem for the societal form of moral relativism. Herskovits, who accepted a cultural or societal form of moral relativism, was quite consistent when he opposed the United Nations Universal Declaration of Human Rights, as he did in the "Statement on Human Rights" that he wrote for the American Anthropological Association Executive Board in 1947. In that statement, directed against the idea of universal and culture-neutral human rights, it was emphasized that "standards and values are relative to the culture from which they derive."[37] We will recall that Herskovits dismissed individual forms of moral relativism but endorsed a societal form of moral relativism. However, culture-neutral human rights present a problem for societal forms of moral relativism as well as for individual forms: if there are universal human rights that are culture-neutral, then these rights will exist independently of both individual and societal standards.

More recently there has been a change in the perspective of many anthropologists on human rights and moral relativism. Elvin Hatch observes that "the efflorescence of ethical relativism among American anthropologists took place in the 1930s and 1940s, when Benedict and Herskovits were its most notable proponents."[38] Some contemporary anthropologists, however, have questioned moral relativism, especially in its cultural or societal form, in the light of claims about universal human rights. In a recent special issue of the *Journal of Anthropological Research,* several anthropologists have reexamined "cultural relativism" understood as a relativistic view in opposition to culture-neutral human rights.[39] In a different issue of the same journal, Merrilee Salmon has argued against moral relativism, or at least for anthropologists' giving up any commitment to the view. After review-

---

37. Elvin Hatch, "The Good Side of Relativism," 277–78, and Ellen Messer, "Pluralist Approaches to Human Rights," 293, both in *Journal of Anthropological Research* 53, no. 3 (Fall 1997).

38. Hatch, "The Good Side of Relativism," 371.

39. *Journal of Anthropological Research,* 53, no. 3 (Fall 1997), the issue in which the articles by Hatch and Messer appear; this special issue has the title "Universal Human Rights Versus Cultural Relativity."

ing and criticizing "ethical relativism," which "identifies the concepts of good and evil, or right and wrong, with what a particular culture approves or disapproves," she says that "since it seems not to be the only way, or even the best way, to achieve tolerance for diversity, and since it has other costs as well, anthropologists might be persuaded to abandon it." In her conclusion she says, "My arguments try to show not so much that ethical relativism is 'false' but that its consequences conflict with our deepest held moral intuitions and that it cannot be held consistently while embracing those intuitions."[40]

Part of the issue, or a closely related issue, is the nature of cultural relativism itself. As we saw in Chapter 1, cultural relativism can be understood in such a way that it entails moral relativism, but also it can be construed as a methodological approach (as Mari Womack and, with some qualifications, John Ladd suggest). Understood in this way, cultural relativism does not entail moral relativism. Terence Turner observes that within anthropology "various forms of cultural relativism" have arisen and that some forms are "overtly incompatible with the idea of universal principles of justice, equity, or rights, but others are consistent with such a notion." And Turner allows that for "many anthropologists . . . 'cultural relativism' is . . . a commitment to suspending moral judgment until an attempt can be made to understand another culture's beliefs and practices in their full cultural, material, and historical contexts," that is, a methodological approach.[41] Salmon makes a similar point about how cultural relativism "in Boas's sense of trying to understand and evaluate the practices of other cultures in their own historical context" is not "ethical relativism," and she is clear that cultural relativism (in Boas's sense) does not entail ethical relativism.[42] John Cook, who would agree with Salmon on the kind of cultural relativism that is recommended by Franz Boas, observes that, nevertheless, Boas's "two most famous students, Herskovits and Benedict" became the "leading proponents of moral relativism." Cook finds this "puzzling"—and, we may add, ironic—if Boas himself "believed that his own views do not support moral relativism," as Cook says.[43]

So, regarding the tension between moral relativism and the idea of universal culture-neutral human rights, cultural relativism, taken as a methodological approach, is not at issue; and to the extent that anthropologists have come to understand

---

40. Merrilee H. Salmon, "Ethical Considerations in Anthropology and Archaeology, or Relativism and Justice for All," *Journal of Anthropological Research* 53 (1997): 47, 58, and 61.
41. Terence Turner, "Human Rights, Human Difference: Anthropology's Contribution to an Emancipatory Cultural Politics," *Journal of Anthropological Research* 53, no. 3 (Fall 1997): 275.
42. Salmon, "Ethical Consideration in Anthropology and Archaeology," 47 and 49.
43. Cook, *Morality and Cultural Differences,* 75.

cultural relativism as a methodological approach to gathering and treating data, they will find no necessity to deny culture-neutral values, including culture-neutral human rights. However, we should not think that the issue of human rights in a setting of cultural diversity is thereby settled.

For one thing, it may be that not all societies recognize rights. Turner says that "some simple stateless societies clearly lack notions of 'rights,' in the sense of specific claims upon, or against, other members of the society or society as a whole, or differentiated social mechanisms for enforcing them."[44] Turner speaks of "notions of rights," not of human rights. Does he have in mind some societies in which there is no practice of making a promise or pledging to do something for a fellow member of the society (which creates a right for the one promised or given the pledge, though not a human right)? But let us allow that Turner is correct. Saying there are universal culture-neutral rights is not saying that they are universally recognized; however, it must be confessed that it would be congenial to the postulation of universal rights if they were universally recognized or, at the very least, if the notion of rights were universally understood. And there is the question: If there are rights, who has them? It is possible for a society to recognize individual rights but to deny that certain members of one's society has them.[45]

Again, once it is agreed that there are human rights, there may be different societal views about what those rights are. Turner observes that it is "possible that such general principles [as fairness, rightness, justice, or equity] might turn out to be shared by cultures and societies with dissimilar rights."[46] A related issue is the priority of rights. Some Asian political leaders, according to Ellen Messer, stress "social and economic over political and civil rights."[47] They might stress the right to have secure employment over the right to express political beliefs. In the "West," on the other hand, the stress might go the other way.

There is also the issue of "group rights," the "collective rights" of a society or some other group, and the connection between such rights and human rights. An example of a group right recognized by the United Nations is the "right to development." Other examples, sometimes mentioned by the proponents of group rights, according to Jack Donnelly, are the right to peace, the right to a healthy environment, the right to share in the exploitation of natural resources, the right to communicate, and the right to humanitarian assistance.[48] Despite how some

---

44. Turner, "Human Rights, Human Difference," 276.
45. Messer, "Pluralist Approaches to Human Rights," 298.
46. Turner, "Human Rights, Human Difference," 276.
47. Messer, "Pluralist Approaches to Human Rights," 301.
48. Jack Donnelly, *Universal Human Rights in Theory and Practice* (Ithaca: Cornell University

think of group rights, Donnelly argues, they are not *human* rights. His thinking seems to be this: a *group* of human beings cannot have human rights because a *group* of human beings is not itself a human being. However, he is clear, this does not mean that collectives or groups of human beings cannot have moral rights—just not *human* rights (145).[49] The International Human Rights Covenants affirm the "right of peoples" to "self determination" and to "freely dispose of their natural wealth and resources." If we are to speak of such collective or group rights as human rights, Donnelly argues, then they "should be interpreted merely as the rights of individuals acting as members of social groups." Thus, he suggests, although we may speak of the right of peoples to "self-determination" as a human right, it should be understood as the right of individuals to act collectively for self-determination (147, 148).The right of peoples to "freely dispose of their natural wealth and resources," as well as the right to share in natural resources and the right to a healthy environment, understood as human rights, then, similarly should be understood as the rights of individuals to act collectively for these ends.

Yet for Donnelly, there are true group rights that are not to be understood as individual human rights. He seems to be right about this, for if it is a "group right" to "develop," and this is understood to mean "grow in number," clearly developing in this sense is something that only a group—such as a societal or ethnic group, and not an individual—could do. Donnelly gives examples of groups that have rights: families, private clubs, ethnic groups, religious communities, states, and more. He sees how individuals may define themselves in significant part as members of a group, and he allows that "to the extent that individuals define themselves and live their lives as part of such collective groups, they will tend to exercise their individual human rights less as a separate individual and more as group members" (150). But also he affirms that there are true group rights, such as the group right to limit contacts with those outside the group. He cites, among religious groups, the Amish and the Hasidic Jewish tradition, and the Indian caste system, as examples of groups that limit contacts with those outside the group (151). That such a group right as this might conflict with traditional human rights is evident.

In addition, Donnelly affirms that there are "cultural rights." By "cultural rights" he understands "rights of members of communities, especially minority communities, to preserve their distinctive culture" (156). Such rights would extend

---

Press, 1989), 144. The right to development was codified in a 1986 United Nations General Assembly Declaration, Donnelly observes.

49. Similarly, it has been maintained that environmental collections, such as ecosystems (like wetlands and forests), have rights appropriate to them, and that animals have rights appropriate to them; see *Relationship Morality,* 355ff. and 376–85.

to various cultural features, notably a culture's language. As rights of *members* of a community they are individual human rights.

It emerges, then, that there are several questions that may be asked about human rights. Are there human rights? What are they? Who has them? Can they take different cultural forms? Are there human rights of individuals acting as members of a group, and are there cultural human rights? What is the priority among human rights? Human relationships, I believe, shed light on all these questions.

The idea that rights are in some way grounded in relationships between persons is now and then found in ethical reflection. For instance, Iris Young, in a book on justice, says that "rights are relationships." But she means that rights are "not fruitfully conceived as possessions"; they are "institutionally defined rules specifying what people can do in relation to one another."[50] Young seems correct that rights are not possessions (although we can give up certain rights, as when we release someone from a promise or give away a piece of property, and can transfer certain rights, such as the right to receive what we are owed by an agreement, we cannot give to another and so "give away" the right to say what we think or the right to religious belief and practice, as we can give away a possession). However, rather than being "institutionally defined rules," human rights are better understood as being defined or explained by relationships between persons.

Another instance of the idea that rights are grounded in relationships is found in Karen Warren's writing on ecological feminism. In her statement of some of the "boundary conditions" of a feminist ethic, she says that a feminist ethic gives a central place to values that are typically not given their due in "traditional ethics," such as care, love, and friendship, in contrast with rights, rules, and utility. But she does not deny that there may be moral contexts in which "talk of rights or of utility" may be appropriate. For instance, she says, talk of rights may be appropriate in regard to "contracts or *property relationships*." Here, then, Warren allows that rights, or our reference to rights, may be grounded in certain kinds of relationships that we enter. It is true that Warren's example of a *property* relationship does not itself apply to rights beyond property rights. She does, however, refer to a wider view that rights—"whatever rights a person properly may be said to have"—are "relationally defined," so that "even rights talk itself is properly conceived as growing out of a relational ethic."[51]

---

50. Iris Young, *Justice and the Politics of Difference* (Princeton: Princeton University Press, 1990), 25.

51. Karen J. Warren, "The Power and the Promise of Ecological Feminism," 140 (my emphasis); she refers to the relational view of rights in a footnote, where she cites Jim Cheney as one who holds this view (141 n. 28).

At the beginning of this section, I suggested that there are culture-neutral human rights but that they are also, in a way, culture-dependent. How this can be is explained, I suggested, by the person/person relationship and other relationships that may be partially molded by societal factors. In Section I of the last chapter, I tried to show how a "rubric" holds for obligation. That rubric, we will recall, is this: obligations have their source in, and are explained by, relationships. This rubric holds as well for human rights, except that the primary relationship that grounds and explains human rights is the person/person relationship, while other relationships may help to define the form that human rights might take in a particular setting.

Human rights are the rights human persons have as persons. They are general rights (holding for human beings generally), and they are moral rights (not bestowed or given by a legal document or by legal action). As I read the Universal Declaration of Human Rights adopted by the United Nations in 1948, there is, in the language of the Preamble and of Article 1, a "recognition" of the equal rights that human beings are "born" with. The *basic* human right is the right to be treated as a person. Understood one way, the source of this basic human right is the inherent worth that persons have by virtue of being persons (the Universal Declaration speaks of the "dignity" of human beings). The inherent worth of persons is the source of the basic right to be treated as a person in the sense that this basic right *requires* the inherent right of persons. Understood in another way that amplifies without contradicting the first way, the source of the basic human right to be treated as a person is the fundamental relationship that involves all persons simply by virtue of their being persons: the person/person relationship. It is this fundamental relationship that is violated when persons are *not* treated as persons and that is respected when they *are* treated as persons.

Persons have whatever other human rights there are, again, by virtue of their status as persons. And when these other human rights are not respected, again, the person/person relationship is violated. In this way the person/person relationship is a broad test for human rights and explains not only the basic human right to be treated as a person but whatever other human rights there are as well. Thus, if there is a human right to liberty (as affirmed in Art. 3 of the Universal Declaration), this is because a denial of liberty would violate the person/person relationship to those denied. Similarly, if there is a human right to own property, or to religious belief and practice, or to freedom of expression, or to education (Arts. 17, 18, 19, and 26 of the Universal Declaration), it is because their denial would violate the person/person relationship. If there is a human right to share in the natural resources of the world, and future generations share in this right, that is because those persons are also in the person/person relationship with us. Many secondary human rights can be given up, as when I give away my property or voluntarily present myself to the authorities to be interned for my own safety. And there can be times when certain human rights must be taken away or overruled, as when a psychotic individual, dangerous to himself and to others, is confined. In these cases the test of the person/person relationship remains in place: when I renounce my right to my property or present myself for internment, or when we confine the psychotic, the person/person relationship must not be violated. The primary human right to be treated as a person is truly inalienable for persons since it exists simply by virtue of one's being a person (and one's participation in the person/person relationship thereby).[52]

These reflections on the person/person relationship speak to the questions: Are there human rights? What are they? and Who has them? The *form* of particular human rights is another matter. The form of respecting various human rights can be importantly determined by other relationships. For instance, the right to own property, the right to religious belief and practice, and even the basic right to be treated as a person may be determined by other relationships, which are themselves partially culturally defined in accord with the rubric we have noted. Thus, what counts as private property may to a great extent be culturally determined. If there is a strong commons tradition, then grazing land may not be open to private ownership; and in the traditional society of the Oglala Sioux, although food, clothing, and livestock could be owned, the land upon which they hunted could not be. The right to religious belief and practice may, in the cultural setting of the Native American Church, extend to the ritualistic taking of peyote—in contrast to a moderately high Episcopal church setting.

As we have seen, the form of various particular *obligations,* such as the obligation to honor one's parents, can vary both intraculturally and interculturally. Similarly, the form of respecting rights, in particular the right to be treated as a person, can vary culturally. As offspring honor their parents, they treat their parents as persons and so respect their right to be treated as persons. However, the *form* of this honor, the way they honor or respect their parents, is in part culturally determined, for the expectations of the parent-child relationship are to an extent culturally determined. The way parents are honored in Japan may be very different from the way they are honored in parts of New York. Thus, respecting the right of persons to be treated as persons, where those persons are our parents, is in part culturally determined.

---

52. For the discussion in this and the preceding paragraph, I have drawn upon my *Relationship Morality,* 214–20.

This point holds when we look at the parent-child relationship from the other end and consider the obligations of parents toward their offspring and the way parents respect the right of their children to be treated as persons. In an Orthodox Jewish community, circumcision of male offspring may be an essential part of parental concern for offspring, as well as a religious observation, whereas this would not be so in other communities. Clearly, similar comments would apply to respecting the right of other persons to be treated as persons by keeping other particular obligations in other particular relationships, such as friendship relationships, the relationship with colleagues, and so on.

Are there human rights of individuals acting as members of a group, and are there cultural human rights? As we have seen, there may be rights of a group (for instance, to develop as a cultural entity or to limit contact between its members and others). If there are such group rights, they are not rights of individuals and so are not human rights. (At the end of this section, I shall take up an instance of a conflict between such a group right and human rights.) On the other hand, there may be rights of *members* of a group (for instance, to meet together), and there may be cultural rights of members of a cultural group (for instance, to preserve their culture or to speak their own language). If there are rights of these kinds, they are rights of individuals and so may be human rights. The test for the human rights of individuals considered as members of a group is whether respect for those persons as persons and as members of that group requires the recognition of the right in question. The test for cultural rights is similar: Does respect for the members of a culture, as persons, require that they can preserve their culture and continue to speak and teach their distinctive language? Does treating persons as person require the preservation of their cultural identity? It may, and if so there is this cultural right. For cultural rights, as for the rights of members of a group, the test is the requirements of the person/person relationship. And in this way, again, relationships—this fundamental relationship in particular—help us understand these rights and what rights of these kinds there are.

A related issue is the *priority* of rights. As I have remarked, according to Messer, some Asian political leaders stress "social and economic over political and civil rights." She also observes that some African leaders have viewed "political and economic freedoms as tied together."[53] Asian leaders might stress the right to have secure employment over the right to express political beliefs, while African leaders might see both as equally necessary. These Asian and African leaders may well claim that economic rights take precedence, or that political and economic

---

53. Messer, "Pluralist Approaches to Human Rights," 300.

liberties/rights are tied together, because they believe that respect for personal worth (in accord with the person/person relationship) requires a prior or collateral respect for economic rights, including the right to employment or a means of livelihood; while in comparatively more affluent countries, employment is not an issue with this importance because of a different perception of what is pressing in respecting the worth of persons (again in accord with the person/person relationship). Whether such economic rights have this priority for groups of persons will depend on what is indeed necessary to respect persons in those groups as persons in accord with the person/person relationship, and it could go different ways for different groups of persons.

Relationships also help us understand another question that can come up regarding human rights: Against whom can rights-claims be made? The answer to this question may not be the same for every human right. Thus the right to education (Art. 26 of the Universal Declaration) may allow a claim that is properly made by an individual against those who make up the nation-state or some polity in which she lives. If so, this is by virtue of the relationship between her and those in the state or polity, a relationship perhaps fashioned in significant part by an implicit social agreement that she has entered with others. A similar comment would hold for the right to employment (Art. 23 of the Universal Declaration). However, the right to a nationality and the right to "social and international order" (Arts. 15 and 28, of the Universal Declaration) are a different matter. These rights, if we have them, require claims against a larger community than those of any one nation-state and would rest on our relationship to those in that larger community. Some human rights could be *in rem* rights, that is, rights that can be claimed against all those in the world.[54] Perhaps the right to liberty and the right not to be tortured are *in rem* rights. The person/person relationship requires us to treat all persons as persons, but whether the right to liberty and the right not to be tortured are *in rem* rights depends in part on the capacity of others in the world to respond and, hence, on a further relationship one has to others in the world, defined in part by their capacity.

If rights derive from relationships, they are not a matter of human invention or creation. Legal rights may be, but moral rights are not. Human rights, as the Universal Declaration says, are *recognized;* they are not created and bestowed. And relationships explain how human rights can be recognized. Donnelly says, however, that the "human rights approach to human dignity . . . was first developed

---

54. James. P. Sterba, *The Demands of Justice* (Notre Dame: University of Notre Dame Press, 1980), 127–28.

in . . . the early modern period [in] seventeenth-century England." For him, Western societies invented human rights.[55] Why, asks Donnelly, were there no human rights in non-Western societies or in Western societies before the seventeenth century? Because, he says, "prior to the creation of capitalist market economies and modern nation states . . . the particular violations of human dignity that [human rights] seek to prevent either did not exist or were not widely perceived to be central social problems."[56] Alternatively, human rights, or basic human rights, existed prior to this time, but they were articulated in a forceful way only in the seventeenth century. It is true that certain human rights of definite focus require a reference to certain "institutions": thus, if there is a right to vote, that right will require a political institution that accommodates voting; and if there is a right to nationality, that right will require nation-states. (Although Young was not right that all rights are "institutionally defined rules," it does seem that certain human rights presuppose certain institutions in the way we have noted.) However, the right to liberty does not require any political institution. And the most fundamental human right of all, the right to be treated as a person, has no institutional requirement.

Now let us examine a contemporary moral issue involving both moral diversity and an apparent conflict between group rights and human rights, in order to bring out the light that relationships can shed on the issue. The contemporary and currently debated moral question to which we now turn is about clitorectomy, also called clitoridectomy or female circumcision, and female genital infibulation. Robert Baker observes that "these operations are indigenous to many African cultures and are performed by older women on younger, prepubescent girls. Unlike male circumcision, these operations are uncommon in the West; they also deprive individuals of more sensations of sexuality than does male circumcision, and they typically have a more deleterious impact on health."[57] Salmon, who like others terms these operations "female genital mutilation," says that "in its severe form, this involves cutting away most or all of the external sex organs (euphemistically called 'circumcision') and sewing or sealing (infibulating) the vagina so as to leave only a pinhole opening for urination and menstruation. The practice affects an estimated ninety-five million or more women in at least twenty-five countries, mostly, but not all, in Africa."[58]

---

55. Donnelly, *Universal Human Rights in Theory and Practice*, 65.
56. Ibid., 63–65.
57. Baker, "A Theory of International Bioethics: The Negotiable and the Non-Negotiable," 245.
58. Salmon, "Ethical Considerations in Anthropology and Archaeology," 55. Salmon cites H. Lightfoot-Klein, *Prisoners of Ritual: An Odyssey into Female Genital Circumcision in Africa* (Binghampton, N.Y.: Haworth Press, 1989).

"Women in cultures that practice genital mutilation," Salmon observes, "claim that it is done for the benefit of men, but women alone are responsible for arranging and performing the operations." She cites the case of a young woman from Togo in West Africa, "who sought and was granted asylum in the United States to avoid genital mutilation." This young woman "became endangered . . . only after her father had died [and her] guardianship [had] passed to her aunt, who attempted to commit the woman to an arranged marriage." Salmon comments that "the practice [of female genital mutilation] is unusual inasmuch as it is intended to control women, it affects them almost universally, and they suffer the greatest harm from it; but they manage and control it almost exclusively."[59]

Baker's comment on the practice is that "insofar as female . . . circumcision is truly a voluntary activity, a rite of passage through which women introduce their daughters to womanhood, Western attempts to prohibit it—essentially because it offends Western sensibilities about the primacy of sexuality—infantilizes Africans by failing to recognize the most fundamental of all human rights, the right to define primacy [of goods] for oneself."[60] People must assert their own "primary goods."

One might wonder if female circumcision is voluntary, as Baker assumes it is, for often it is performed on children.[61] And one might question the role he sees for autonomy, given our earlier reflections on whether autonomy is a recurring basic value (in Sec. II above). However, that female circumcision and infibulation are widely practiced by women in Africa is not in question. And it very often may be done for the good of the young woman who is subjected to these operations. Salmon observes that "marriage within the culture *as things now stand* may not be an option for an uncircumcised woman. Moreover, for females in that culture, marriage is a prerequisite for obtaining any other rights. So being able to marry is a clear benefit and may outweigh the harm of circumcision from the point of view of the girl."[62] Jomo Kenyatta, the former leader of Kenya, who was a member of the Kikuyu tribe and had a Ph.D. in anthropology, said, "No proper Kikuyu would dream of marrying a girl who has not been circumcised."[63] The aunt who sought an arranged marriage for the young Togolese woman may have had her good in mind.

---

59. Salmon, "Ethical Considerations in Anthropology and Archaeology," 56.
60. Baker, "A Theory of International Bioethics: The Negotiable and the Non-Negotiable," 245–46.
61. Salmon, "Ethical Consideration in Anthropology and Archaeology," 57; and Carole Nagengast, "Women, Minorities, and Indigenous Peoples: Universalism and Cultural Relativity," *Journal of Anthropological Research* 53, no. 3 (Fall 1997): 361.
62. Salmon, "Ethical Considerations in Anthropology and Archaeology," 57 (Salmon's emphasis).
63. Ibid., 56. Salmon cites Lightfoot-Klein, *Prisoners of Ritual: An Odyssey into Female Genital Circumcision in Africa*, 71.

There is, it appears, a parallel with medieval Byzantium. In the medieval period a number of court positions were filled mainly by eunuchs. Although it was not necessary to be a eunuch to fill these positions, eunuchs had the advantage that they were excluded from the throne and thus posed no threat as usurpers. So it was that ambitious parents might enhance the prospects of a son in civil service by making him a eunuch.[64] Paul of Aegina (615–90 C.E.) describes a technique of eunuchism whereby the testicles could be crushed in a hot bath, which was recommended in the case of children.[65]

As the Byzantine parents were seeking the benefit of their sons, one may say, so African women are seeking the benefit of their daughters. However, although there clearly is widespread support for the practice of female mutilation in African culture or cultures, it would be hasty to conclude that there is no indigenous opposition. Elizabeth Zechenter points out that "the assertion, often made by relativists, that indigenous women are indifferent to, or offended by, Western notions of human rights is factually erroneous." She observes that there are "ever-growing women's movements across the globe," and cites as an example that "African women have organized educational campaigns to combat the brutal sexual surgery of clitoridectomy."[66]

Carole Nagengast explicitly raises the issue of the conflict between group rights and individual human rights: "What *do* we do when group rights to cultural principles and traditions mean that women's rights to be free of violence and to realize their human and bodily integrity are violated?"[67] The issue posed here is not between cultural rights and human rights, for cultural rights are individual human rights, but between a group right to follow a cultural practice and human rights that conflict with that cultural practice. On the one hand, Nagengast argues that there is a "pitched battle" over "the very meaning of 'culture.'" On the other hand, she argues that "among the questions that must be asked before any practice is assigned the status of inviolate cultural principle [which a group has a right to follow] is this: Does it undermine human integrity?" Following A. J. M. Milne, she suggests that "human integrity" be understood in terms of various rights, including the rights to life, justice, aid, freedom, and civility. To which, Nagengast says, others would add the right to bodily integrity.[68]

64. *The Cambridge Medieval History,* vol. 4, *The Byzantine Empire,* pt. 2, *Government, Church, and Civilization,* ed. J. M. Hussey (Cambridge: Cambridge University Press, 1967), 20–22 and 85.
65. Arturo Castiglione, *A History of Medicine,* trans. and ed. E. B. Krumbhaar (New York: Alfred A. Knopf, 1941), 254.
66. Zechenter, "In the Name of Culture," 339–40.
67. Nagengast, "Women, Minorities, and Indigenous Peoples," 360 (Nagengast's emphasis).
68. Ibid., 360. Nagengast cites A. J. M. Milne, *Human Rights and Human Diversity* (London:

Thus, to the extent that Nagengast regards the human-integrity question, construed in terms of individual rights, to be the decisive question, she regards the deeper principle to be respect for the rights of individuals, essentially human rights. In support of the idea that the rights of individuals are more fundamental than the rights of groups, one might add the following reasoning: group rights are rights of groups of individual persons and derive from, or in some manner rest upon, the rights or interests of the persons who constitute the group; arguably, then, group rights should not take precedence over those individual rights or interests from which they derive, in the event that they should be in tension with them. However, I do not think that this reasoning will conclusively settle the issue about female mutilation—if only because it could be argued that there is a *cultural right* to practice female mutilation, which, as opposed to a group right, is an individual human right. But in any case, it seems to me that this reasoning and Nagengast's appeal to human rights does not go deep enough.[69]

The deeper appeal is to relationships. If there is any hope of understanding and resolving this and like issues, that hope rests upon understanding the various relationships that come into play. Recall again the young woman from Togo. As she was described by Salmon, she was granted asylum by the United States to be protected from genital mutilation, apparently with her father's support or approval. And then, when her aunt became her guardian, her aunt sought an arranged marriage for her. Let us add some details to this historical case, thus fictionalizing it but also making it more useful for our purposes. Let us allow that the father, a Togolese, had been living in the United States and was well acquainted with Western or American ways of raising daughters. He hoped that his daughter might study

---

Macmillan, 1986), 139. Cf. Martha Nussbaum's list of the ten central human "capabilities" that she sees as providing a basis for universal norms of justice: "being able to live to the end of a human life of normal length," "being able to have good health," "being able to move freely from place to place," "being able to use the senses, to imagine, think, and reason," "being able to have attachments to things and people outside ourselves," "being able to form conceptions of the good," "being able to live with and toward others [and] being able to be treated as a dignified being," "being able to live with concern for and in relation to animals, plants, and the world of nature," "being able to laugh, to play, to enjoy recreational activities," and "being able to participate effectively in political choices that govern one's life [and] being able to hold property." *Women and Human Development: The Capabilities Approach* (Cambridge: Cambridge University Press, 2000), 78–80.

69. In the same way Onora O'Neill's suggestion that "principles of action that hinge on victimizing some . . . cannot be adopted as fundamental principles [of justice] by any plurality [of potentially interacting beings]," while it may be right, and while it may be applicable to female mutilation (though O'Neill does not explicitly apply it), does not go deep enough—if only because the issue of whether victimization occurs in these cases is not addressed and so is left open by O'Neill's suggestion ("Justice, Gender, and International Boundaries," 315).

at a university in the United States and become used to the ways of American society. Let us allow, too, that the young woman's aunt, who is proud to be a part of a traditional African culture, is well acquainted with the necessity for a young woman to be circumcised if she is to marry and to participate in the benefits that are reserved for married women. The young woman herself has been in the United State for several years, attending elementary school, but after her father's death she returns to Togo to live in her aunt's home in a rural setting.

With no more details than these, we can begin to see that there may be a number of relationships with their moral demands at work in our imagined setting. Her father, in his relationship to her, his daughter, would be obligated to care for her in the best way he could, which he might judge to be to find asylum for her in the United States. Her aunt, especially as her guardian, would have a similar obligation in her relationship to the young woman, but her judgment about what is in the young woman's interest would be very different from that of the young woman's father. The young woman, in her relationship to both her father and her aunt, would have an obligation to honor them—and the extent to which that honor or respect would require obedience would depend on the nature of the relationships, which in part would be culturally determined. Also the young woman would be related to her society (those persons in her society). And here the question arises whether she is related to her Togolese society or to her American society or to both, and about just what she owes to each. A similar question could arise regarding her father in our scenario. With only a little imagination we can see how some of the obligations that those in our scenario might have, arising from their various relationships, might conflict, including those that the young woman might have. However, there is one more relationship: the person/person relationship. This relationship requires that all in the relationship—which means all of the persons in our scenario, including the young woman—be treated as persons, with the respect due to a person. In respecting the obligations of other relationships, we cannot go counter to this fundamental relationship. Here is the touchstone, I submit—not an appeal to human rights, as Zechenter suggests—for human rights are themselves grounded in relationships. If we live in a culture that encourages the practice of female mutilation, do we in following that practice respect our person/person relationship to young women who face these operations? And to ask a different question: How do those of us who are not in that culture, and hence in a different relationship to those young women, respect our person/person relationship to them?

It may be facile to say that there is a violation of human rights or of the person/person relationship in these cases, just as it may be presumptuous to say that there is none. And it complicates matters when we realize that respect for the person/

person relationship that we have to these young women—and hence the *way* we are called upon to respect their worth as persons—may vary with the other relationships we have to them. Here again, as earlier, it is a strength of an appeal to relationships to explain our moral obligations and the status of moral issues that it leaves in place whatever moral indeterminacy there is.

But we can be clear that the person/person relationship requires that persons be treated as persons, with the respect persons deserve as persons; and we can be clear that that respect can take different cultural forms, which is not to say that cultural practices cannot violate the person/person relationship. The person/person relationship remains as a broad test, even if questions remain about whose judgment is definitive regarding that test.

VII. The Person/Person Relationship and Moral Pluralism

Although in the earlier discussion of human relationships and incommensurability (in Sec. VII of the last chapter) I did not bring it into relief, the person/person relationship bears on the question of incommensurability. Crosby's form of moral pluralism, we will recall, has it that moral perspectives are incommensurable. I suggested that when two moral perspectives are incommensurable, it may be because the *forms* of certain relationships, and hence what is demanded and allowed by those relationships, are foreign to the understanding of one or the other perspective. Thus, to use my earlier example, the cultural perspective of the predominant societies of North or South Americas or Europe on marital fidelity might be incommensurable with the Eskimo perspective on marital fidelity due to a lack of appreciation of the *forms* of the marital relationship and their varied demands. So much we saw earlier. Now we can observe that what would remove that lack of appreciation is seeing that different forms of the marital relationship can be in accord with the person/person relationship, and that the respect of persons—in this case, spouses—can take various forms. However, the person/person relationship bears on other issues that come up regarding moral pluralism, and in this section I shall address several others.

At the end of Chapter 5 I raised several questions for moral pluralism, Kekes's form specifically, although some apply to other forms as well. Here again, with brief introductions in some cases, are the five main questions or question sets. (The questions themselves are in italics.)

1. For Kekes, we will recall, every good life must give a place to the "primary values," such as food and life. But once the primary values are accommodated, a wide range of other "secondary values" remain. Will any of the remaining secondary values that might be chosen as a part of a particular good life be as good as any of the others that they exclude? As I asked earlier, *Will gormandizing or miserliness do as values in a good life? Why not?*
2. Values are ranked within the conception of a good life. *Will any conception of a good life do? Is every conception of a good life a conception of a good life?* Such conceptions often come out of a tradition, but they need not. Are all conceptions, if they recognize all primary values, equal or "equally reasonable"? If the pluralist replies that, to avoid a "defective" conception of a good life, the values chosen must be "suitable" for the individual, and the range of chosen values cannot be "too narrow" or "too wide," why, on pluralistic grounds, is this so?
3. *Just what are the primary values, those values required by our shared human nature?*
4. For Kekes, living in a civilized way is a value, apparently a primary value. *Allowing that there is a value to being civilized, why is it a value? And if there is a value to "the appreciation of beauty, playfulness, and nonutilitarian relationships, as well as tackling difficult projects that require hard work," all of which Kekes sees as essential to good lives, why is there?*
5. *Granting there is no "highest value" like life, justice, love, friendship, as pluralists like Kekes say, might there nevertheless be a different kind of morally significant factor that could have relevance in value conflict situations, irrespective of the conception of a good life?*

Pluralism cannot answer in its own terms the questions posed above. However, if we appeal to the person/person relationship, we can provide an answer to each.

Will gormandizing or miserliness do as values in a good life? Why not? The first (being overindulgence in eating, in contrast with refined taste in food) will not do, because it violates the person/person relationship that one has to oneself, and the second violates that relationship to others as well as to oneself.

Will any conception of a good life do? Is every conception of a good life a conception of a good life? Are all conceptions, if they recognize all primary values, equal or "equally reasonable"? If the pluralist replies that, to avoid a "defective" conception of a good life, the values chosen must be "suitable" for the individual, and the range of chosen values cannot be "too narrow" or "too wide," why, on pluralistic grounds, is this so? Depending on what all the "primary values" turn out to be, not all conceptions of the good life may turn out to be "reasonable" or even good, such as a "good life" that features gormandizing or miserliness. And the test for a value's being "suitable" for the individual is, again, the person/person relationship. As Kekes says, self-knowledge is important here. But it is knowledge about how to give oneself proper respect. It is not merely knowledge of one's "character and circumstances." Thus, one way for a paraplegic to show herself self-respect is to master rock climbing, even though "circumstances" indicate otherwise. Similarly, whether a "narrow," intensely focused life, like that of a dedicated artist or writer, is a good life, or a "wide," expansive, and diversified life is a good life, will depend on whether such lives are in accord with the person/person relationship one has to oneself and to others.

Just what are the primary values, those values required by our shared human nature? Primary values, I argued earlier (Sec. VI of the last chapter), cannot be wholly accounted for by needs, as Kekes suggests. But if there are universal values deriving from our "human nature" in some way, then this is because when any person goes counter to such a value, or fails to incorporate respect for such a value in his or her life, the person/person relationship is violated. "Primary values," then, are open to our understanding in reference to the person/person relationship in something like the way that the basic human rights are.

Allowing that there is a value to being civilized, why is it a value? And if there is a value to "the appreciation of beauty, playfulness, and nonutilitarian relationships, as well as tackling difficult projects that require hard work," all of which Kekes sees as essential to good lives, why is there? Being civilized is a value, and even a primary value, as Kekes strongly suggests, if any person's not living in a civilized way violates the person/person relationship to others or to herself or himself. For Kekes, we will recall, our being civilized allows us "leisure, choices, and the security to go beyond necessity." If we must have these as a part of our lives, and respect others' having them, then this is because they are a general requirement of our person/person relationship to all others and to ourselves. Having the discipline to "tackle difficult projects" and complete them seems more dubious as a *primary* value in this sense, for it may be that some of us do not have this ability and yet do not fail to respect others and ourselves as persons, although clearly such an ability *could be* one way that a person might respect himself or herself, just as developing an appreciation of beauty could be.

Granting there is no "highest value" like life, justice, love, friendship, as pluralists like Kekes say, might there nevertheless be a different kind of morally significant factor that could have relevance in value conflict situations, irrespective of the conception of a good life? By now it should be clear how this question is to be answered. In value conflict situations, relationships—and ultimately the person/person relationship—can be appealed to. Thus, in a conflict between justice and friendship, one's relationship to those who are in need of justice and one's relationship to one's friend would be looked to. The demands of these relationships would be weighed and compared, and much, of course, would depend on the specificity of the relationships (the severity of the need for justice, the expectations of one's friend). In coming to a determination, of course, no one in these relationships would have his or her value as a person discounted or ignored, for that would violate the basic person/person relationship.

In his criticism of moral pluralism, Callicott says this: "Here . . . is the crux of what I think is wrong with moral pluralism. It severs ethical theory from moral philosophy, from the metaphysical foundations in which ethical theory is, whether we are conscious of it or not, grounded."[70] His criticism is directed against Stone's moral pluralism, which, we will recall, posits a plurality of ethical theories that an individual might rightly use in different spheres of his or her moral life. However, Callicott's criticism can be applied to other forms of moral pluralism. Part of Callicott's concern is that without such a "foundation" there is no way to begin to decide between ethical theories when they conflict.[71] Applied to Kekes's moral pluralism, there is no way to choose between conflicting, or incompatible, values. I should say, though, that such a foundation need not be "metaphysical," unless that term merely means "real." The relationships that form the foundation of morality—and to which we can appeal to resolve conflicts—are real enough, but they are given in our human moral experience.

Before Callicott leaves the subject, he considers a criticism offered by Jim Cheney. Cheney objects to the effort to develop a "totalizing theory" or a comprehensive conceptual framework. Rather, we should accept it that there has occurred a "shattering into a world of difference, the postmodern world."[72] LaFleur registers the same kind of point. Ethical thought "is almost invariably . . . moral *bricolage,*" he says—that is, a creation of an assemblage out of "leftover bits and pieces" (as opposed to following a single, primary principle). He finds that the process of "moral *bricolage*" well describes the Japanese Buddhist approach to the moral issues

---

70. Callicott, "The Case Against Moral Pluralism," 113.

71. Ibid., 112. Callicott is clear, however, that his complaint is not that moral pluralists cannot "articulate a *criterion* for choosing among several inconsistent courses of action" (120; my emphasis).

72. Ibid., 116–17. Callicott cites Jim Cheney, "The Neo-Stoicism of Radical Environmentalism," *Environmental Ethics* 11 (1989): 302 and 310.

73. LaFleur, *Liquid Life,* 12. LaFleur cites as the source of this idea Jeffrey Stout, *Ethics After Babel: The Languages of Morals and Their Discontents* (Boston: Beacon Press, 1988), 74.

of abortion.[73] Callicott endeavors to reply to this kind of criticism by advancing a "single moral philosophy" that will "unit[e] multiple moral communities."[74] This moral philosophy regards "the community concept" as the "root moral concept." I referred to it at the beginning of Chapter 6, where I suggested that Callicott was among those moral thinkers who in some way recognize the fundamental moral importance of relationships.

To pay heed to relationships is to respect the "bits and pieces" of morality, for it is to heed the myriad relationships between persons in all their types and in all their diversity, within and across cultures, without stipulating any fundamental moral principle or criterion like, say, Mill's Principle of Utility. But also it is to put in place a basic structure or foundation, namely, that of relationships, which can be appealed to for its explanatory power and for the light it sheds on moral issues and decisions.

I have, in this section, criticized moral pluralism; but as I said at the end of Chapter 5, it is to our profit to note how pluralists like Kekes and others have recognized a plurality of values, or a plurality of moral perspectives. It is time to acknowledge that we live in the midst of moral diversity across and within cultural settings, and a recognition of the moral importance of relationships does not deny this acknowledgement. Rather, it enhances it (as we shall see in Chapter 9).

VIII. Is There the Person/Person Relationship?

One may want to say that there surely is the person/person relationship, for after all, there are persons. However, to say that there is the person/person relationship is to say more than that there are persons who are related in *some* way. It is to say more than that there are persons who are related as, say, physical entities arranged in space. It is to say that there is a relationship that exists between persons *as persons*. If the person/person relationship exists, it, like other relationships between persons, has a moral dimension. It can be violated, and it is the source of binding obligations, in particular the obligation to treat persons as persons. And although I am inclined to agree that *if* there are persons (as of course there are), then there is the person/person relationship, I must allow that many might grant that there are persons and yet reject the idea that they are bound in a moral rela-

---

74. Callicott, "The Case Against Moral Pluralism," 120–24.

tionship to persons as persons.

One thing we should be clear on is that the person/person relationship does not itself contain a particular conception of a person. For instance, it does not require or deny that persons are created by God or can attain Buddhahood. It does not require a definition of persons in terms of some such property as rationality or sociability or self-consciousness. It does not presuppose any particular definition of *person,* or even that *person* can be defined. For there to be any in the person/person relationship, there must be persons, but the person/person relationship allows that the category of *person* can be "primitive" in that it is not itself definable in terms of some essential feature or features. Persons are those we meet, love, envy, sympathize with, toward whom we have duties, and with whom we have relationships of many kinds—including the person/person relationship. Persons as persons have the worth of persons, but the person/person relationship can allow that persons change, so that one can say truly, "I am no longer the person I was." However, there are various ways of thinking of persons. Is the person/person relationship compatible with them all?

For instance, there is the concept of a person as a *social self,* as an entity constituted by social relationships. Part of the impetus for formulating this notion of the self or person is a sense of the inadequacy of conceiving of human persons on an "atomistic model." This atomistic model, Elizabeth Wolgast suggests, is found in "Hobbes's picture of equal autonomous agents, [in which] people can be likened to molecules of gas bouncing around in a container. Each molecule proceeds independently, is free to go its way, although it occasionally bumps into others in its path." On this view, persons "are a collection of unrelated units." "This fundamental picture" Wolgast calls "social atomism." Locke shared this picture, she says, for although he did not share Hobbes's dismal view of human nature, he too sees "men being . . . by nature all free, equal, and independent." Kant, Hume, and others, stressing moral autonomy, developed the idea that "the source of moral authority lay in the individual—in one's conscience, moral sense, or reason"—an idea Wolgast calls "ethical atomism."[75] Charles Taylor refers to "political atomism," citing Hobbes and Locke again, using the term *atomism* to mean "doctrines" that "inherited a vision of society as in some sense constituted by individuals for the fulfillment of ends which were primarily individual."[76] The primary problem with the

---

75. Elizabeth H. Wolgast, *The Grammar of Justice* (Ithaca: Cornell University Press, 1987), 4–5 and 6–7.
76. Charles Taylor, *Philosophy and the Human Sciences: Philosophical Papers 2* (Cambridge: Cambridge University Press, 1985), 187.

atomistic model, for Wolgast, is that "in it one cannot picture human connections and responsibilities. We cannot locate friendliness or sympathy in it any more than we can imagine one molecule or atom moving aside for or assisting another."[77]

One can get a sense of this complaint about atomism and its leaving out "human connections and responsibilities." The corrective, we might think, is heeding relationships to human persons, and how they fashion values and the responsibilities we have to and for one another, for which it is not necessary to deny the right to equal treatment or the right to freedom, which could still qualify as human rights.

However, one reaction to atomism has been to suggest an alternative concept of the self: the social self. Iris Young, for instance, says that "societies do not simply distribute goods to persons who are what they are apart from society, but rather constitute individuals in their identities and capacities."[78] Karen Warren says: "Humans are who we are in large part by virtue of the historical and social contexts and the relationships we are in, including our relationships with nonhuman nature. Relationships are not something extrinsic to who we are, not an 'add on' feature of human nature; they play an essential role in shaping what it is to be human. Relationships of humans to the nonhuman environment are, in part, constitutive of what it is to be human."[79] The idea here is that what it is to be a human person is defined by society or a social context, even if Warren might construe our "society" to include relationships to nonhuman beings in a way that Young would not.

The idea of a person as "constituted" by society (Young), or the idea that human persons are who they are "in large part by virtue of the historical and social contexts and the relationships" they are in (Warren), has been found by anthropological study to be at work in at least one society. Richard Shweder and Edmund Bourne, in an essay with the title, "Does the Concept of the Person Vary Cross-Culturally?" draw attention to K. E. Read's work on the Gahuku-Gama people of New Guinea. Citing Read, they say, "The Gahuku-Gama conception of man 'does not allow any clearly recognized distinction between the individual and the status which he occupies.'"[80] For the Gahuku-Gama, people "are not conceived to be equals in a moral sense: their value does not reside in themselves as individuals or persons; it is dependent, rather, on the position they occupy within a system

---

77. Wolgast, *The Grammar of Justice*, 25–26.
78. Iris Young, *Justice and the Politics of Difference*, 27.
79. Warren, "The Power and the Promise of Ecological Feminism," 143.
80. Richard A. Shweder and Edmund J. Bourne, "Does the Concept of the Person Vary Cross-Culturally?" in *Culture Theory: Essays on Mind, Self, and Emotion*, ed. Richard A. Shweder and Robert A. Levine (Cambridge: Cambridge University Press, 1984), 167; K. E. Read, "Morality and the Concept of the Person Among the Gahuku-Gama," *Oceania* 25 (June 1955): 256.
81. Shweder and Bourne, "Does the Concept of the Person Vary Cross-Culturally?" 168; Read, "Morality and the Concept of the Person Among the Gahuku-Gama," 260. Parenthetical page numbers in the following paragraphs refer to Read's work.

of inter-personal and inter-group relationships."[81] Read says that for the Gahuku-Gama, "moral obligations are primarily contingent on the social positioning of individuals" (260). So "a younger brother, for example, is expected to be mindful at all times of his elder brother's superior status" (258). There are "common obligations," but they are determined by the social status "of husband and wife, of brothers, age mates, of parents and children, of members of linked clans and so on" (257).

Read perceives a difference between the Gahuku-Gama concept of person and the "Western" concept of person. From "the Western point of view" individuals have an intrinsic value apart from being in a certain social status and "there is an identical moral responsibility towards all other individuals" (257); "there are minimum responsibilities which apply to all circumstances [and] this common measure of rights and responsibilities depends on the intrinsic ethical value which we attach to the individual" (259). For the Gahuku-Gama there are no minimum responsibilities that apply in all circumstances to all individuals regardless of social status. Read tells us that for the Gahuku-Gama "it is wrong to kill a member of his own tribe, but commendable to kill members of opposed tribes" (262), that how people outside their tribal system of relationships behave is a "matter of indifference" to the Gahuku-Gama, and that, moreover, moral obligations do not extend beyond the tribe, so that the Gahuku-Gama regard it as justifiable to kill, steal from, and seduce the women of those outside their tribal system (256–57).

I find two distinguishable ideas here, both of which are implicitly accepted and followed by the Gahuku-Gama if Read is correct. The first idea is that persons are social selves defined by their social roles; and the second idea is that individuals are not equals in a moral sense, so that it is allowable for the Gahuku-Gama to treat those outside the tribal system with moral indifference (to treat them essentially as nonpersons).

First Idea

This idea—that a person is socially determined by his or her social status—is essentially the idea of the social self found in Young's thinking and in Warren's. Read sees it as contrasting with the "Western" concept of person. For the Western concept, as he sees it, persons are beings with internal worth irrespective of societal arrangement, with responsibilities to all others. Notice that this concept is *like* the atomistic concept of a person, the concept rejected by Wolgast and Young, but different in focus. The "Western" concept, as Read presents it, has a stress on the individual's moral responsibility/duty to *all*, as opposed to the stress of the atomistic model on the individual's autonomy/freedom to do as he pleases. So just what the

"Western" cultural concept of a person is (if there is such a concept) may be in some doubt. However, that, strictly speaking, is not our concern. Our concern is with the concept of a person as a social self, and whether it would deny the person/person relationship.

This idea that one is essentially or importantly a social self with a status defined by a social role (or roles), or by relationships, is recognizable, and in a way right. "Who are you?" may at times be adequately answered with "I am John's father" or "I am the Mayor of Casterbridge." In different settings each of these answers can tell another "who I am." These roles—father, mayor—and others, such as offspring, older brother, spouse, or clan member, arise from or express relationships that themselves determine obligations and have moral demands in ways we have discussed. Moreover, the *form* of the responsibilities one has in these roles is shaped by the *particular* relationship. Thus, the responsibilities one has as a father are shaped to an extent by the particular relationship between oneself as a particular father and one's particular child, as we have seen; while at the same time, a society's expectations of parents can also shape the requirements of the parent-child relationship, as we have allowed.

Read speaks of the "distributive" character of morality for the Gahuku-Gama. He says that for the Gahuku-Gama "moral obligation . . . is distributive in the sense that it is . . . dependent on and varies with [the] social positioning of individuals" (260) and that "the distributive morality of the Gahuku-Gama explicitly recognizes significant differences in the individual's moral obligations and responsibilities to other people" (257). Again, this to an extent sounds right. In fact, we see the same thing in "our" culture and in other cultures, as Read comes close to acknowledging when he says that "we may argue, of course, that the historical forms of Western European morality have also been distributive" (257). Parents have duties to their children that they do not have to the children of others, and (to use Read's own example) parents have duties to their children that employers do not have to their employees. However, at the same time, "we" recognize duties to all others, such as the general duty not to harm others. As Read says, "we recognize that there is—or at least that there should be—a certain common measure of ethical content in all our relationships" (259).[82]

This much is compatible with the person/person relationship and welcome to moral thinking that looks to relationships. The person/person relationship, then,

---

82. From this last point, Read wrongly concludes that "the diversity in our moral obligations is more apparent than real" (259). The Gahuku-Gama too, Read acknowledges, recognize "common moral obligations," but only for the "group at large," as opposed to those not in the tribe (257).

can allow that what makes one the person one is importantly involves a social role. But if that role should change, one would remain a person, even if a "different person." So the father of John would remain a person if he had had a daughter instead of a son; and the Mayor of Casterbridge remains a person though he should lose that status.

An appreciation of the importance of social roles and relationships for one's having a sense of who one is, and for proper behavior, is found in various cultures. In discussion, Yoko Arisaka pointed out to me that there are different terms in Japanese for the English *I*. Which Japanese term is used depends on the relationship one has to the person addressed in conversation: for example, one term would be used in addressing one's wife, another in addressing one's professor as a student.[83] This linguistic usage indicates an awareness of different roles in different relationships and, by extension, an awareness that what is appropriate interactive behavior in one relationship may not be appropriate in another. To some extent, the same sensibility is to be found in other cultures, expressed in the manner of speech (whether it is "familiar" or not), if not in the semantics of the first person pronoun.

Granting all of this is not to deny the inherent worth of persons or that there are human rights, and it is not to deny that there is the person/person relationship, even if it does correct the "atomistic model." Only if it is an essential part of the social-self concept of the person that there are *no* obligations toward all others or that persons do *not* have worth as persons (so that there would be no person/person relationship) would the social-self concept of the person deny the relationships view we have elaborated; and as far as I can see, this is not the intent of thinkers like Young, Wolgast, and Warren. In any case, these moral propositions are not a part of the social-self concept itself, even if they are incorporated into the morality of the Gahuku-Gama, as apparently they are, in accord with what I termed the "second idea."

Second Idea

The second idea is that individuals are not equals in a moral sense, so that it is allowable for the Gahuku-Gama to treat those outside the tribal system with moral indifference (to treat them essentially as nonpersons). Extended, this idea would have it that it is allowable for those in a given society to treat those in other societies with moral indifference. Clearly, the second idea contradicts the per-

---

83. These comments were made by Yoko Arisaka during a discussion session on my book *Relationship Morality* at the 1998 Pacific Division Meeting of the American Philosophical Association.

son/person relationship in that it denies that those outside the tribe need to be treated morally, or as persons. It should be noted, then, that the first idea does not require the second. The first idea allows the person/person relationship and its moral requirements, whereas the second idea does not. So the first idea cannot entail the second.

That the Gahuku-Gama do not treat those in opposed tribes as persons who must be treated morally is a phenomenon that is hardly limited to the Gahuku-Gama people. Nor is it limited to tightly circumscribed tribal societies. Sadly, this moral phenomenon is repeated regularly in human history. It occurred when the Nazis in Germany in the 1930s designated Jews and others as *Untermenschen* and then treated them as subhumans in concentration camps and conducted medical experiments on them. It occurred in North America in the last century in the treatment of Native Americans in the period of westward expansion, and it is to be found in America in the attitude of nineteenth-century Southern slave owners toward their slaves. This phenomenon is a part of the war mentality that characterizes the enemy as "devils" or as "animals" or as in some way subhuman. It is to be found in the commercial attitude that, although it is wrong to cheat those in one's own ethnic group in a business transaction, it is all right to cheat those not in one's ethnic group. On the contemporary scene, this phenomenon is expressed in white supremacist groups regarding other races as subhuman.

There is a tendency on the part of human groups—at least some groups in at least certain settings—not to recognize the moral status of at least some persons, that is, to deny that they are persons in the full moral sense. In the language of relationships, it is denied that some individuals are included in the person/person relationship. This, of course, does not mean that the person/person relationship, with its moral requirements, does not in fact obtain and include those individuals. It means only that it is not recognized or acknowledged that it does so by different human groups in various settings. And it is noteworthy that the persons focused on as excluded from the full moral status of persons varies from setting to setting: those excluded by the Gahuku-Gama form one group, those excluded by the Nazis

---

84. The phenomenon associated with the second idea—a tendency on the part of human groups to exclude at least some persons from full moral consideration—is related to, though distinguishable from, Michael Gelven's observations about our use of the "we-they principle." Gelven believes that this principle has validity and contributes to our self-understanding. However, Gelven is clear that the use of this principle in the way we regard others should not lead us to moral prejudice. In accord with Gelven's comments, we can observe that there is nothing wrong with recognizing that we belong to various groups (family, nation, ethnic community, etc.). This recognition does not deny either that we have real but different obligations to those in various groups by virtue of our differ-

another, and those excluded by American slave owners another.[84]

Before we leave the topic of the social-self view of the person, let us look briefly at another rather different version of the social-self view, one that apparently endeavors to give us a definitional theory. Wayne Booth offers such a variant of the social-self view in his effort to provide a new understanding of the "self," a concern he pursues in the context of seeking new support for Amnesty International's affirmation of a universal human right not to be tortured. Like others, Booth is suspicious of the "atomic" idea of the person, and he argues that "a new version of an older *social* or *rhetorical* self can provide a much more secure platform for Amnesty."[85] In the definition of person that Booth develops, "what is essential" to the self is found in "its freedom to pursue a story line, a life plot, a drama carved out of all the possibilities every society provides" (89). On this account, though "each person is . . . unique [since] nobody will undergo precisely *my* sequence of experience from birth to death" (86), the value of persons does not depend on their uniqueness (as opposed to the view of persons as "atomic isolates," as Booth sees it). Human lives "are narratable as *plot lines*," several plot lines, and "the plots are plotted not just outside us but within us," so that "my father and mother are in me, encountering one another there . . . meet[ing] my playmates from infancy, my schoolmates, my teacher, my various friends and enemies, my favorite literary characters and their authors" (90). In the story line one pursues, all of these characters may figure, and they "form a society," so that the self *is* "a society" (90, 91).

As Philip Quinn says, commenting on Booth's concept of the social self, "Metaphorically speaking, then, each self is a society of selves."[86] Each self in the life drama it carves out creates a story with its cast—its society—of characters, we may say. Torture is wrong, for Booth, because "the tortured one is no longer able to plot, once the torture goes beyond the moment when some degree of choice still seems possible": torture takes away one's freedom to pursue a story line of one's own making, which is the source of a human being's value.[87]

A consideration of Booth's argument for the right not to be tortured, or the wrongness of inflicting torture, is beyond our concern—which is with whether Booth's concept of a person as a social self is compatible with the person/person

---

ent relationships, or that we stand in the person/person relationship to all persons (*War and Existence: A Philosophical Inquiry* [University Park: Penn State Press, 1994], 179).

85. Wayne C. Booth, "Individualism and the Mystery of the Social Self; or, Does Amnesty Have a Leg to Stand On?" in *Freedom and Interpretation: The Oxford Amnesty Lectures, 1992*, ed. Barbara Johnson (New York: Basic Books/HarperCollins, 1993), 80 (Booth's emphasis in quotations). Parenthetical page numbers in the following paragraphs refer to this work.

86. Quinn, "Relativism About Torture," 160.

87. Booth, "Individualism and the Mystery of the Social Self," 93–94, and 92.

relationship. It may not be, not if his concept is a *definition* of person, and the person/person relationship includes *all* persons (as it does). The problem is one that Quinn sees: "normal humans" all possess the freedom to plot their own stories, but others, like the severely retarded, do not. Thus, as Quinn says, they would have to be "set aside."[88] But this is to set them aside from personhood and from the person/person relationship. The problem that arises here for Booth's view of the social self is a problem that generally arises when a definitional theory of persons or personhood is formulated. Such theories propound some essential feature of persons, and invariably some persons lack that feature. Whether we try to define person in terms of consciousness, self-consciousness, rationality, or some other "natural property," we shall be able to find example of persons who will be excluded—the example of a severely retarded person, for instance. The same comment applies to the feature of autonomy, understood as having the capacity to make decisions for oneself, and even to the feature of having a social role, if being able to enact that role is required. It also applies to the feature of uniqueness. A strength of Booth's discussion is that he sees that uniqueness is not essential to having the value of a person. Allowing that clones are not unique, we would all still be persons if we were all clones of one individual (just as identical twins are persons).

We should observe that the way we find counterexamples to all such definitions of person is *not* by standing back and contemplating the question "Is this feature essential to being a person?" It is by putting ourselves in the setting of a human relationship to one such. Thus, when a father discovers that he can react with love toward his severely retarded child, he thereby becomes undeniably aware that not being severely retarded is not necessary for being a person; and the same holds for the other well-worn candidates for the essential property of personhood.

To sum up this section so far: the person/person relationship is compatible with any number of conceptions of person, including the conception of person as a creation of God and the conception of a social self, according to which we are "who we are" by virtue of our social roles. However, if some such feature as plotting and enacting a narrative, or having rationality or consciousness, is put forward as *defining* what a person is so that one must possess that feature to be a person, there would be an incompatibility if—as seems unavoidable—such a definition excluded some persons.

At this point let me return to an issue that Harman raised for us back in Chapter 4: the issue of "inner judgments," as we may call it. The issue and its resolution bear on the question of whether there is the person/person relationship. We will

---

88. Quinn, "Relativism about Torture," 162.

recall that Harman affirmed a special form of moral relativism in that, if he is right, an inner moral judgment may be correct in relation to, or relative to, one agreement, and incorrect in relation to another. Beyond making sense only in relation to some agreement, inner judgments have two further important characteristics for Harman, we will recall: first, "they imply that the agent has reasons to do something"; and second, "the speaker in some sense endorses those reasons and supposes that the audience also endorses them." Those in the agreement recognize the reasons appealed to by inner judgments as reasons. For, after all, what counts as such a reason in Harman's account is a function of a specific agreement. Harman acquainted us with his example of "a contented employee of Murder, Incorporated," who was "raised as a child to honor and respect members of the 'family' but to have nothing but contempt for the rest of society." He is given the assignment to kill a bank manager. Our reasons why it is wrong to kill the bank manager ("It is wrong to harm others"), Harman observes, are not reasons for him because they do not operate within his agreement.

As I said earlier, I think it can be maintained that Harman's version, as an account of the logic of "inner judgments," is unassailable. That is, it is consistent as an internal account of his defined categories. But although Harman can spell out the logic of his concept of "inner judgment," it is another thing for the concept to apply significantly to morality and to our moral lives. The question to ask is: Why should we think any moral judgment is an inner judgment? At issue here is whether we can offer a reason that supports a judgment like "You were wrong in doing that" when that reason is not recognized as a reason by the hearer. It is this last issue that I said we would return to in Chapter 7.

Harman (as we noted in Chapter 2) says that "criminals" are given no "sufficient reason" not to harm others by an appeal to caring about or respecting others. He means criminals like members of Murder, Incorporated, who among themselves have an agreement to respect only members of the "family" and no one outside the "family." This is surely the way it goes on Harman's "inner judgment" account. Moreover, it may actually be that a Murder, Incorporated member (if there were such a group) cannot be given anything that *he* would accept as a reason why what he is preparing to do—kill the bank manager—is wrong.

But we can, nevertheless, give him a sufficient reason why the killing he intends to commit is wrong. It harms the bank manager, it harms you, the would-be murderer, it violates the bank manager's right to live, it manifests a lack of the kind of concern or respect one person ought to have for another, and, at bottom, it violates the person/person relationship. True, the member of Murder, Incorporated (as conceived by Harman) will not be moved by these reasons, but they are nevertheless sufficient reasons for his not committing the murder. *Sufficient reasons need not register on everyone as sufficient reasons.* We can give a middle-aged eater of fast foods a reason why he should stop eating fast foods even if we cannot give him a reason he will accept as a good reason.[89]

So we may reply to Harman that his criminals and the member of Murder, Incorporated can be given and do have a sufficient reason not to harm those outside the group *even though they do not appreciate it,* and that this is a reason that they themselves would see to be sufficient if their hard-heartedness changed and they came to see the humanity of their intended victims and related to them with sympathy—if, that is, they came to appreciate their person/person relationship to their intended victims.

I find here support for the person/person relationship. If there is a reason for the would-be murderer not to kill the bank manager (and there is), that reason is not accounted for by anything in Harman's scheme. But it is accounted for by the person/person relationship.

Matilal observed of Harman's "inner judgment" relativism: "The argument is sound, but is this plausible?" I said that a part of Matilal's point might be that it is one thing for the logic of "inner judgments" laid out by Harman to be internally consistent, and it is another for it to apply significantly to our moral lives. It does not apply to our moral lives, we can now say, because it leaves out relationships and the fundamental person/person relationship in particular. Matilal may concur. He says this: "The Harmanian assumption is that one through rational choice has to be exclusively and solely a member of a group, that is, simply a Ksatriya or a Murder, Inc., member, not anything else, not a father, or a son, or a lover."[90] What Matilal sees, I think, is that Harman leaves out of account the moral weight of these relationships—and of the person/person relationship, upon which they rest.

In responding to Harman in this way we are not, of course, rejecting as false moral relativism (the idea that there is no single true morality), only the relativistic thinking advanced by Harman, with its dependence on "inner judgments."

---

89. In other words, Harman must have it that the only sufficient reasons that can be given to a person (at least regarding the wrongness of his action) are "internal reasons" in something close to Bernard William's sense of that term. See Bernard William, "Internal and External Reasons," in *Moral Luck* (Cambridge: Cambridge University Press, 1981). Harman maintains what is *basically* the same idea about sufficient reasons in "Moral Relativism," 48–49.

90. Matilal, "Ethical Relativism and Confrontation of Cultures," 347. In the *Bhagavad-Gītā* Arjuna is a member of the Ksatriya caste, and Matilal presents Krishna's main argument that Arjuna ought to take up arms and fight as an appeal "to the *agreed upon* moral code of the Ksatriya caste," parallel to Harman's moral relativism (346, Matilal's emphasis).

Finally, what should we say about the person/person relationship? Donald Cochrane has said, "Respect for persons is not found in the world as a discernible characteristic of people, but is imposed on the world as a way of seeing them. We do not discover that people are persons, we make them so." He says this is so because "my being a person from the moral point of view is not contingent upon a description of my character or personality being such and such." "Nor," Cochrane says, "can my right to be seen as a person depend upon superlative achievement."[91]

Cochrane's supporting reasons are correct, but his claim that "we make" people persons is not established by his reasons. Yes, one's being a person is not contingent on any feature of one's character or personality. This is a corollary of the point I made earlier when I criticized definitional theories of persons that propound some essential feature of persons. Invariably they suffer counterexamples. In the same way, one's value *as a person* is not dependent on one's value as, say, a mathematician or a tennis player, or on any other achievement. On all this Cochrane is right. But this does not mean that we invent persons, or make people into persons. Persons *are* persons, whether we recognize them as such or not—just not by virtue of some feature of their character or some achievement or some other "natural property." If there are persons with the worth of persons, it is not because they have some feature that we are called upon to assess or evaluate. Wong sees this fairly clearly when he says, "To truly adopt the attitude that human worth is groundless and unconditional, we need to be able to care for people independently of our evaluation of them."[92]

To be sure, as we have seen, there is a sense that "we are who we are" by virtue of our social roles—being a mother, a husband, a medical practitioner, a firefighter. But our worth as a person is not contingent on any of these roles: take any or all of them away and a person yet remains.

Can we *discover* persons? I believe we can because we sometimes do. We do when we discover that those beyond our acquaintance, or hitherto dismissed from moral consideration, or regarded as evil, do count morally by virtue of the worth they have simply by being persons. To react to persons in this way, with sympathy or concern, *is* to discover them as persons and to discover that one is related to them in the person/person relationship. And typically we recognize the inherent worth of those near to us—in our tribe or in our family—and so, implicitly, our person/person relationship to them.

---

91. Donald Cochrane, "Prolegomena to Moral Education," in *The Domain of Moral Education*, ed. Donald B. Cochrane, Cornel M. Hamm, and Anastasios C. Kazepides (New York: Paulist Press, 1979), 79.

92. Wong, *Moral Relativity*, 206.

However, we may recognize the worth of those near us or in our ken, and so implicitly our person/person relationship to them, but not recognize and even deny a *universal* person/person relationship. I have no proof that there is this universal relationship involving all persons. But clearly, we can reason that as we all have discovered *some* persons to have the worth of persons—and thus in effect discovered our person/person relationship to them—so there is the possibility of discovering this in the instance of *all* persons. As we have acknowledged the person/person relationship to some persons, so we ought to acknowledge at least the strong possibility of our being in this relationship to all persons, including ourselves. To do so is to acknowledge more than the possibility that there are other persons in the world whom we now and then encounter. It is to acknowledge the strong possibility that we are *related* to one another in a relationship that has moral requirements that we can either violate or try to live up to.

IX. Conclusion

In this chapter and the last I have tried to show how relationships between persons can address the moral diversity we experience in our multicultural world. In the last chapter I appealed to many common and familiar relationships, such as the relationships we have to our friends and marital relationships. In this chapter I have focused on the person/person relationship, which I argued in the last section we should acknowledge as a universal relationship embracing all persons, or, at the very least, we should acknowledge the strong possibility of this universal relationship.

Even where our attention to the role of relationships cannot make out which course of action is morally right, as in the case of inveterate moral issues like abortion, heeding relationships can shed light on the way such issues are understood in different settings. Similarly, relationships can account for our sense that certain moral issues are indeterminate.

What do relationships tell us about the correctness of moral relativism? They help us to understand how there can be moral diversity *and* recurring moral values. I have argued that relationships give us a way of understanding how diverse moralities can be equally true, and at the same time there can be a "single true morality." What this understanding of relationships implies about what is right and wrong in moral relativism we shall pursue further in the next chapter. What this understanding of relationships implies for moral diversity we shall pursue further in the last chapter.

EIGHT

What Is Right/Wrong About Moral Relativism?

In Chapter 1 we accepted David Wong's definition of moral relativism—*there is no single true morality*—as our working definition. We said that moral relativists are those who find something insightful in this claim, while those who reject relativism, moral absolutists, are those who find this claim to be misguided. But what if one finds the claim to be both insightful *and* misguided, and to be both fundamentally? Such ambivalence is not beyond the realm of possibility.

In the last two chapters we laid the groundwork for the claim that moral relativism is right: relationships of various kinds—marital relationships, friendship relationships, and so on—take different forms across cultures and within cultures, and hence the obligations they create take different forms. And so we may say: "There is no one true form of morality."

Also, however, *types* of relationships recur across cultures and within cultures, and the underlying person/person relationship may be appealed to as an explanation of the recurring values of, for instance, loyalty and fidelity in basic types of relationships *and* as a test for forms of relationships. And this allows us to say: "There is one true form of morality."

I. Moral Relativism, Right and Wrong

Several authors have been aware of something right *and* wrong about moral relativism, of something right about relativism and something right about the view it opposes, absolutism. When relativism is differently defined, so that it is seen as opposing pluralism, there is again at least one author, John Kekes, who allows a strength and even a rightness to some forms of relativism.

As I noted in Chapter 4, Damien Keown, writing on Buddhist ethics, says that Buddhism "steers a middle course" between relativism and absolutism, so that Buddhism's absolutism is "attenuated and qualified," although a "position of extreme relativism" is ruled out, given Buddhism's appeal to human nature and the "inalienable characteristics of the world." Harold Schulweis, speaking of the Jewish tradition of revealed law, says: "Conservative interpreters of the tradition tend to stress the absolute character of revealed law. Liberal interpreters of the tradition point to the qualifications which beset the abstract law once it is contextually applied. On closer examination, the tradition appears as a 'relative absolutism.'"[1] The anthropologist Robert Redfield recounts:

> When once I mentioned the Eskimo practice of assisting to death an aged parent as an instance of very common or universal human care for old parents, my remark was greeted with laughter. Those who laughed were right in so far as they were thinking of the difference between trying to preserve the life of an aged parent and destroying that life. But I too was

---

1. Schulweis, "Judaism: From Either/Or to Both/And," 29.

right, for I thought of the common human tenderness for the old and helpless parent, as Freuchen shows it to us in the Eskimo also. Morality is both relative and universal.²

True, Redfield is contrasting relativism with the "universal," and, as we have seen, universally accepted values are compatible with moral relativism. However, he comes close to endorsing the idea of morality having both a relativistic and an absolute aspect, as he would if he explained universally accepted values in terms of absolute values.

Among philosophers, Amélie Oksenberg Rorty—in a passage I quoted in the Introduction—says, "The claims of relativists and their opponents are, when sanely and modestly construed, each plausible and mutually compatible." Relativists are right, she says, "to insist that even such dramatically basic activities as birth, copulation, and death . . . are intentionally described in [cultural] ways that affect phenomenological experience," and "antirelativists . . . rightly insist that there are events and facts—some of them intentionally described by reference to social practices—whose truth is not culturally determined." Birth and death may have both a cultural significance and a significance not dependent on cultural determinants. Although Rorty is commenting on *cultural* relativism and the view that opposes it, cultural relativism, as we have seen, can be construed as involving moral relativism.

John Kekes's pluralism opposes both moral monism and moral relativism, although his pluralism agrees with each of these two opposing views on certain points, as we saw in Chapter 5. His pluralistic thinking agrees with monism on the "objectivity" of judgments about conflicting values. But he also allows that relativism has a strength. Kekes understands relativism as denying "objective" and "context-independent" moral considerations (in contradistinction to denying that there is a single true morality). So understood, relativism stands opposed to moral pluralism. For Kekes, we will recall, relativism goes wrong for not recognizing the proper limits to morality, and for not allowing "objective" considerations for resolving moral conflicts and "context-independent" bases for some moral judgments. But still he sees that a strength of the form of relativism he calls conventionalism is "its insistence on the richness and variety of human possibilities and its reluctance to condemn moral possibilities from a point of view alien to them."³ Furthermore, as I noted in Chapter 5, he says of two of the forms of moral relativism

---

2. Robert Redfield, "The Universally Human and the Culturally Variable," reprinted in Ladd, *Ethical Relativism*, 142.
3. Kekes, *The Morality of Pluralism*, 131.

that he distinguishes, conventionalism and perspectivism, that if they allow an appeal to "objective," "context-independent" reasons, then "there may be no substantive disagreement between pluralists, on the one hand, and [these two forms of relativism], on the other" (52). Kekes's pluralism and these forms of relativism as well as the third form he distinguishes, radical relativism, are together in rejecting the claim that there is a single true morality.

Others too have tried to heed what is right and what is not right about relativism, or what is right about it and right about the view it opposes, the philosopher Richard Brandt and the anthropologist Clyde Kluckhohn among them. However, not all in this group have gone further and, like Kekes, sought to grasp a structural explanation of how it can be that there is both something right and something not right about moral relativism.

II. The Intuitive Basis of Moral Relativism

By the "intuitive basis" of moral relativism, I mean what in our pretheoretical general awareness of moral phenomena inclines us toward relativism. I do not mean anything that logically compels us to accept moral relativism, or even what is necessarily good evidence in its support, although it may be at least prima facie support.

One element is our encountering different cultural groups and individuals in our shrinking world in one way or another, through travel or communication, and our encountering different cultural groups and individuals in our own multicultural society. These encounters lead to a simple, growing awareness of the diversity of values among human beings, in the broadest sense of "values." We come to appreciate that different people value very different things. There are different values relating to food, dress, and manners, which can themselves have a moral significance; and there are different values relating to more obvious moral concerns, such as the proper attitude toward parents and toward one's spouse. The recent heightening of this appreciation is in part due to a lessening of parochialism, thanks to ubiquitous instant world communication and in part due to the increased physical proximity of cultural groups in the multiple diasporas of the last century continuing into this century. One does not have to be a relativist to appreciate this diversity, even in its moral dimension, but this pretheoretical appreciation *inclines* us more toward relativism than toward absolutism, if only because absolutism, more than relativism, would be called upon to explain the phenomenon of moral diversity.

Another element of the intuitive basis for moral relativism is our having the sense that diverse values—particularly moral values—are not merely seemingly different but are truly different, in conjunction with our seeing how these different values are fitting and natural for those who follow them. Related to this is our having the empathy to see that if we were in their shoes we too would have those values. Of course, there is plenty of room for misunderstanding, and it may be, as Rorty observes, that for "the most part . . . we live in the interesting intermediate grey area of partial success and partial failure of interpretation and communication . . . among neighbors as well as abroad among strangers [and] between the self of yesterday and the self of tomorrow."4 Still, we may with empathy be able to understand how neighbors and strangers have other moral values, and even how the "self of yesterday" held different moral values and beliefs.

I believe that another element of the intuitive basis of moral relativism, also found in our moral experience, is a sympathy for others in their moral predicaments and a related tolerance for the moral values and decisions of others. My appeal is not to the misguided argument for relativism on the grounds of an absolute duty to practice tolerance. Rather, I am citing what I think is the widespread pretheoretical moral judgment that we *ought* to practice moral tolerance toward one another. In our contemporary world of moral diversity, there seems to be a quickening sense that tolerance is an appropriate initial response toward the moral values of others. Joseph Runzo has suggested that the "roots of relativism" are "anti-authoritarianism both secular and religious, the empowerment of traditionally disenfranchised groups, awareness and appreciation of human diversity, and in general an increasing tolerance."5

III. The Passional Basis of Moral Relativism

By the "passional basis" of moral relativism, I mean desires and fears and other psychological reasons that attract us to moral relativism or repel us from its opposite. In some cases, such psychological reasons may spring from deep-seated needs (what William James called a "passional need").6 But that does not make them any the less potent. If the intuitive basis of relativism consists of what we are *aware of* or

---

4. Rorty, "Relativism, Persons, and Practices," 418.
5. Runzo, "Reply: Ethical Universality and Ethical Relativism," 171.
6. William James, "The Will to Believe," in *Essays in Pragmatism,* 106.

perceive to be the case, the passional basis consists of what, broadly, are *emotional* reactions to what we perceive. However, the two may be entwined; and indeed it may be that some perceptions, as when they amount to an appreciation, themselves involve an emotional or affective element. Still, with this disclaimer, I think that the distinction between intuitive and passional bases will be of use to us.

Rorty observes that the controversy between relativists and absolutists (she uses the term "antirelativists") "carries the baggage of personal and cultural psychology, with both parties speaking to central but archaic desires and convictions." She goes on to say that an item on "the hidden agenda" of the relativist "is the horror of being judged or evaluated. . . . The relativist voices our conviction that only our intimates have the right to evaluate us, along with the certainty that those who judge us harshly have failed to understand us."[7] Related may be the desire to be free of moral constraints not of our own making. Geertz observes that "what the relativists, so-called, want us to worry about is provincialism—the danger that our perceptions will be dulled, our intellects constricted, and our sympathies narrowed by the overlearned and overvalued acceptances of our own society."[8] His comment is about cultural relativists, but it can be applied to moral relativists. His observation cites a desire of relativists, or a fear, and hence qualifies as a passional basis, although it is connected to the *judgment* that we ought to be less provincial and so more tolerant, which is an element of the intuitive basis for moral relativism.

IV. The Intuitive Basis of Moral Absolutism

A chief element of the intuitive basis of moral absolutism is the perception of the authority of morality—its capacity to lay a claim on our actions, or its bindingness—and how this authority transcends our individual preferences, societal attitudes, and the agreements individuals make. This basis of absolutism is perceived when we judge that in certain cases individual preferences, societal attitudes, and agreements ought to be resisted and opposed and thus are not morally binding.

Another part of the intuitive basis for moral absolutism is the recognition and acknowledgment of shared and even universal values. This pretheoretical basis for absolutism is not the fallacious argument that absolutism must be true because there are universally accepted moral values. It is the pretheoretical recognition that

---

7. Rorty, "Relativism, Persons, and Practices," 421–22.
8. Geertz, "Anti Anti-Relativism," 15.

there are shared values and that certain moral obligations recur across and within cultures. One does not have to be an absolutist to recognize this moral commonality, but (mirroring the point I made about an appreciation of moral diversity inclining us toward moral relativism) *this* pretheoretical recognition and appreciation inclines us more toward absolutism than toward relativism.

Another element is the sense that at least *some* general moral judgments cannot be less than absolute: they must be exceptionless. Of course, there may be differences about which general moral judgments or which moral rules are exceptionless. But to the extent that we perceive that some moral rules are exceptionless—not just universally accepted, but universally binding—we have a perception that inclines us toward absolutism. Thus to the extent that we believe it is without exception wrong to take a life, or without exception wrong to torture, we will be inclined toward absolutism. Such a perception may or may not be allied with a religious belief that God's laws are to be understood as exceptionless commands (which is a recognizable theological position, but not the only way to understand God's commands religiously). As we noted in the last chapter, Philip Quinn, in his discussion of torture, held the belief that torture is always wrong. Accordingly, he was, as he allowed, an absolutist "of a sort" in holding that "the moral prohibition of torture is binding on absolutely everyone and at all times."

A last element of the intuitive basis for moral absolutism is a peremptory sense of responsibility for persons beyond our ken and outside our society or immediate circle of concern who are in need of help, perhaps due to a natural disaster—a sense that morally we ought to do what we are able to do to help, which may be marked by sympathy and the perception that care or concern is appropriate for these "strangers." As the recognition of shared moral values does not entail moral absolutism, so the sense of moral responsibility for those we do not know does not necessitate accepting moral absolutism; again, however, it inclines us more toward absolutism.

V. The Passional Basis of Moral Absolutism

For Rorty, both relativism and absolutism have a "hidden agenda." Absolutism's is "the pleasure of judging and evaluating."[9] Related is the sense of moral superiority, and of power and pride, in having the moral truth by which we can judge others.

---

9. Rorty, "Relativism, Persons, and Practices," 422.

Geertz says that the fear of the absolutist (or "anti-relativist") is of "spiritual entropy." "What the anti-relativists, self-declared, want us to worry about, and worry about and worry about, as though our very souls depended upon it," Geertz says, "is a kind of spiritual entropy, a heat death of the mind in which everything is as significant, thus as insignificant, as everything else."[10] Here again, Geertz's comment relates to cultural relativism, or rather, in this case, to its opposite. But once more we can easily transfer his point and apply it to the opposite of moral relativism, moral absolutism. So applied, his point draws to our attention the fear of a moral loss of bearings.

Perhaps we should not have some of the emotional reactions that constitute the passional bases for relativism and absolutism. My concern here has been merely to identify the fears, desires, and so on that provide a passional basis for moral relativism and absolutism, not to evaluate them.

VI. What Is Right About Moral Relativism

What is right about moral relativism? Drawing upon the discussion of the last two chapters, I can answer this question directly. Moral relativism recognizes that there is a moral diversity—not just a diversity of moral beliefs, but a diversity of moralities themselves. It recognizes, that is to say, a diversity of *true* moralities. Moral relativism recognizes, not just that there might be different moral beliefs about, say, the propriety of having more than one wife, but that having more than one wife may *be* right in one morality and *not be* right in another. It allows that there might be a diversity of moralities, with different, even incompatible obligations, relating not just to marriage but to friendship, ownership of property, and other matters in the range of human affairs. Thus, it can recognize the propriety of Eskimo marriages that do not involve sexual exclusivity and the propriety of the Dinka sacrifice of the spear-master. Moral relativism can recognize that autonomy in making medical decisions may or may not be a value among members of different societies or ethnic groups.

The moral diversity that moral relativism recognizes may be intercultural, or it may be intracultural. Thus, it can understand that the obligations of one friend-

---

10. Geertz, "Anti Anti-Relativism," 15. Geertz comments that he himself finds "provincialism," the fear of the relativists, "altogether the more real concern" (16).

ship are not obligations in another friendship within a culture. It allows for equally valid diverse values, ranging from love to patriotism and from spelunking to esthetic appreciation. It can allow that there are different equally valid conceptions of a good life, just as Kekes's pluralism does (Kekes did not object to moral relativism on this score). In fact, although Kekes's pluralism is opposed to relativism, given his characterization of it, his pluralism *is* relativism under Wong's definition. On all these points it seems to me that moral relativism is right.

Furthermore, it seems to me that moral relativism is right in rejecting at least two forms of moral absolutism (the idea that there is a single true morality). In one form, absolutism asserts that *moral rules are absolute:* they are rules to which there are no exceptions. When Quinn allowed that he is an absolutist "of a sort" because he holds that the moral prohibition on torture holds absolutely, he was allowing that he was this kind of absolutist—at least regarding the rule prohibiting torture. Moral relativism is right, I think, in rejecting the absolutist view that all or even many moral rules are exceptionless. In another form, absolutism asserts that there must be an *absolute standard* for moral rightness, a test for moral rightness, consisting of a simple or complex feature that is necessary and sufficient for moral rightness and that we can use to identify right actions. John Stuart Mill, as I observed in Chapter 1, advanced an absolute standard for moral rightness but rejected the idea that moral rules were absolute. So he allowed that there might be times when it is right to lie or steal but only because lying or stealing might maximize happiness and so meet his proposed absolute standard for moral rightness. Moral relativism is right to reject the idea that there must be an absolute standard in this sense. (Relationships, by contrast, on the view I have been developing, do not provide such a standard; rather relationships provide a source or basis for obligation and an explanation of moral rightness, although, in addition, the person/person relationship, among other things, provides a negative test for permissible relationships and a broad test for human rights.)

So, we may say, *moral relativism is right in saying there is no single true morality.*

What Relationships Explain About the Rightness of Moral Relativism

Relationships account for what is right about moral relativism and account for the intuitive basis of moral relativism. They explain how there can be a diversity of true moralities—just as there can be a diversity of true friendships. They explain the diversity of values and obligations, intercultural and intracultural. Marital relationships may again be cited as illustrative: a requirement of many marital relationships is sexual exclusivity, whereas of others, as in traditional Eskimo societies, it is not. Within a culture, one friendship may require long listening sessions on the glories of the Harley-Davidson; another may not. The recognition of a variation in the obligations that persons might have is what is correct in Harman's conviction that there is "no single true morality," but it is relationships, not implicit agreements or participation in a convention, that account for this.

Relationships explain the fittingness of different values: for instance, those in a marriage relationship that requires sexual exclusivity can still understand how nonexclusivity may be fitting in another marital relationship in another social setting—even as they see that it would be wrong for themselves to be in such a relationship, for they do not have the expectations of a marriage that others in other cultures have. For them, marital fidelity, in any marital relationship they would enter this side of a complete cultural transfer, takes the expression they are familiar with. Moreover, entering such a different marital relationship would violate existing relationships to other persons, such as parents and one's society at large. As we gain an appreciation for the other forms of the marital relationship, we may gain enough empathy to see that if we were in the cultural shoes of others, we too would be able to express the marital value of faithfulness as they do in their marital relationship, and yet we may understand that it would be wrong for us to try to wear their shoes.

A similar comment can be made about autonomy. In some settings, as in "mainstream American society," medical practitioners may have an obligation to fully inform their patients about their condition and the risks of possible procedures. But in other settings, as when treating those from traditional Navajo society, their obligation may be not to do so. The explanation is that in these different social settings there are different relationships between practitioner and patient, with different requirements—and, as we saw in Section II of the last chapter, different ways of respecting persons and honoring the person/person relationship. The same kind of point holds for privacy, although regarding privacy the issue may be more complex. Ruth Macklin reflects on "the common practice in some developing countries" of "publicly posting . . . highly personal information about the individual's health status, inoculations [and] women's menstrual cycles." Macklin recounts that some years ago, when a physician widely known for his work in public health asked a Chinese colleague, "Don't people consider this an invasion of their privacy?" his Chinese interpreter replied that the concept of privacy did not have a Chinese equivalent, so the interpreter could not translate the question. When there is no operative principle employing the concept of privacy or confidentiality, Macklin asks, "can such practices be wrong?"[11]

---

11. Ruth Macklin, "Universality of the Nuremberg Code," in *The Nazi Doctors and the Nuremberg*

In his discussion of the issue of privacy, Baker addresses the question of what "Western" biomedical scientists should do in different cultures. He says that in the "West" they should respect privacy "because they, their subjects, their peers, and their culture accept it as a primary good." And, he says, "outside the West" they also should respect privacy "because a failure to respect privacy is a failure to respect their own values."[12] He sees a similarity between this case and the case of the puritan on the nudist beach: "Were a puritan inadvertently to visit the beach on a day designated for naked sunbathing and swimming and were the puritan then to join the nudists in naked sunbathing and swimming, the puritan's acceptance of puritan values would be suspect."[13] About the puritan's acceptance of puritan values, Baker is surely right. Moreover, Baker is aware that matters of etiquette can be different: the "norms of etiquette are held to be binding out of respect for the groups that accept them," he says.[14] As we might put it, one should be polite in the way that is understandable. In many cultures, including African cultures, when one is offered something to drink or eat, it would be impolite not to accept it. If one is a woman in a Muslim country, one should not go out in public wearing shorts. In these cases the dictum "When in Rome do as the Romans do" holds. However, when it comes to respecting one's "own values" the matter is different, as Baker sees it, and surely there are differences here.

But Baker's explanations are not complete. He says that Western biomedical researchers should respect privacy *inside* the West "because they, their subjects, their peers, and their culture accept it as a primary good." But what if privacy is a bad thing that should not be valued? Not that it is. If it is not a bad thing, it is not bad because it does not violate the person/person relationship; and if we ought to respect privacy, it is because the person/person relationship requires us to. On the other hand, *outside* the West, Baker says, Western researchers also should respect privacy because not doing so is a failure to respect their own values. But this cannot be the

---

Code, ed. George Annas and Michael Grodin (New York: Oxford University Press, 1992), 249; quoted by Baker, "A Theory of International Bioethics: Multiculturalism, Postmodernism, and the Bankruptcy of Fundamentalism," *Kennedy Institute of Ethics Journal* 8 (1998): 211. Although there may be no term for privacy in the Chinese language being used, I find it dubious that there is no way to express the *concept;* however, given our concern, we need not deal with this question.

12. Baker, "A Theory of International Bioethics: The Negotiable and the Non-negotiable," 244. Baker subscribes to a contractarian view of morality, about which more shortly. Let me note here in passing that *not failing to respect your values* would not be a contractarian value unless it were agreed to; moreover, it appears that those "outside the West" have *not* agreed to the negotiated morality that, on Baker's view, would make respecting privacy a value.

13. Ibid.

14. Ibid., 243.

final explanation. Again, what if the values are wrong? If so, in *not* respecting them they do what is wrong, but also in respecting them they do what is wrong. In *not* respecting them they go against their own conscience in doing what they believe to be wrong. Baker says that they fail to respect their own values; more pointedly, they do what they feel they *ought not to do* because they owe it to themselves not to do what they feel is wrong. That is, they violate a duty to themselves, and so violate the person/person relationship to themselves. But if the value is wrong—or wrong in its application to some others—then they violate that same relationship to those others. (In such a dilemmatic case it is time to reexamine the value in question.)

And what of matters of etiquette? Baker says that the "norms of etiquette are held to be binding out of respect for the groups that accept them." This seems all right, as far as it goes. But what makes dress a matter of etiquette and privacy a moral matter? Once again, it is the different relationships we can be in. If I am a woman and dress in shorts in a Muslim country, I offend my hosts and violate both my relationship of visitor-host and the underlying person/person relationship I have to them. By contrast, if privacy is a value I hold, which my self-respect requires me to observe, then I have a good reason to respect it in a non-Western country, if only because I have a duty to myself to do so.

Notice what happens if *how I dress* is a matter of my self-respect: then, in order to respect myself and my person/person relationship to myself, perhaps I ought to avoid demeaning myself by dressing as others dictate. Perhaps, if I cannot resolve the conflicting requirements of these relationships—to my hosts and to myself—I may be faced with an indeterminate issue, which is also explained by the person/person relationship in conjunction with these relationships (as we saw in the last chapter).

Something similar may happen regarding the issue of privacy. If there is not only a universal *human right* to privacy but also a universal requirement of the person/person relationship that privacy always be respected and practiced in research settings, then this gives researchers an obligation to practice privacy in China. It is different if privacy is required by the person/person relationship and other relationships researchers have to those in America, but not required by the person/person relationship and other relationships researchers have to those in China. This would make privacy rather like autonomy in mainstream American society and in traditional Navajo society, but with a difference. In the case of autonomy, where autonomy involves a person making his or her own informed medical decision, in the Navajo culture it was the practice *not* to impose the burden of hearing bad news on people. In the case of privacy, in China it does not seem that practicing privacy in research settings is forbidden; rather, the matter of privacy is not deemed important enough to consider or even to identify. Notice, however, what happens if a Western researcher's practicing privacy is taken as nothing consequential by individual Chinese, but as an affront by her host colleagues in China. Then, perhaps, the Western biomedical researcher should not practice privacy in China, contrary to Baker's suggestion. Or if practicing privacy is a value she respects, and she has a duty to herself to practice it, then perhaps there is indeterminacy—again explained by the person/person relationship in conjunction with other relationships.

For Baker, "moral norms are binding by virtue of the acceptance of the persons whom they bind; consequently, they have no jurisdictional boundaries." He says this because he has accepted a contractarian ethical theory, according to which morality is "negotiated" and then, when agreed to, that acceptance makes it binding on those who accept it.[15] This view has the problems of "agreement views" (discussed in Chap. 6, Sec. V and Chap. 7 Sec. I). In particular, it has the problem that agreements can violate relationships, including the person/person relationship, and so ought not to be entered; and if such agreements are made, if they egregiously violate other relationships, they ought not to be adhered to. However, the present point is not that Baker's contractarian theory is wrong, it is that it does not provide a deep enough explanation of when and how the value of privacy is to be observed.

In this way it is finally an appeal to relationships that explains the fittingness of diverse values as well as the indeterminacy of value questions when fittingness comes into question or conflicts arise.

Lastly, under this heading, it is relationships that explain the quickening sense of sympathy and tolerance we seem to see in our contemporary world of moral diversity. As we become acquainted with the ways different people are differently related to their friends, children, spouses, family, and larger ethnic community—as we come to appreciate the various forms these relationships can take, with their different expectations and requirements and their different forms of trust and emotional attachment—the ways of others in other cultures and in what may be our own multicultural society no longer seem odd but become understandable.

VII. Where Moral Relativism Goes Wrong

A primary way that moral relativism goes wrong has been long recognized and often alluded to in this discussion. Moral relativism, depending on the form it takes, does not allow for, because it cannot recognize, evil societies, evil personal

---

15. Ibid., 243 and 234ff.

values, or evil agreements. The cultural or societal form cannot recognize evil social practices. In the last chapter, I mentioned several: slavery in the American South, contemporary racial and gender discrimination in the United States, John Cook's examples of "honor killings" in certain rural Arab societies, and the Sicilian social practice that allows a rejected suitor to kidnap and rape the woman who rejected him. Other examples abound. The "standard counterexample" to the societal form of moral relativism is the Nazi treatment of *Untermenschen* earlier in this century.[16] The individual form of moral relativism, for which personal feelings or "attitudes" determine moral rightness, cannot recognize evil personal values. And the form of moral relativism that sees morality as relative to agreements, the form advanced by Harman, cannot recognize evil agreements.

Although moral relativism is right in rejecting the idea of an absolute standard for moral rightness, it goes wrong in not recognizing bases for moral judgments that are different from "conventions" (societal practices, personal attitudes, and agreements). As John Kekes saw, unreconstructed moral relativism does not recognize "context-independent" and "objective" moral bases. Ultimately, the bases that go unrecognized are relationships: the moral demands of the many relationships that make up our individual and collective lives, especially the demands of the person/person relationship. These relationships together, along with the understanding of what would violate them, give us the means to morally evaluate judgments based on any set of "conventions." Although what counts as persons living up to their relationships can vary greatly, and may do so even within *types* of relationships (like friendship), respecting the requirements of our relationships, including the person/person relationship, remains as the unchanging basis and condition of morality in all its diverse forms.

At this point, then, we may say that *moral relativism goes wrong in not seeing that there is a single true morality.*

What Relationships Explain About How Moral Relativism Goes Wrong

Relationships account for what is not right about moral relativism and account for the intuitive basis of moral absolutism. I have just said that respecting the requirements of our relationships, including the person/person relationship, is the unchanging basis and condition of morality, a claim that rests on the discussion of the last two chapters. Let me now turn to the intuitive basis of moral absolutism, the view opposing moral relativism.

---

16. Salmon, "Ethical Considerations in Anthropology and Archaeology," 49. Salmon rightly calls this case the "standard counterexample." It is so precisely because it so clearly is a counterexample to the societal form of moral relativism.

A chief element of the intuitive basis of moral absolutism is the perception of the authority of morality—its capacity to lay a claim on our actions, or its bindingness—and how this authority transcends societal practices, individual attitudes, and agreements. This perception is explained by an implicit appreciation of the requirements of various relationships. The requirements of the relationship I have to my friend account for my special obligations to my friend as a friend, independently of societal practices. The requirements of the relationship I have to my employer account for my obligations to my employer, independently of my individual attitudes. The requirements of the relationship I have to my young children account for my obligations to my children as a parent, independently of any agreement I have with my children. And the requirements of the relationship I have to persons as persons account for my obligation to persons in general to be just in my dealings with them, independently of the practices of my society, my personal attitudes, and any agreements I may have made with any persons.

It is true that societal attitudes may contribute to determining the requirements, or the forms of requirements, of many of our relationships—such as marital relationships—in ways we have noted. Also societal attitudes as expectations may help fashion the social relationship that persons have to others in their society. But although societal practice or attitudes may play these roles vis-à-vis relationships, societal practice or attitudes per se cannot themselves adequately account for obligations—if only because some things approved by some societies are things that ought not to be done.

It is also true that one's individual attitude or preference may mark an important moral value for one to pursue, a value that is important for one's self-respect. When this is so, it is because of a relationship one has to oneself that would be violated if that value were not pursued. The person/person relationship that one has to oneself explains how a preference can take on such a moral significance. My valuing spelunking over other activities and devoting time to it may contribute to my self-respect by helping me to develop my ability to do what is challenging, alone and with a kind of quiet courage. My pursuing spelunking, then, becomes a duty to myself—but not merely because it is my preference. My preference for vanilla ice cream does not mark a duty to myself that I would violate if on occasion I chose chocolate. What makes the difference is a requirement of the person/person relationship I have to myself. What does *not* explain the moral value of spelunking for me, and its being a duty to myself, is my preference per se.

It is true that making an agreement can create an obligation, but to do so is to enter a certain kind of relationship. It is not the agreement per se that finally explains the obligation. In fact, some agreements fail to create a moral obligation. Finally, then, it is an appeal to our relationships, including the person/person relationship, that explains the source of our obligations and how its authority or bindingness transcends societal practices, individual attitudes, and agreements.

Another element in the intuitive basis of absolutism is the sense that at least *some* general moral judgments cannot be less than absolute, such as Quinn's sense that the prohibition of torture must be absolute in the sense of being exceptionless. Notice that in the case of the judgment that torture is always wrong there is a connection to the person/person relationship. What explains the sense that torture is always wrong is the perception that torture *must always* treat persons in a way that violates their status as persons. This holds as well, I think, for other candidates for exceptionless general moral judgments about, for instance, capital punishment, abortion, and war. True, we might ask if these perceptions are correct. However, whether they are correct is not relevant to the present point, which is that these perceptions—right or wrong—explain the sense that these judgments are absolute.

A last element of the intuitive basis for moral absolutism is a sense of responsibility for persons beyond our ken, outside our society or immediate circle of concern, a sense perhaps marked by sympathy and the perception that care or concern is appropriate. What explains this sense of responsibility is an implicit recognition of the requirements of the person/person relationship as it applies to persons we may never have seen. This recognition may not be articulated, except inchoately, as when we reflect that all of us are bound together, or are in the same "family," or that we need not send to know "for whom the bell tolls," in that each death affects and diminishes us all. It is true that a sense of responsibility for other persons beyond our acquaintance could be partially explained by respect for the authority of morality or for moral principle. But the authority of morality and moral principles (as statements of general obligation) are themselves explained by relationships. And when our sense of responsibility for others is marked by a sympathy or caring for them as persons, the explanation must be deeper than respect for the authority of morality or for moral principle.

VIII. The Principle of Ascent Explained

In Chapter 3 I introduced and discussed what I called "the Principle of Ascent." This principle affirms that "ascending values tend toward universality: as the level of abstraction of a moral value increases, the breadth of its application and acceptability increases." I illustrated this principle with two primary examples: Eskimo marriage and sacrificing the spear-master by the Dinka people of the southern Sudan. Many other examples might be used, including those we have discussed in the intervening pages, such as female genital mutilation.

Moral relativism in some forms may have to deny the Principle of Ascent. For instance, a societal form that insisted that moral values and obligations are established by the societal attitudes of a particular society and do not hold outside that society would have trouble accepting this principle, if we understand the principle as saying that values of greater levels of abstraction apply to and hold across societies. But other forms of moral relativism—other ways of understanding and affirming that "there is no single true morality"—would not. In this section I want to show how relationships account for the Principle of Ascent and explain why it is often applicable to moral values, and how this principle can be embraced by moral relativism.

In Chapter 3, in regard to the Eskimo marriage and Dinka sacrifice cases, we saw that if our descriptions of what was done become fuller, then the actions can be seen to be in accord with a more widely shared value. In the Dinka sacrifice case, at one level of description the action is "sacrificing the spear-master," and though the Dinka may see this as a moral value, we observed, many will not see this action, thus described, as morally valuable. However, the same action may be described as "trying to conserve the life of the community," and many will agree with this more abstract moral value. As our characterization of the action becomes fuller, we ascend, or our description ascends, toward a more abstract value that is more widely acceptable.

We made a similar point regarding the Eskimo marriage case. On traditional Eskimo hunting trips the man and woman, though they are married to others, may have sexual relations. At one level of description they are having sex with one not their spouse, and though the Eskimo society may see this as in accord with moral value and thus morally permissible, many will not see this action as morally permissible. Again, however, what they are doing can be differently described as acting in a way that does not violate marital trust. This description connects their action with the more abstract value of marital trust, and under this description the Eskimo practice is more widely acceptable in accord with the Principle of Ascent.

The same basic point can be applied to the case Redfield draws to our attention, again from Eskimo culture, that I referred to earlier in this chapter. In his words, it is "the Eskimo practice of assisting to death an aged parent," which he suggests is "an instance of very common or universal human care for old parents." Redfield, of course, has in mind the same Eskimo practice that in Chapter 3 we saw Richard Brandt referring to in his discussion of Eskimo parricide, which he contrasts with early Roman parricide. Brandt brings it to our attention that the

Eskimos' action, more fully described as "the merciful cutting short of a miserable, worthless, painful old age" (and the intended opening of the way into a more comfortable existence in the spirit world, we should add), is quite different from the Romans' action, more fully described as "the getting rid of a burden, or a getting one's hands on the parent's money." For Redfield, although we may describe the Eskimo act as "assisting to death an aged parent," the more revealing description is giving "care for old parents." The second description, drawing upon the intention of the Eskimo agents, ascends toward the more abstract moral value of giving care to aged parents, which, as the Principle of Ascent indicates, applies more broadly as a moral value.

One more example. Herodotus reports that

> Darius, after he had got the kingdom, called into his presence certain Greeks who were at hand, and asked—"What he should pay them to eat the bodies of their fathers when they had died?" To which they answered, that there was no sum that would tempt them to do such a thing. He then sent for certain Indians, of the race called Callatians, men who eat their fathers, and asked them. . . . "What he should give them to burn the bodies of their fathers at their decease?" The Indians exclaimed aloud, and bade him forbear such language.[17]

At one level of description, the values of the Greeks and Indians are very different: for the Greeks, their deceased fathers should be cremated, not eaten; for the Indians, their deceased fathers should be eaten, not cremated. Both groups may yet agree that their dead fathers should be honored and their bodies treated with due respect.

Now let us see how a consideration of relationships explains the Principle of Ascent. In the case of the Dinka sacrifice of the spear-master, if this action is described in terms of its goal—that is, what the Dinka are trying to do, which is to conserve the life of the community—then very many of us will recognize this value as one we share; for we understand our being, and others' being, in a *relationship to the community* that requires us to do our part to maintain the community. If the action is described as sacrificing the spear-master (by burying him in dung), then, very few of us outside the Dinka community will initially see that kind of action as a shared value. Even though sacrificing the spear-master is a *form* of trying to conserve the community, few of us outside the Dinka culture under-

---

17. Herodotus, *History of Herodotus*, Book 3, Chap. 38; adapted from trans. by George Rawlinson in Ladd, *Ethical Relativism*, 12.

stand a relationship to the community as requiring such an action, just as few of us outside that culture believe in the efficacy of the sacrifice. On the one hand, we fail to understand or share the value of sacrificing the spear-master because we do not recognize such an act as a *form* of meeting the obligation of a relationship to a community or society. On the other hand, we do understand the general moral responsibility to conserve a community that we and the Dinka have, because we recognize the demands of the *type* of relationship that members of a community have to their community or society. In this way relationships explain the Principle of Ascent: the less abstract value—sacrificing the spear-master—is a value by virtue of being the specific form of a relationship's requirement, but not a form of value shared by others; the more abstract value—conserving the community—is a value by virtue of being the requirement of a *type* of relationship, and many can recognize it as a shared value.

Analogous comments hold for the value of marital fidelity. On the one hand, we may fail to understand or share the value of the Eskimo *form* of marital fidelity; but, on the other hand, we do understand the general and more abstract moral responsibility of marital faithfulness and devotion because we recognize the demands of the *type* of relationship that marriage is. Similarly for the values of caring for the aged and respect for the dead.

The Principle of Ascent functions in a fairly clear way. What appears to be its near cousin is appreciated in anthropological research. Richard Shweder and Edmund Bourne refer to it as "the higher order generality rule." This principle or rule, in their formulation, says: "Emphasize general likenesses and overlook specific differences." It has been applied in anthropology inside and outside the moral domain. As Shweder and Bourne note, it can lead ethnologists and sociobiologists to regard the "conversation" of humans and the "barking" of canines as "equivalent," each being "an example of a universal 'signaling' function of communication systems." Their implicit criticism of following this rule is that differences are *ignored* or *overlooked* when it is followed.[18]

Applying the Principle of Ascent, like applying the higher order generality rule, requires us to emphasize certain likenesses. However applying the Principle of Ascent does not require us to ignore or overlook differences. For instance, the difference between sacrificing the spear-master and other forms of trying to conserve the community are to be appreciated as the less abstract and unshared values. Such differences are not denied. As our descriptions of what is done become fuller, we set certain differences aside in the sense of not emphasizing them. For instance, we

18. Shweder and Bourne, "Does the Concept of the Person Vary Cross-Culturally?" 159–60.

set aside a description of the *means* by which members of the community try to conserve the community or society. In this way our description connects to values that "ascend" in abstraction. In our giving a fuller description, we bring in facts *left out* of the less full description (such as beliefs and motives). In this way the fuller description, which connects the action to the more abstract value, brings into the action's description facts "overlooked" by the less full description.

Relationships, then, explain why the Principle of Ascent may be applied to different recurring values, such as marital fidelity, friendship, respect for the aged, and so on. This is not to say that this principle entails that friendship, say, can take just any form: in accord with what we have seen, morally it cannot take a form that does not treat persons as they deserve, that is, that violates the person/person relationship. However, it remains that in many if not all cases of moral diversity, it is pertinent to apply this principle to see if, in addition to that diversity, there is, in the light of a fuller description of the actions, a shared value—which is made understandable by the presence of comparable relationships.

Levels of Description of Actions

At this point we should return to, and take up, an issue that arises in connection with the Principle of Ascent. An application of this principle requires that we can describe actions at different levels. In the Eskimo and Dinka cases, we can describe the actions before us at a "lower," less full level of description, or we can describe those actions at "higher" or fuller levels, incorporating into our description, for instance, background beliefs and the goal of the action. In the light of such fuller levels of description, we can see that actions that initially appear to be the same are different, and actions that initially appear to be different are the same. And we can invite a wider agreement on the morality of what is done by ascending toward a more abstract moral value.

As I said in Chapter 3, I think the notion of levels of description is unproblematic in itself. It is a notion often employed in our thinking about what people do. Thus, we may think initially that two individuals we know have both "done the same kind thing" when we learn that each donated a large amount of money to famine relief; however, when we learn that one of the individuals donated the sum he did at the instruction of the court in order to get a lesser sentence for the fraud he practiced in obtaining the funds in the first place, our judgment may well change. That is, when we learn that what he did was to donate money *in order to get a lesser jail sentence,* we no longer feel comfortable saying that he and the other individual, whose goal was to relieve people from starvation, did the "same thing."

In all the cases we have considered, both the less full and the fuller levels of description provide descriptions of something persons did, some action that was performed. In fact, each level designates the same action, although one description is, of course, *fuller* than the other. Many ethical thinkers have accepted this commonplace notion that when we go to a fuller description, and incorporate into our description of comparable actions the *motives or goals or beliefs* of the individuals, we will find that *different* actions are involved (or the corollary that when we incorporate into our description of apparently different kinds of actions the *motives or goals or beliefs* of the individuals, we will find that *the same* action is involved). Brandt accepts this idea, as we have seen. So does A. C. Ewing when he says that "what can externally be classified as the same kind of act, when performed in a society with a different psychology and different institutions, is not really the same." As an illustration he says that it "might without self-contradiction be maintained that slavery and polygamy were right in ancient Egypt and yet wrong in the United States in the nineteenth century A.D."[19]

As I remarked in Chapter 3, it seems to me that in many cases we display a moral insensitivity when we regard the actions of those in other societies—or for that matter, intraculturally, the actions of others in our own society—at "lower" or less full levels of description. We are more sensitive in our moral understanding of what the Eskimos are doing and what the Dinka are doing when we regard their actions in the light of a fuller description that includes the background beliefs and the goal of the action. This in itself does not mean that all actions with a worthy goal or motive, or informed by background beliefs that are understandably accepted, are necessarily right actions. But it does mean that, if the action is right, we will have a better chance of appreciating the action's rightness if we consider its fuller description.

What is involved here, as far as intercultural perceptions go, is related to overcoming a form of ethnocentrism. Herskovits, as I noted in Chapter 1, thought of ethnocentrism as "the point of view that one's own way of life is to be preferred to all others." If ethnocentrism is instead *looking at other cultures in terms of one's own culture,* then ethnocentrism can cause an inability to perceive the underlying similarity of actions in other cultures, for we would see actions in other cultures in terms of what they would be in our culture—which is to discount differences in beliefs, motives, and goals.

John Cook draws to our attention what he calls "the Projection Error." "It occurs," he says "when, having witnessed (or perhaps read about) certain actions of an alien people, one misconstrues their actions because of the following

---

19. A. C. Ewing, *Ethics* (New York: Free Press, 1953), 113.

circumstances: (a) one is ignorant of the actual motivation of those people, and (b) their actions appear similar in some way to actions of a sort that might occur in—or that one is familiar with from—one's own culture." Cook continues: "The error itself consists of thinking, on account of their similarity, that the actions of an alien people are actions of the *same* sort as actions that might occur—or that one is familiar with from—one's own culture."[20] This kind of error would occur if we regarded an Eskimo husband's having sexual relations with a woman not his wife on a hunting trip as the same thing as a husband in "our culture" having an extramarital affair with his secretary at a hunting lodge. As Cook sees, the corrective is to go to a fuller level of description, bringing in motives (and perhaps more), which requires not looking at the other culture in terms of one's own. Cook seems concerned about a failure to see that actions are *different,* as opposed to a failure to see that actions are the *same*. But both failures may be ethnocentric or projection errors. In short, a number of thinkers have seen a good reason for allowing that we should consider a fuller description of actions, including motives, in considering whether comparable actions are different or the same action.

However, some have questioned the correctness of this idea. For example, for John Ladd it is important to keep apart the "action" and the "reasons for doing it." The proper way to think about my case of two individuals donating money to famine relief is to regard each individual as performing the same *action* and then to point out how they had different *reasons* for their actions.[21] As Ladd sees it, Brandt goes astray in his presentation of Eskimo and Roman parricide to the extent that he suggests different actions are involved, and so too, for Ladd, regarding the other cases we have discussed.

Ladd's concern is that "moral discourse is put into confusion when actions are fused with the wherefore of them." He substantiates his concern by citing the case of Adolf Eichmann, the Nazi chief of the Jewish Office of the Gestapo who was responsible for organizing the mass extermination of millions, mainly Jews, in the Holocaust. Eichmann, Ladd points out, "described his actions as obeying the orders of his superiors." Rather, for Ladd, his action was what he *did,* organizing the extermination camps and bringing about the death of millions, and the *reason* for what he did was obedience to his superiors.[22]

Is Ladd right? I want to say that he is not wrong—and that my earlier account also is not wrong. Each way of understanding the sameness or difference of actions

---

20. Cook, *Morality and Cultural Differences,* 93 (Cook's emphasis).
21. Ladd, "The Issue of Relativism," 116–17.
22. Ibid., 117.

is coherent and is an alternative way of representing the facts about actions. For the purposes of overcoming ethnocentrism and seeing the moral value of practices in other cultures, and finally, for our purpose of understanding what is right about moral relativism and where it goes wrong, either account can be pressed into service (although the "levels-of-description" account, along with the Principle of Ascent, may make the shared values more evident).

Consider an analogy. In the dagger scene in Act II of *Macbeth*, Macbeth asks, "Is this a dagger which I see before me . . . ?" It is, we appreciate, in Shakespeare's words, a "dagger of the mind, a false creation proceeding from the heat-oppressed brain." So what is it Macbeth sees before him? We can answer, "He sees a dagger, but it is not a real dagger"; or we can answer, "He doesn't really see anything; he's hallucinating a dagger." Neither is wrong. Each may invite elaboration, but each is correct in what it says. The analogous point applies to the issue Ladd raises.

Let me illustrate how the analogous point applies to the issue Ladd raises. Recall the example I used in Chapter 3 to illustrate levels of description of actions. Two people are standing on the corner of a busy intersection. One is waiting for his wife, the other is waiting to set off a bomb. We may say of them, I suggested, that they are both doing the same thing at one level of description (standing on the corner), but at another, fuller, level of description their actions are very different things (one is waiting for his wife and the other is waiting for the optimum time to detonate a bomb). Saying that in the light of their intentions or motives they are doing very different things is coherent and understandable. But Ladd is right that we could as well communicate what the two people are doing by saying that they are doing the same thing, performing the *same action* (standing on the corner), but for very different *reasons*.

This point holds for more complex moral cases as well. We can see how by using one of the cross-cultural cases we considered: the Eskimo practice of killing, or allowing to die of exposure, their aged parents (a case Ladd, in fact, considers).[23] On the "levels-of-description" account, in conjunction with the Principle of Ascent, as we go from the description of the action as *allowing aged parents to die* to its description as *allowing aged parents to die in order to care for them*, we ascend toward a shared value, that of giving care to aged parents, and we see that the action of the Eskimos is the same action we in "our culture" perform using a different means informed by different beliefs. On this account, the action of the Eskimos is in its fuller description not merely allowing aged parents to die, and it is distinguishable from the action *allowing aged parent to die to be relieved from a burden or to gain*

23. Ibid.

their wealth. On this account, the Eskimos' action and our action in trying to care for aged parents are the same action. On Ladd's account, the Eskimos' allowing aged parents to die in order to care for them and one's allowing aged parents to die for selfish reasons are the same *action,* but they are done for different *reasons.* On the other hand, although for Ladd the Eskimos' action and our own action in trying to care for aged parents are *not* the same action (for we do not allow our aged parents to die), the *reasons* for these actions are the same reason. It seems that we could communicate the basic facts about Eskimo practice and the practice in "our culture" using either approach.

What about seeing the value of the Eskimo practice using either approach? Following the "levels-of-description" approach, along with the Principle of Ascent, we can come to see that the action of the Eskimos in its fuller description has the same value as our own efforts to care for aged parents because each action, as the same action (trying to care for aged parents), is an instance of the same value. Following Ladd's approach, we would say that the action of the Eskimos is not the same action we in our culture perform as we try to care for the aged, for the Eskimos' action is an instance of allowing aged parents to die, whereas our own action is not; rather, the Eskimos' action is the same action that a selfish person performs when he kills or allows to die his aged parents for their wealth. *However,* Ladd's account must allow, the reason for the Eskimo's action is *trying to care for aged parents,* whereas the reason for the selfish act is *trying to gain parents' wealth.* Thus, on Ladd's account too, the action of the Eskimos can be seen as having the same moral worth as our action—not because the actions are the same, but because they are done for the same moral reason, in accord with the same value.[24]

The explanatory force of relationships remains in place for either approach. Just as relationships can explain why the *action of caring for aged parents* is an action with value, so it can explain why *caring for aged parents as a reason for an action* is a moral reason: in each case the explanation is that caring for aged parents is in accord with the requirements of the parent-child relationship and the underlying person/person relationship. We could work through the other cases we discussed, drawing attention to the relationships relevant to those cases—the Dinka sacrifice and the Eskimo marriage cases, and so on—and show the same thing. There is an advantage to the "levels-of-description" account, however. For when we use it, we keep before ourselves how the things other people do can at once be different from, and the same as, what we do (interculturally and intraculturally), and how, being the same, can have the same moral value we believe our own actions to have.

---

24. *Ceteris paribus,* of course. It must be, for instance, that the Eskimos and those in "our culture" act in good faith on their beliefs about the benefits to their aged parents of their respective actions.

But what then of Ladd's concern about moral discourse being "put into confusion when actions are fused with the wherefore of them," and his concern with the Eichmann case in particular? Ladd's concern, or one moral concern, might be that if we allow Eichmann to describe his action as "obeying the orders of his superiors" and so say that he was doing the same thing that others in the war did when they obeyed the orders of their superiors, we will end up with the moral confusion that Eichmann was as morally justified as any soldier. However, we can allay this concern. Granted, on the "levels-of-description" account Eichmann is doing the same thing as others who obeyed their superiors *as far as obeying commands go*. But there are fuller descriptions available. What orders was Eichmann obeying? What were their effects on innocent people? When we complete the fuller description of what Eichmann did, it is that he "obeyed orders to establish extermination camps and to bring about the deaths of millions." In the light of this description, it is evident that Eichmann's action is *not* the same action of many who followed orders and does *not* share a value with their actions. Thus, we need not resort to Ladd's account of the sameness and difference of actions to reflect adequately on Eichmann's case.

It remains, then, that either account can be used in reflecting on the sameness or difference of actions (with some preference for the "levels-of-description" account), and that in any case heeding motives, whether as a part of the action fully described or as a reason for the action, helps us to understand the moral status or value of the action.

A Small Paradox

Before I quite end this section, as I will do by saying how moral relativism relates to the Principle of Ascent, I need to return briefly to a paradox that surfaced in Chapter 3. In one form it relates to "moral rules" that most of us find to be familiar. As we have seen, we are more sensitive in our moral understanding of what the Eskimos are doing and what the Dinka are doing when we regard their actions in the light of a fuller description that includes their motive or goal. What, then, should we say about stealing per se, when there is no consideration of the agent's motive? "Stealing is wrong" *tout court* is a moral rule that ethical theories endeavor to accommodate. Most of us share the pretheoretical judgment that in some sense it is a moral rule that "Stealing is wrong," stated without reference to motive. How can *both* the sense that we are more sensitive morally in the light of fuller descriptions of actions *and* the pretheoretical judgment that certain rules are right *tout court* be correct? We also raised the paradox in connection with the Hopi "game" called the "chicken pull," the game in which a chicken is buried up to its neck in sand and contestants playing the game ride by on horseback, trying to grab the chicken and yank it from the sand. Chicken pulling, with no gloss, seems to be an instance of extreme cruelty to an animal. On the other hand, if we more fully describe the actions of the Hopi in playing this game, filling in a possible motive, it seems we can say that chicken pulling, like watching American boxing, is a means of attaining a needed and replenishing relief from the burdens of life. Chicken pulling and watching American boxing, then, would both be ways of *trying to* maintain a stability in one's life. At this level of description, chicken pulling seems to be the same thing we do in our society in various ways and even to be morally permissible. But how can it be that on the one hand the cruelty of chicken pulling is wrong and, on the other hand, Hopi individuals trying to maintain a stability in their life (which they do through playing the game of chicken pulling) is morally permissible?

Relationships can once again be appealed to for an explanation. Consider the stealing version of the paradox. What accounts for the wrongness of stealing *tout court* is that stealing per se violates the relationship we have to persons who own property: when we take someone's property without that person's permission we violate the relationship we have to that person by virtue of her owning that item of property. Because there is this general relationship to persons as property owners, we have a general moral rule "Stealing is wrong." However, when stealing is the only way to relieve the starvation of our children, or of strangers, other relationships become relevant. In this sort of case, the fuller description of one's act of stealing is *stealing in order to save another from starvation*. This description connects the action, via the person's motive or goal, to a value other than respect for property, namely, the obligation to prevent harm to others, which we have by virtue of the person/person relationship, and, if the one starving is our own child, by virtue of the parent-child relationship as well. Notice that in saying this much we have not claimed that the overriding duty *is* to steal in order to feed those who are starving. Although this may be the case, that judgment requires comparing the demands of the various relationships and considering how best to treat all persons affected as persons, in accord with the person/person relationship. Still, as much as we have seen gives us a way of understanding the stealing paradox: different relationships can create competing moral demands.

Something similar holds for the paradox in its chicken pull version. Chicken pulling in itself is wrong because it violates our relationship to a living being by inflicting pain on an animal in a cruel way.[25] But just as stealing without qualifi-

---

25. This relationship is not a relationship *between persons;* it is a relationship *between persons and*

cation should be distinguished from stealing to save a life, so chicken pulling without qualification should be distinguished from chicken pulling *while trying to maintain a stability in one's life* (which Hopi do through playing the game of chicken pulling). Chicken pulling in this fuller description may be morally permissible, as morally permissible as watching American boxing, which those in mainstream American culture may do to release aggressive energy and maintain a stability in their lives. This fuller description connects the chicken pulling to other relationships, such as the relationship one has to oneself. Again, noting this does not automatically make the Hopi practice right—that depends on the relative moral demands of the relationship Hopi individuals have to the living animal that is sacrificed for the sake of the game in comparison to the moral demands of the relationship Hopi individuals have to themselves and perhaps to others in the Hopi society.

Finally, let me say something about moral relativism and the Principle of Ascent. That principle is: "Ascending values tend toward universality: as the level of abstraction of a moral value increases, the breadth of its application and acceptability increases." As I observed above, moral relativism in some forms may have to deny the Principle of Ascent. A societal form of moral relativism that asserted that moral values and obligations are established by the societal attitudes of a particular society and that there are no values of greater levels of abstraction that apply to and hold across societies would have trouble accepting this principle. Absolutism in some forms, we should observe, would have a problem at the other end of the principle, if we understand the principle as allowing that less abstract particular *forms* of a value may hold *less* than universally. What we should particularly note here, though, is that at least one form of moral relativism—at least one way of understanding and affirming "there is no single true morality"—would not have trouble with this principle. The form that would not is the form that relationships explain.

IX. Conclusion: Stopping the Pendulum

With the issue of moral relativism, there is a pendulum swing. At times within the circle of reflective thought, moral relativism seems intellectually right—and then,

---

a nonhuman animal, and so persons are in the relationship. I explore how morality, understood in terms of relationships, extends to nonhuman animals and the environment in Chapter 15, "The Worth of Persons and Animal Rights," in *Relationship Morality.*

with the next swing, it seems wrong. Harman, who accepts moral relativism, recounts how in the 1960s various teachers of ethics rejected moral relativism.[26] At that time, and for several decades, the swing of the pendulum in philosophy was away from moral relativism. But today thinkers like Harman and Wong represent an incipient swing back toward relativism. There is something similar in anthropology: Herskovits and Benedict represented what was perhaps the extreme in anthropology in the direction of moral relativism, and now there appears to be a movement back the other way. Of course, the metaphor is not perfectly applicable. For one thing, not all are carried along in the predominant direction of thought. For another, there may be more than one pendulum in the circle of reflective thought—so that when the philosophical pendulum was tending away from relativism, at the same time the anthropological one was tending the other way. And in the broader intellectual culture there may be yet another pendulum, at present swinging toward postmodernism, which in one manifestation is relativistic. Nevertheless, it seems there are times when moral relativism is in the ascendancy and times when it is not.

The issue of moral relativism may seem to be resolved, but then it returns—and is given a different resolution. The pendulum swings. That the issue keeps coming back to be addressed anew in new ways suggests that there is something that appeals to our sensibilities in the positions that define the issue—in both the extremes. Going further, we may say that there seems to be something in both the positions that is right. This means that moral relativism is not all wrong. To finally come to a rest in our reflections on this issue, we need to see what is right about moral relativism and what is not right about it. But we need more. We need to find the *explanation* for what is right about the view and for what is not right about the view. It has been our effort to find that explanation.

The keystone of our explanation is relationships. Moral relativism is right that "there is *no* single true morality," for there are various *forms* of relationships between friends, between spouses, between speakers and hearers, between individuals and their societies; and these various relationships can generate different and even opposed duties in what are truly different moralities. But moral relativism is also wrong in that these *types* of relationships invariably do generate duties of friendship, marital fidelity, truth telling, and societal loyalty, and in that the person/person relationship generates the duty to treat persons as persons without being dependent on societal or cultural attitudes or on individual attitudes or on conventions or agreements. So it is also true that "there *is* a single true morality."

So is it, then, that both relativism and absolutism are right, and both are wrong?

26. Harman, "Is There a Single True Morality?" 364.

Isn't this merely a resolution of the sort we would offer if we followed the pattern of William James's resolution of the man-going-round-the-squirrel issue? In the Introduction I suggested that simply offering a clear and sweet distinction, which allows both parties to be right, does not go that far. My earlier suggestion, I believe, is correct. I am not merely drawing a lucid distinction and saying, "If you mean A, then you on this side of the issue are right" and "If you mean B, then you others on the other side of the issue are right." Nor am I, as Amélie Oksenberg Rorty did, pointing to elements on each side that are true. I am pointing to an underlying structure of relationships that *explains* how both relativism and absolutism are right in a fundamental way. It is a structure that accounts for the reasons each has for saying the other is wrong, and explains how their respective ways of being right connect to profound pretheoretical intuitions, themselves grounded in our shared experience of living in relationships.

NINE

Diversity and Morality

As a matter of descriptive fact, there is cultural diversity about us in the world and, depending upon where we live, to a greater or lesser extent in our immediate surroundings. In Singapore or London or Los Angeles, cultural diversity is and has been familiar; and now, in other cities and towns not known as multicultural crossroads, a new cultural diversity is manifesting itself. In various contemporary settings we find about us diversity in dress (ranging from the Sikh turban to the Iranian chador to blue jeans), diversity in food (ranging from garam masala to gefilte fish to "fast food"), diversity in grooming

grooming (ranging from uncut hair to a shaved head), and diversity in language (ranging from Farsi to Tagalog to the versions of English). There is also moral diversity. As a matter of descriptive fact, there are differences that we can observe in different cultures about what people value and what they regard as obligatory. At an easily accessible descriptive level, we can observe differences in what different people and different peoples count as respect for parents and as proper expressions of friendship. Moreover, we should allow, beyond what different people and peoples *regard* as right and obligatory, there are actual different moralities.

So it is that what in one relationship is an offspring's duty toward her parents will not be an offspring's duty in another child-parent relationship in another culture *or* within a single culture. Intraculturally, how a child honors a parent, or a parent nurtures a child, or a friend is loyal to a friend, or one spouse respects the other may vary from particular relationship to particular relationship. Interculturally, what may count as etiquette at table in one society may not qualify as acceptable in another society, and what may be a proper expectation of a marital relationship in one society may not be allowable in another marital relationship in another society. Good manners are importantly determined by societal practice, and beyond etiquette, societal expectations can importantly contribute to determining the expectations and requirements of various close relationships. In the same way, societal practice and traditions can contribute to the proper implementation of values such as autonomy or privacy in other relationships. In short, we consistently encounter the phenomenon of moral diversity—a diversity of actual moralities—both intraculturally and interculturally.

Samuel P. Huntington, the political scientist I drew upon in Chapter 2 for his views on universal values, is concerned with "cultural coexistence." He offers this advice: "In a multicivilized world, the constructive course is to renounce universalism, accept diversity, and seek commonalities." As a political scientist, Huntington's primary concern is a political concern with world order. He is concerned with the "clash of civilizations," and the threat of chaos in world affairs, for which he sees much evidence: "a global breakdown of law and order, failed states and increasing anarchy in many parts of the world, a global crime wave, transnational mafias and drug cartels, increasing drug addiction in many societies, a general weakening of the family, a decline in trust and social solidarity in many countries, ethnic, religious, and civilizational violence, and rule by the gun prevalent in much of the world." "Civilization," he observes, "seems . . . to be yielding to barbarism," with the prospect of "a global Dark Ages possibly descending on humanity." For Huntington, approaching this concern as a political scientist, "an international order based on civilizations is the surest safeguard against world war."[1]

Our concern is with the phenomenon of moral diversity itself and with gaining a better understanding of it. Our coming to understand moral diversity better does not ipso facto create a new "international order." But coming to understand why and how there is moral diversity and thus more than a single true morality, and also how amid the diversity there can yet be a single true morality, is not hurtful to the enterprise of seeking an "international order based on civilizations" and the intercultural communication it presupposes. Let me comment on Huntington's advice that in our multicultural, "multicivilized" world "the constructive course is to renounce universalism, accept diversity, and seek commonalities" in the light of what we have seen about morality and relationships.

The "universalism" that we are to renounce, for Huntington, is that which would insist upon the "supposedly universal features of one civilization." We can agree that there is a sense of "universalism" that should be rejected. In the terms of relationships, using a formulation that follows Huntington's, we should reject the idea that the *form* of various obligations arising from various relationships that we are familiar with in our culture or civilization must have a universal application. We should reject the idea that the form of the obligation of marital fidelity arising from the marital relationships we are familiar with coincides with an unvarying universal demand of all marriage relationships. Even within a culture or civilization, this point has an application: the form of the obligations of friendship arising from friendships that one is familiar with may or may not coincide with the obligations of friendship in another friendship within one's culture.

The "diversity" that Huntington wants us to accept is cultural: "Cultures . . . prescribe institutions and behavior patterns to guide humans in the paths which are right in a particular society."[2] By putting it this way, Huntington commits himself to that form of societal moral relativism that says societal practices or attitudes define moral rightness for a society. This idea is open to correction, as we have seen. Rather, the diversity we should accept is the diversity of *forms* of relationships—such as the marital relationship, which, like other relationships, is found in different forms, with different demands, in different cultures. Again, this point holds *within* a culture as well.

The third element of Huntington's advice is that we should seek "commonalities." He has in mind what is "common to most civilizations," their shared values,

---

1. Huntington, *Clash of Civilizations*, 318 and 321.
2. Ibid., 318.

which, he allows, following Walzer, constitute a "'thin' minimal morality [deriving] from the common human condition."³ As we saw in our earlier comments on Walzer, he distinguishes between a "thin" sense of justice and a "thick" sense of justice. The "thin" sense of justice represents the transcultural value of justice, which applies across cultures. And it is the person/person relationship that accounts for the demands of justice in this sense (justice requires that persons, regardless of culture, be treated as persons, that the person/person relationship to them not be violated—as it is by tyranny and oppression). In this way, one implicitly recognized "commonality" of all civilizations or cultures is the person/person relationship, which, among other things, accounts for justice as a transcultural value as well as other transcultural values. Another "commonality" consists of all the various relationship *types* that recur from society to society: child-parent relationships, marital relationships, friendship, and so on.

We may, then, seek to find both moral diversity *and* moral commonality; moreover, we may seek to find moral commonality *within* moral diversity if we heed the moral role of relationships. We have seen this point amply illustrated by the various examples of relationships and their requirements that we have discussed in this book. In this chapter we shall first examine an especially divisive instance of the phenomenon of moral diversity to see the particular way commonality, in this case, nevertheless resides within diversity. We shall then examine the danger of diversity seen as difference, the form of moral principle and practice in a multicultural world where there is understanding of moral diversity, and the form of moral progress that should be looked for in a multicultural and a multimoral world.

I. A Case of Diversity

In 1995 O. J. (Orenthal James) Simpson was brought to trial and charged with the 1994 murders of his wife, Nicole Brown Simpson, and her friend Ronald Goldman. The murder trial, which lasted eight months, was given intense coverage by print and broadcast media. Many around the world followed the trial, and many who did so formed an opinion about the guilt or innocence of O. J. Simpson. On October 3, 1995, the jury found Simpson not guilty.

In a newspaper editorial published two days after the jury's verdict had been rendered, Clarence Page cited polls showing that "two-thirds of white Americans

---

3. Ibid.

believed Mr. Simpson was guilty while two-thirds of blacks thought he was innocent."[4] Johnie H. Scott and James Dennis, in their examination of the news media's coverage of the Simpson murder trial, cite newspaper articles that report how the white and black publics had different views on whether justice was served by the jury's verdict. One article refers to the "almost unanimous racial division" in the reaction to the verdict.[5] Scott and Dennis observe that pictures in the print media of African Americans taken after the verdict showed them to be "elat[ed]," while pictures of white American showed their "anger, disgust, or both." They pose the question: "If a picture is worth a thousand words, then what does this observation say about race relations and the racial divide in America today?"[6] In another article, reporting on the results of a 1994 telephone interview of Los Angeles County residents, it is disclosed that 77 percent of blacks, as compared with 32 percent of whites, believe that the jury system is unfair. This finding, Scott and Dennis comment, "tells us . . . that African Americans have a long history of distrust in the jury system simply based on an inability to win in that situation."[7]

In the first article referred to above, it was reported how an African American man interviewed by a television station said, "Now white people can understand what an unjust decision feels like."[8] His implicit reference is to the 1992 verdict acquitting the four arresting officers in the Rodney King beating case. Scott and Dennis, who are alive to media bias, register some concern that the media chose this particular quote, with its apparent concession that the Simpson verdict was unjust.

As a result of their examination of the news coverage of the O. J. Simpson murder trial, Scott and Dennis conclude that the media allowed racial bias to get in the way of objective reporting in their rush to find "scoops" and "leaks."[9] Our concern here is not with the issue of media bias, or with the different opinions about O.J. Simpson's innocence, or even with racial bias as such, but with a phenomenon of moral diversity brought into relief by Scott and Dennis and by Page.

---

    4. Clarence Page, "An Entire Deck of Race Cards," *Baltimore Sun,* 5 October 1995.
    5. Johnie H. Scott and James Dennis, "'Rush to Judgment': A Mediated Analysis of the Politicizing of the O. J. Simpson Murder Trial by the American News Media," paper presented at the annual convention of the National Association of African American Studies, Houston, Texas, February 1996, and at the Ethics and Values Colloquium, California State University, Northridge, April 1996, 2.; the article cited is Ray Richmond, "Immense TV Audience Tunes In, Hears 2-Word Outcome," *Los Angeles Daily News,* 4 October 1995.
    6. Scott and Dennis, "'Rush to Judgment,'" 6.
    7. Maura Dolan, "Jury System is Held in Low Regard by Most," *Los Angeles Times,* 27 September 1994. Cited and commented on by Scott and Dennis, "'Rush to Judgment,'" 6–7.
    8. Richmond, "Immense TV Audience Tunes In," quoted by Scott and Dennis, "'Rush to Judgment,'" 2.
    9. Scott and Dennis, "'Rush to Judgment,'" 11.

There are two issues of justice involved in the O. J. Simpson murder trial. Both white Americans and black Americans, in Los Angeles and elsewhere, had a concern with justice. But their primary concerns with justice were different. Page observed in his editorial: "There were two trials here. There was the inside trial that the jurors saw in which O. J. Simpson was being judged. And there was the outside trial that the rest of us saw, in which American society, particularly its system of justice, was on trial." And he goes on to say that the polls he cited were "about the outside trial . . . the fairness of the criminal-justice system."[10]

The two issues of justice may be approached with this observation: on the one hand, many in the white population thought justice was not served with an acquittal, for they thought that a guilty man, or one the evidence strongly indicated was guilty, had escaped being found guilty and a proper punishment; and on the other hand, many in the black population thought justice was served with an acquittal, for a black man had gotten the same chance to make the system work for him as a white man with comparable wealth would have gotten. The concern among white Americans was with the requirement of justice that those innocent be acquitted and those guilty be found guilty. The concern among black Americans was with the requirement of justice that there be equality of treatment within the legal system. It should be noted that one could believe that O. J. Simpson was guilty, or that the evidence strongly indicated that he was, and yet celebrate the justice of equality in access to the resources available in the system of legal justice.

Both of these concerns are with *moral* justice, although each concern is with the moral justice to be found in the legal system of a governmental entity. And the objects of these two concerns are compatible: both are requirements of moral justice in its larger dimension. Nevertheless, these concerns are distinguishable and are very different in emphasis. Here, in these different concerns about different issues or aspects of moral justice, is the diversity. It is an intracultural diversity, we may say; or, if we wish to emphasize the cultural or ethnic differences between the black population and the white population in America—as perhaps we should when we consider the different historical experiences of these two populations— we may say that it is an intercultural diversity. But there is no reason to say that different conceptions of justice are being appealed to. If we follow Walzer and say that there are "thin" and "thick" meanings of justice, it is but one "thick" meaning that both concerns appeal to, or, alternatively, both concerns appeal to the shared "thin" meaning of the general concept of justice.

10. Page, "An Entire Deck of Race Cards."

Still, there is a diversity, and what helps us to understand that diversity is to see that the two groups stand in different relationships to the larger society. Those in the black population have experienced racial discrimination and bias in many forms in their individual lives, and this fact to a great extent fashions the relationship they have to the larger society in which they live. In that relationship, black Americans have learned to expect a presumption of guilt and have realized that they have to work harder than those who are white to gain what their society has to offer, including legal justice. Given this relationship, many in the black population have a special concern about African Americans' receiving equal treatment. Many of those in the white population may have experienced hardship, but they have not experienced a steady discrimination based on their race. Their relationship to the larger society, consequently, is different in significant ways from that of black Americans. Their relationship leads them to expect that they will receive from their society what they earn or deserve, *ceteris paribus*. Given this relationship, many white Americans see the primary concern of justice to be that individuals get what they deserve by virtue of their actions.

To appreciate the difference between the relationship of African Americans and the relationship of white Americans to the greater society, we need not think that each relationship is in order morally. In fact, the first, being informed by racial discrimination, goes counter to the demands of the person/person relationship. Consequently, as I argued in Section I of Chapter 7, it is a relationship that ought not to exist. It ought to be rectified. Nevertheless, it does exist, and it provides an understanding of the concern with justice that issues from it.

In both cases, though, there is an underlying commonality, marked by there being no ultimate disagreement about *all* that justice requires. This underlying commonality is more fully explained by the fact that all in the society, black or white, are in the same fundamental relationship, the person/person relationship. It is this relationship that explains both of the requirements of justice, for if either is not respected, the person/person relationship is violated. This is so even though what violates that relationship in the two cases is different. When a person does not get what he or she deserves, then the person/person relationship between that individual and others who are in a position to provide what is deserved is violated, as when an innocent person is found guilty (especially when that person is known to be innocent). Or, if the person is guilty and found to be innocent, then the person/person relationship between that individual and others in society, including the crime's victim or survivors is violated (especially if there is a strong case for the person's being guilty). In the other case, when a person is not given equal treatment, then that person is not being treated as a person equally with other persons, and the person/person relationship that person has to others who are in a position to help provide equal treatment is violated.

In this way, by heeding the different relationships between the black population and the larger society on the one hand, and the white population and the larger society on the other hand, we can understand their diverse moral reactions in the name of justice; and by heeding the underlying person/person relationship we can see how each is understandable in terms of a violation of that underlying relationship. I am not ruling it out that other relationships may have made moral claims on the reactions of black and white Americans. For instance, the relationship a person has to one's ethnic group may require an expression of loyalty. Nor am I ruling it out that a sense of identity or solidarity with one's own ethnic group may be an important motivating factor, regardless of, or in addition to, any moral requirement of one's relationship to that group. Nor do I mean to dismiss either a seeking of revenge or a sense of the sweetness of the tables' being turned as possible motivating factors. Our concern here, however, is with the diversity and commonality of the *moral* values and claims of African Americans and white Americans in their reactions to the O. J. Simpson murder trial, not with the mixture of their motives. And it remains that the concerns of these populations with justice are diverse and at the same time have an underlying commonality that is understandable in the light of the person/person relationship and what violates it.

II. Familiarity with Diversity

There is cultural diversity in the world, social diversity within our culture, and moral diversity both beyond and within our culture. We are all *aware* of these kinds of diversity, and in this sense they are familiar to us; however, we may not have that level of familiarity with them that allows us to be comfortable with them. We all often and regularly seek the quiet harbor of the familiar with which we feel comfortable. Although we may enjoy adventure if it is adequately controlled, finally we return to what is familiar. Our friends tend to be like us, sharing our profession or our interests or our neighborhood. Americans abroad seek out other Americans. Nationals of various countries who live in a foreign country form expatriate communities. It is, after all, easier to communicate with those who share our idiom, recognize our common references, and do not think our gestures odd. For whatever reason, we often seek the culturally familiar.

This is not to say that we cannot negotiate and enjoy the new and culturally unfamiliar, as on a vacation to another country. However, we would like the new and culturally unfamiliar not to be threatening or inimical. Sometimes when we live among others who are culturally different from ourselves and who seem comfortable with ways that are not familiar to us, we come to feel perplexed, and other times we may come to feel anxious. As one ethnic group comes into contact with the unfamiliar ways of another group, a tension may develop; and this can happen particularly when the diversity is in the moral sphere.

In the last section we saw an instance of such a tension over a moral matter. The moral concern of the African American population regarding the O. J. Simpson murder trial seemed to miss the point for the white population; and the moral concern of white Americans seemed off the mark, if not perverse, to African Americans. I have tried to bring out the underlying commonality of their two concerns, but when such a commonality is not appreciated in a deep way, the very difference of the moral reaction of the other group can be a source of tension. Multiplied across a range of moral issues or instances, such a tension can become pervasive and general, so that African Americans feel uncomfortable interacting with white people and vice versa.

When exacerbated, this tension can strongly affect behavior. As an effect of this tension, an African American man standing in a public building waiting for an elevator with a number of white men and women may feel uncomfortable and out of place; a white person may be afraid to speak to a black person whom he sees every so often at their shared work place, lest he say the wrong thing and unknowingly give offense. Jack Miles makes observations along the same lines in his essay on the impact of the Latino immigration on the black population in Los Angeles. Several families who live on his street hire gardeners. Miles observes: "All the gardeners are Latino, and when a slight brown man walks down a driveway, he is understood to be there for a good reason. Were a tall black man to do the same, there is not one of us who would not be immediately on the *qui vive*."[11] The point of Miles's observation is not simple, for some of his neighbors are themselves black, and the reaction he describes has much to do with the well-known fact that gardeners in Los Angeles are Latino, not African American. He goes on to observe, however, that "black men complain that they cannot shop without being shadowed by a suspicious shopkeeper. The same in effect goes for the black teenagers who

---

11. Jack Miles, "Blacks vs. Browns," reprinted in *California Dreams and Realities: Readings for Critical Thinkers and Writers,* ed. Sonia Maasik and Jack Solomon (Boston: Bedford Books/St Martin's, 1995), 91–92.

show up unannounced on our block."[12] In these cases especially, we can detect the kind of moral tension that I mean to draw attention to. The shopkeepers are suspicious of black men who are shopping, thinking they are likely to be shoplifters. Those living on the block think the black teenagers may be up to thievery. In the first case, the shopkeepers see as the most important moral concern the prevention of theft, while their black patrons complain about being denied equal courtesy with other patrons. Although in these examples Miles illustrates the white reaction to African Americans (as opposed to Latinos), we should appreciate that the tension I am referring to may be between any of very many ethnic groups—and may occur within an ethnic group between genders, say, or between generations. All that is required for the distinctly moral tension that I am referring to is the perception on each side of a difference in moral concern or behavior, a difference in what is morally approved of or taken to be the more important moral concern.

What we see in such examples is not a difference over a matter of moral principle: there may be complete agreement on moral principles, and it may be that the right principles are accepted by all concerned. What we see in these examples is a kind of moral unease or malaise. It is closer to the heart of moral behavior than moral principle, closer to virtue—yet even deeper than virtue; for generosity, justice, temperance, and consideration may all be in place in the dispositions of those on the opposing sides but may be vitiated by this moral malaise, which itself derives from the moral tension we have identified.

A factor that contributes to this moral tension is that our sense of our value as persons can be expressed by emphasis on our particularity. To proclaim the value we have as a person we may, for instance, proclaim our blackness ("black is beautiful") or our Jewishness or our Asian-American or Italian-American or Chicano identity, or our Ibo or Irish identity, or our gender identity. Take this identity away, and we are still a person, we appreciate. Yet to stress our value as a person, we may have no way other than to stress such a particularity.[13] In fact, if our self-respect is at risk, it may be a duty to ourselves to stress a particularity about ourselves, such as our blackness, that proclaims our value as a person.

Yet when others see us exclusively in terms of our ethnic identity, problems may ensue. Stories abound to illustrate this concern. Here is one, relating to an episode in Strangers' Quarters in Kumba, a township in West Cameroon, in the early 1960s. A young white man, a "European," was walking through Strangers' Quarters in the evening. As he passed a house, he heard an African woman on the porch of the

12. Ibid., 91–92.
13. Discussions with Tamara Benefield have helped me appreciate this point.

house speaking to her very young child in pidgin, the lingua franca of West Cameroon. She was telling her child to be good or the white man would eat him. The child was crying in fright. She did not know that the young white man could "hear" pidgin enough to understand. He objected, saying in effect, "Now why do you say that?" The African woman was somewhat taken aback, but his pidgin was too limited for much more of an exchange. And what did he have to say anyway? Many white mothers in the past in his own country must have said something similar to their children about the boogie man, the black boogie man, to get their children to be good.

Amartya Sen cites the eleventh-century writer Alberuni (al-Bīrūnī), an Iranian Muslim, who, in India, observes that the Hindus "differ from us to such a degree as to frighten their children with us, with our dress, and our ways and customs, and as to declare us to be devil's breed, and our doings as the very opposite of all that is good and proper." Alberuni continues, however, "We must confess, in order to be just, that a similar depreciation of foreigners not only prevails among us and the Hindus, but is common to all nations toward each other."[14]

Nevertheless, anecdotally I can report this: on the ethnically diverse campus where I teach, it seems to me that my students are friends in an easy and natural way across ethnic and racial lines. Keith Ward remarked (at a 1997 conference on world religions at Chapman University) that nothing contributes to the ecumenical effort as much as people from the different religions sharing a meal together. Being together in a university setting can bring about the kind of familiarity and understanding of others' moral ways and concerns that address the moral tension and malaise I spoke of.

This increased understanding can happen in a university setting, but in other multicultural settings as well. The contemporary world is itself such a multicultural setting—the one that includes all the others. When the kind of moral understanding I have described happens, what is it that we come to understand? It is not a universal resolution to the moral problems we face, ranging from justice in college admissions to world famine. Nor do we come to understand that there is, in fact, no moral diversity—for there *is* moral diversity. I suggest that there are two things we come to understand and appreciate. First, in great part it is how relationships one is familiar with in one form can be expressed in other forms. We come to see that as we try to fulfil our family commitments, to meet our commitments to our friends, and to obtain just treatment for ourselves through a certain set of actions, so others may try to do the same things through a different

14. Sen, "Human Rights and Asian Values," 38.

set of actions—and that at a higher level of description the actions may turn out to be the same. The second thing we come to understand is that these other persons, who recently may have been "other" to us, are with us in a relationship that we all share by virtue of our being persons.

III. Moral Principle and Practice

What are we hoping for in the new multicultural world? Certainly we are hoping for more moral understanding of one another. But there is more to be hoped for in the moral sphere. It is to be hoped that moral understanding will bear its fruit in moral practice. In this section I want to examine the form of such practice and what it might be, fully realized.

For nearly everyone, at the level of pretheoretical understanding, there are moral principles. This holds for moral philosophers as well as for those of us who are not moral philosophers but who are moral beings in the quotidian sense that we often in our lives face moral questions about what we ought to do, make moral decisions, and think well or poorly of others and ourselves for our actions. For some of us, moral principles are moral rules like "It is wrong to steal" or "Everyone ought to be treated fairly." It is possible to think that there is one fundamental moral principle, as Mill thought, and then to hold that the familiar rules of morality are secondary moral principles.[15] And it is possible to think that the virtues are morally more important than principles, so that *being* honest—having the virtue of honesty—is more important than conforming one's overt behavior to the moral principle or rule "It is wrong not to tell the truth." For all of these approaches, however, there are moral principles in some sense and with some degree of moral importance.

The first thing we should appreciate is that the moral practice that we may hope for as the result of an understanding of moral diversity is not merely morally principled behavior; at least morally principled behavior should not do as our highest aspiration. For one thing, it is possible that an adopted moral principle would be a wrong principle; for instance: "It is permissible to subjugate those peoples who do not convert to our religion [or, in another variant, are not citizens of our nation]." Today perhaps no one would confess to believing that this is a right principle, but in the past it has been followed.

---

15. John Stuart Mill, *Utilitarianism*, chap. 2.

However, even if the moral principles that are followed are right principles, the resulting moral practice is not the best we can hope for. Let us allow that a right moral principle is the principle of moral justice that requires us to treat everyone with equality. If everyone diligently followed this principle, the world might well be a better place. Still, though everyone was dedicated to following this principle, there could be questions about what following the principle entailed. It might be unclear what "equal treatment" in different settings—hiring, job advancement, college admissions, health insurance—amounted to, and against whom specific claims to the right of equal treatment should be made. These questions are answerable, but not by the principle in its bare form. There is another consideration. Say that all these questions are answered or resolved. Even so, the most we would have is everyone carefully and correctly following the proper moral principles. Though this much may well mean that everyone's moral rights (or many of them) are respected, it would not mean that the resulting moral behavior is informed by any sense of caring for other persons or of human solidarity with them. Although on some views of what morality involves, such as Kant's, such "feelings" are not a part of morality, a view of morality that sees relationships between persons as fundamental to morality cannot fail to acknowledge a necessary place for feeling and sentiments. In accord with common intuitions, if friends do not in some way care for each other, and if married partners do not in some way trust one another, those relationships are not lived up to. Merely following moral principles in an assiduous but mechanical way would leave out an essential element of moral behavior.

The moral practice that we may hope for in our multicultural world is a moral behavior, both external and internal, that is in accord with the moral demands of our relationships. But which ones? We all have a sense of the demands of our close relationships, and often—at least briefly—we have a sense of our relationship to those in the world who are in special need, like those in Bosnia, Bangladesh, or Sierra Leone. In a multicultural world, we are coming to have a greater appreciation of those who are culturally different from ourselves, interculturally and intraculturally, and I have suggested that we gain a moral understanding of the moral diversity we encounter by coming to understand how relationships familiar to us may find expression in different *forms* among different cultural groups, and by coming to understand how we all, irrespective of our cultural ways, are in one person/person relationship to one another.

If we realize what the person/person relationship requires, we will appreciate that we always ought to treat persons as persons. Moreover, we should recognize that we are in a *further relationship* to those whose cultural ways differ from our own and with whom we live in a multicultural setting. This is a new relationship we have to others not by virtue of our being related as persons, but by virtue of our all living together in a morally diverse world, in a multicultural setting within a larger culture, or in the contemporary world, shrunk by rapid travel and instant electronic communication. Like other relationships, this new relationship has requirements. As we all try to live together and to understand one another, this relationship requires the active effort of those in morally diverse groups to understand the moral ways of their various neighbors. There is a further positive implication of this new relationship. We should treat those with diverse moral ways in a way that expresses our appreciation of our joint need to understand one another, which is to say with some sense of solidarity. This new relationship, then, requires an extension of the way we morally treat those close to us with whom we have a familiar relationship. As opposed to merely treating our morally diverse neighbors with a respect that is based on moral principle that we feel it our duty to follow, our relationship to one another requires our solidarity.

IV. Moral Progress

What will count as moral progress in our new multicultural world? This question is closely related to that of the last section. Or rather, what answers the question of the last section, about what we may and should hope for in the new multicultural world, is closely related to what answers the question of what we should look for in seeking moral progress in this multicultural world.

Perhaps all moral philosophers and all moral theories would allow that there can be moral progress *in some form*. Some variants of moral relativism must deny some forms of moral progress, but they can allow others. Thus societal forms of moral relativism that regard the moral customs or beliefs of a society as defining moral rightness in a society would deny that there can be progress in a society's moral beliefs, but they could allow that more people in a society's following their society's moral beliefs constituted moral progress. Moral thinkers who are not relativists, however, speak of moral progress with more alacrity. Among these thinkers we may find several conceptions of moral progress.

1. Moral Progress in the Consistent Application of Principles: A. C. Ewing articulates a classical and clear concept of moral progress when he says, "One of the chief lines, perhaps the chief line, of moral progress through the ages has lain in making our ethics less and less inconsistent by applying the same principles more and more thoroughly to our conduct towards more and more people."16 Assuming that the principles being applied are *right* moral principles, this would seem to be a kind of moral progress. For this kind of moral progress, the progress is not in the principles themselves or in our moral understanding, but in the consistency of our applying principles presumably already understood; and the locus of the progress is the agent, the person applying the principles with more consistency.

2. Moral Progress in Ideas (Moral Beliefs, Principles): Moral progress of another kind occurs when there is improvement in our moral principles themselves. Moral progress of this kind occurs when, for instance, the principle "It is right to treat those who have our ethnicity with fairness" gives way in our thinking to the principle "It is right to treat all with fairness." Moral progress of this kind would have occurred if the German Nazis had rejected the principle that "*Untermenschen* do not deserve to be treated as human beings," or if Sicilian society had rejected the principle (embodied in the societal practice) that allows a rejected suitor to kidnap and rape the woman who rejected him.

3. Moral Progress in Behavior: It is possible to think of moral progress solely in terms of moral behavior. This notion of moral progress is closely related to Ewing's, but with a difference. For Ewing moral progress is a matter of a growth in the *consistency* of moral behavior. Here the idea is that there could be moral progress if there were, say, a widening of our sympathy for others, or if by intermarriage or by some other means our attitude toward others was changed. Franz Boas observes that "it is difficult to define progress in ethical ideas . . . [and it] is still more difficult to discern universally valid progress in social organization." However, he does allow that "progress in social forms" can take place. "It is," Boas says,

> based fundamentally on the recognition of a wider concept of humanity, and with it on the weakening of the conflicts between individual societies. The outsider is no longer a person without rights, whose life and property are the lawful prey of any who can conquer him, but intertribal duties are recognized. However these are developed, whether the tribe wishes to avoid the retaliation of neighbors, or whether friendly relations are established by intermarriage or in other ways, the intense solidarity of the tribal unit and its subdivisions is liable to break down.17

16. Ewing, *Ethics*, 125.
17. Franz Boas, *Anthropology and Modern Life* (New York: Norton, 1962), 228–29.

Although Boas casts his point in terms of *tribal* societies, in principle it applies to nontribal societies as well. The form of the advance Boas describes includes the recognition of both rights and duties; but the advance itself is not the better appreciation of how widely moral principles apply or the rejection of old principles, it is a behavioral change seen in the recognition of a wider concept of humanity and a weakening of conflicts.

4. Moral Progress in Ideas and Behavior: Ruth Macklin proposes a conception of moral progress that embraces both moral beliefs and behavior. She suggests that the "concept of moral progress" is "explicated as resting on two basic normative principles," which can be used to judge the comparative degree of moral progress across cultures or eras. The "principle of *humaneness*" is that "one culture, society, or historical era exhibits a higher degree of moral progress than another if the first shows more sensitivity to (less tolerance of) the pain and suffering of human beings than does the second, as expressed in the laws, customs, institutions, and practices of the respective societies or eras." The second principle, the "principle of *humanity*," is that "one culture, society, or historical era exhibits a higher degree of moral progress than another if the first shows more recognition of the inherent dignity, the basic autonomy, or the intrinsic worth of human beings than does the second, as expressed in the laws, customs, institutions, and practices of the respective societies or eras."[18]

Macklin concedes that "these two principles are admittedly somewhat vague" by virtue of the use of such terms as "sensitivity to," "tolerance of pain and suffering," and "recognition of the dignity, autonomy, or intrinsic worth of human beings." Nevertheless, she observes, "The application of the principles is based on clear observable evidence" drawn from societies and eras. Thus, under the principle of *humaneness,* the "prohibition of cruel and unusual punishment is a sign of moral progress over earlier eras when the hands of thieves were cut off," and further evidence of moral progress is found in "the sorts of arguments used to justify changes in laws and allowable practices." Similarly, under the principle of *humanity,* she cites the Bill of Rights, fair employment legislation, child labor laws, equal rights amendments, and judicial decisions against discriminatory practices as evidence of moral progress.[19]

Thus, though the focus of Macklin's discussion of moral progress seems to be on modern societies like that of the United States, in contradistinction to the focus

---

18. Macklin, "Universality of the Nuremberg Code," 242. She cites her "Moral Progress," *Ethics,* 87 (1977): 371–72, where there is an earlier statement of these two principles.

19. Ibid., 242 and 243.

of Boas's comments on "progress in social forms," and though the examples of evidence she cites relate more easily to the judgment that there has been moral progress in a particular society over time (from era to era) than that one society shows "a higher degree of moral progress" than another society, clearly, for her, the field of possible evidence for moral progress includes both behavior (customs and societal practice) and ideas (constitutional amendments, legislation, and judicial decisions).

We should note Macklin's special debt to Kantian thinking, as when she appeals to "the inherent dignity, the basic autonomy, or the intrinsic worth of human beings." As we have seen, autonomy may not be a value in some cultural settings, and respect for persons in those setting may require that they not be treated as autonomous agents. And we might note as well that there is no reference to the treatment of animals or care for the environment in her criteria for moral progress, both of which, more and more, are being recognized as moral concerns.

Nevertheless, even if her formulation of the principles she cites might be open to emendation or additions, it remains that Macklin gives us a clear notion of moral progress and that if there were changes in accord with her two principles, arguably it would be moral progress by virtue of developments in ideas *and* behavior. Of course, those who characterize moral progress essentially in terms of ideas or essentially in terms of behavior need not deny moral progress in the other dimension. For Boas, although progress is in "social forms," still it is "associated with advance in knowledge" and based on a "recognition of a wider concept of humanity."[20] Conceivably, there could be progress in moral ideas alone (in a society's moral beliefs or principles) or in moral behavior alone (with no accompanying rationale). Over the long range, though, the one would need the other; and moral progress in the full sense would involve both spheres.

Before we go on to a fifth way of understanding moral progress, let me connect what we have so far seen with relationships and their explanatory power. Relationships explain moral progress as progress in applying principles, or as progress in ideas, or as progress in behavior, or in behavior and ideas together. Moral progress as progress in behavior is explained as progress in meeting the practical requirements of relationships. Some of these relationship whose requirements are being lived up to better may be relationships not acknowledged heretofore, and some may be newly entered relationships. Boas's example of intermarriage is an example of such a new relationship for those in a cultural setting which had forbidden intermarriage. If what I said earlier is correct, we today in our contemporary world are, by virtue of the physical and electronic proximity of moral diversity, in another

---

20. Boas, *Anthropology and Modern Life*, 228.

new relationship with people and peoples who have moral ways different from our own. Moral progress as progress in ideas is progress in identifying principles (or beliefs or laws) that flow from relationships, including the person/person relationship with its implications for human rights and for the proper demands of familiar relationships. Progress in applying moral principles to more and more persons, where doing so is a matter of moral recognition (Ewing), is explained by an implicit or explicit recognition of how widely general relationships extend, especially the person/person relationship, which is, in essence, what occurs when we come to a wider concept of humanity (Boas) or come to have respect for the inherent dignity or intrinsic worth of more persons (Macklin).

5. *Moral Progress in Allowing a Greater Range of Concepts of a Good Life:* Moral pluralists acknowledge that there is a moral diversity in the world. For some it is a diversity of moral systems, for some a diversity of moral perspectives, and, for John Kekes (as we saw in Chap. 5), it is a diversity of values and of reasonable conceptions of a good life. Moral pluralists do not despair over moral diversity; they accept it and accommodate it in terms of their pluralism. However, at the same time, they need not see an *increase* in diversity as progress. It is distinctive of Kekes's pluralism that he does see an increase in diversity as an "ideal." For traditions and for individuals, the ideal for Kekes, we will recall, is a "form of life in which the widest range of specific values may be pursued." It is progress for traditions to provide a wider range of conceptions of a good life, and it is progress for individuals to have a wider range of values from which to construct a good life. Earlier (in Sec. VII of Chap. 7) I argued that there are limits on, and opportunities for, the values and conceptions of a good life that Kekes's pluralism does not recognize. A "good life" that violates one's person/person relationship to oneself or to others, or "values" that do so, are not good or valuable after all. A "value" like gormandizing may be included as a central feature of one's life, but that does not take away its demeaning character and demoralizing effect. If this is correct, then there are some increases in the diversity of accepted values, or conceptions of a good life including such values, that would not constitute moral progress.

Others, of course, have seen a value in *cultural* diversity. Some have held that human beings have a cultural right to maintain their cultural identity, and I argued earlier (in Sec. VI of Chap. 7) that if respect for members of a culture, as persons, requires that they preserve their culture, then this is among their rights. Again, if one's maintaining one's cultural or ethnic identity is a requirement of self-respect, then doing so may be a duty to oneself, as I argued above. However, this kind of diversity is *cultural,* and although cultural diversity may often involve moral diversity, in some cases diverse cultures may have essentially the same morality.

Furthermore, what such cultural rights and a duty to oneself to assert one's cultural or ethnic heritage show—assuming there are such rights and duties in and for several cultures—is that diversity has a value, but not that it has a value *for itself*. Cultural diversity and the moral diversity it may entail have a value just so long as maintaining or asserting cultural identity is a requirement of respect for members of a culture or of persons' self-respect as persons. It may be, then, that others who have seen a value in the melting of peoples into one homogeneous culture or way of life are also right, as they would be if such a merging of cultural ways can, in other settings, also be a means to the realization of self-respect.

6. Moral Progress in Tolerance for Diversity: However, if there is a question about whether an increase in moral diversity per se is moral progress, this question does not apply to progress in *tolerance* for diversity, including moral diversity. Kekes and other moral pluralists would surely recognize a growth in the tolerance for moral diversity as moral progress, as would others.

Elizabeth Wolgast understands moral diversity as a plurality of moral perspectives. In a world of such moral diversity, tolerance is of special value, she believes:

> How people treat one another in a heterogeneous culture will reflect the members' capacities as individuals to offer respect to one another despite their moral differences. In this sense toleration must rank high among public virtues, and it is particularly precious for the respect of individual conscience. Although one may wish for a simpler world where such a virtue is unnecessary, a homogeneous moral community, there is surely a particular worth in the practice of toleration as I describe it."[21]

She means a toleration for persons' moral perspectives, their "individual conscience[s]," as she says, and their "steadfast moral commitment," which we can understand as like our own if we have our own moral commitments. Sometimes we may judge that a moral perspective with which we disagree is still deserving of respect, so that we acknowledge its "moral persuasiveness without subscribing to it." However, not all viewpoints may be open to understanding and toleration, Wolgast suggests. She rejects the idea that "there is a general obligation to tolerate others' views when the judgments they yield, albeit intensely held, are wrong."[22]

Wolgast's concern with tolerance is developed in particular reference to the current debate about abortion. She laments the fact that an effort "to understand

---

21. Wolgast, "Moral Pluralism," 115.
22. Ibid., 114.

the moral force of, and another's commitment to, a moral perspective is notably missing in most debates about abortion." Such an effort would be an effort "to imaginatively see inside another's moral universe." However, she does not maintain "that we must hold all perspectives as equally worthy," or that we are morally committed to tolerating views that yield wrong, though sincerely held, moral judgments. A perspective that approves of infanticide, she allows, "may not be morally credible to us."[23]

She has in mind, then, two kinds of conflict cases, both of which are intracultural: first, cases that we (in Chap. 7, Sec. IV) identified as morally indeterminate in the sense that they either resist careful and sincere efforts at resolution or in principle can have no satisfactory resolution (such as the abortion debate); and second, cases where one moral perspective approves of what is more straightforwardly wrong (her example of infanticide). In addition there are other instances of moral diversity that involve moral differences in practice and judgment but typically do not give rise to moral debate about the right course of action, and that may be either intercultural or intracultural. These are the instances of moral diversity that I have discussed, such as the intercultural case of the difference between the demands of Eskimo marriage and the demands of marriage in the cultures of the predominant societies of North or South America or of Europe, and the intracultural case of different friendships with different moral demands.

In all of these cases, relationships help us to understand the possibility and the appropriateness of tolerance and hence how tolerance can be a value and a virtue. Consider the two kinds of conflict cases that Wolgast draws to our attention. We have seen how reflecting on the different relationships involved in morally indeterminate cases helps us to understand those issues and why people are divided on them. In our own discussion of the abortion issue (in Sec. II of Chap 7), I tried to bring out how reflecting on relationships helps us to understand the disagreements within the abortion issue. Each side looks to different relationships and to different understandings of relationships and their demands. There may be disagreement over our relationship to the fetus as a person and, allowing that the fetus is a person, about whether the rights of the woman or the rights of the unborn fetus are more stringently demanded by the person/person relationship. Relationships in this way help to explain the indeterminacy of this issue.

Understanding this much should enhance our understanding of the two opposed views or perspectives. Moreover, if one is opposed to abortion and appeals to the rights of the fetus, and so to our person/person relationship to the fetus, one should

23. Ibid., 113, 114, and 115.

be able to understand the perspective of those who are not opposed to abortion, who appeal to a woman's right to have an abortion, as making the *same kind of appeal* ultimately to the person/person relationship. And it would go the other way as well, so that one who is not opposed to abortion should be able to understand the perspective of one who is. Such understanding, it may be hoped, will lead to the form of tolerance that, in Wolgast's words, leads each side to acknowledge of the opposing perspective its "moral persuasiveness without subscribing to it."

However, realistically, this may not happen. Those opposed to abortion and those not opposed to it may continue to regard their own view as right and the opposing view as straightforwardly wrong. Each side, in other words, may see the abortion debate as a conflict case of the second sort that Wolgast identifies. In this kind of case, one side approves what is patently wrong—even evil. Wolgast does not regard the abortion debate as this kind of case, but she does allow that there can be such cases. A moral perspective that approved of infanticide is one of her examples, and we could bring forward other examples, such as the Sicilian practice that allows rejected suitors to resort to rape. Is tolerance appropriate in such cases? Here too, an appeal to relationships can be helpful. Although it may be wrong for us to approve or even withhold disapproval in such cases, still the person/person relationship allows, and even requires, our respect for the person. Respect for persons does not require us to agree with their moral judgments or to tolerate their moral views or action, but it does require us to tolerate them as persons, granting them the civility that they may deny to others even as we disapprove of their actions.

Finally, there are the kinds of intercultural and intracultural differences that we have discussed in several contexts in this book—differences, for instance, over the demands of marriage and over the demands of friendship. Here our reflections on relationships give us the means to understand how diverse moralities can be equally right morally (for different moralities, with their different *forms* of such relationships as the marital relationship, can nevertheless equally be in accord with the demands of that *type* of relationship and the demand of the person/person relationship that persons be respected as persons). At the same time, our reflections give us the means of understanding how some moralities can be wrong (for instance, a morality that embraced abusive relationships would be wrong in that it allowed a relationship in which persons are *not* treated as persons). It is an implication of thinking of the different forms of relationships in this way, including the marital relationship, that we should wean ourselves away from asking such general and unqualified questions as "Is it right to have more than one spouse?" In some forms of the marital relationship it is, and in others it definitely is not. Again, the question "Is it right to disagree with your parents?" is ill-conceived as a general and unqualified question. So too are various analogous questions directed to the general requirements of relationships that may have different forms. Rather, an appreciation of the different *forms* that relationships can take gives us the means to understand how diverse moralities can be equally right morally, and this understanding opens the way to a tolerance for those moralities that are different from our own.

Thus, in order to accommodate fully the ways of tolerance open to us, and to encourage their growth, we need to have in place respect for all persons *as persons*, and not only tolerance for the moral perspectives of seriously committed moral agents. This respect for persons is entailed by the person/person relationship, and the kinds of tolerance that Wolgast and others recognize as valuable should be seen as forms of the respect for persons that the person/person relationship requires.

Related to an increase of tolerance for diversity is an increase in certain cognate moral feelings, such as the feeling of fellowship. We drew upon Boas's thinking in his *Anthropology and Modern Life* in discussing moral progress as progress in behavior. In his *Mind of Primitive Man,* which he wrote earlier but revised later than *Anthropology and Modern Life,* Boas says "We can trace the general broadening of the feeling of fellowship during the advance of civilization. The feeling of fellowship in the horde expands to the feeling of unity of the tribe, to a recognition of bonds established by a neighborhood of habitat, and further on to the feeling of fellowship among members of nations. This seems to be the limit of the ethical concept of fellowship of man which we have reached at the present time."[24]

John Cook sees Boas's reference to this "gradual broadening of the feeling of fellowship" as his "citing ... an example of 'progress'"—and we need not disagree. Boas says that "at the present time" (he revised *The Mind of Primitive Man* in 1938), "members of nations" mark the limit of the feeling of fellowship. If it is progress for our feeling of fellowship to be extended beyond our immediate group to members of our nation, then it should be further progress for that feeling to be extended to the diverse peoples of our larger culture and of the world. Of course, this sense of fellowship is different from tolerance for diversity in that tolerance can exist without a feeling of fellowship (based on considerations of mutual security or self-interest, say), but, conversely, the feeling of fellowship cannot exist without a spirit of tolerance. This feeling is a feeling that accompanies, or forms the affective part of, an appreciation of being in the person/person relationship to other persons in the world. Its growth marks a widening realization of the compass of the person/person relationship in which we stand.

---

24. Franz Boas, *The Mind of Primitive Man* (New York: Free Press; London: Collier Macmillan, 1938), 202.

V. Conclusion

In our new world of moral diversity, there are many moral voices. Some are intercultural, some intracultural. Some speak for rights: women's rights, ethnic rights, gay rights. Some appeal to "family values." Some that are less militant we may barely be aware of, but we discover as the voice of a distinct morality. This polyphony may at times cause us to feel confused or anxious. "Things fall apart," we may think, as Yeats thought in his Europe and as Achebe thought in his Africa. Huntington, viewing the world scene, is concerned about the emergence of global chaos and barbarism.

Yet there is in our moral diversity an underlying commonality. Neither the diversity nor the commonality should be denied, and what explains the one explains the other. There is in our human affairs, and in our moral diversity itself, the basis for a sense of solidarity. However, our reacting to moral diversity as something threatening or merely exotic undermines human understanding of both our diversity and our solidarity. Appreciating the validity of various moralities and how they in their diverse ways reflect the commonality of the underlying values of relationships that are familiar to us all upbuilds our understanding and our sense of solidarity. One important form of moral progress is progress in tolerance for other moral perspectives and other moralities. When tolerance is binding, it is based on understanding. And perhaps the deepest understanding occurs when we come to see in different moral perspectives and in different moral behaviors a respect for relationships that we do not stand in, but in which we might have stood in another kind of life—especially when we see simultaneously that these relationships that we do not stand in are, in fact, different forms of the same types of relationships that we respect in our own lives.

We can appreciate that at one level of description there may be moral differences in practice of such a sort as to bring an initial shudder to those on either side—as in the funeral story by Herodotus. At the same time, keeping in mind the lesson of the Principle of Ascent, we can appreciate that at a fuller level of description there may be no moral difference. To be sure, it is too simple to reason that if a society or culture or individual is sincerely committed to a practice, then that practice is morally allowable. The Nazi death-camp policy, the Pol Pot policy of the Khmer Rouge, and the Sheridan policy toward American Indians are among the counterexamples that press forward to show that the forms of moral relativism that propose such a criterion contradict the morality they mean to represent. This is why we need the test of the person/person relationship. But many distinct moralities with their distinctive forms of human relationships are in accord with the person/person relationship.

We have come to the conclusion that there is no one true morality (for different relationships, or forms of relationships, can create different moralities with different obligations) but also that there *is* one true morality (for respecting the proper requirements of our relationships is an unchanging basis of morality in all its forms, and the requirement of the person/person relationship is that persons in the various relationships in which they stand always be treated as persons). We have also come to the conclusion that there is both a moral diversity and a moral commonality. If I am right, what is needed is not a recognition of moral relativism alone, but a recognition of both the rightness and the wrongness of the idea that there is no single true morality, and—even more importantly—a recognition of the underlying explanation of why this is so. That explanation involves the moral functioning of the myriad relationships that bind us one to another, including the person/person relationship, which itself binds us as beings with the groundless and unconditional worth of persons. It is this understanding of relationships that stills the pendulum swinging between moral relativism and moral absolutism; and it is this explanation, at the turning of the millennium, that encourages us to accept moral diversity along with its grounding in moral commonality.

Works Cited

Aquinas, St. Thomas. *Summa Theologica.*
Aristotle. *Nicomachean Ethics.* Trans. W. D. Ross. In *Introduction to Aristotle,* ed. Richard McKeon. New York: Modern Library, 1947.
———. *Nicomachean Ethics.* Trans. J. A. K. Thomson, rev. by Hugh Tredennick. In *The Ethics of Aristotle.* New York: Penguin Books, 1976.
Austin, J. L. "A Plea for Excuses." In *Philosophical Papers,* ed. J. O. Urmson and C. J. Warnock. Oxford: Clarendon Press, 1961.
Baker, Robert. "A Theory of International Bioethics: Multiculturalism, Postmodernism, and the Bankruptcy of Fundamentalism." *Kennedy Institute of Ethics Journal* 8 (1998): 201–31.
———. "A Theory of International Bioethics: The Negotiable and the Non-Negotiable." *Kennedy Institute of Ethics Journal* 8 (1998): 233–73.
Beauchamp, Tom L., and James F. Childress. *Principle of Biomedical Ethics.* Third edition. New York: Oxford University Press, 1979.
Benedict, Ruth. *Patterns of Culture.* Boston: Houghton Mifflin, 1934.
Blackhall, Leslie J., Sheila T. Murphy, Gelya Frank, Vicki Michel, and Stanley Arzen. "Ethnicity and Attitudes toward Patient Autonomy." *Journal of the American Medical Association* 274, no. 10 (13 September 1995): 820–25.
Boas, Franz. *Anthropology and Modern Life.* New York: Norton, 1962.
———. *The Mind of Primitive Man.* New York: Free Press; London: Collier Macmillan, 1938.
Booth, Wayne C. "Individualism and the Mystery of the Social Self; or Does Amnesty Have a Leg to Stand On?" In *Freedom and Interpretation: The Oxford Amnesty Lectures, 1992,* ed. Barbara Johnson. New York: Basic Books/Harper Collins, 1993.
Bradley, F. H. *Appearance and Reality.* Second edition. Oxford: Clarendon Press, 1897.

Brandt, Richard B. *Ethical Theory: The Problems of Normative and Critical Theories.* Englewood Cliffs, N.J.: Prentice-Hall, 1959.
———. *Hopi Ethics.* Chicago: University of Chicago Press, 1954.
Bringa, Tone. *Being Muslim the Bosnian Way: Identity and Community in a Central Bosnian Village.* Princeton: Princeton University Press, 1995.
Callicott, J. Baird. "The Case Against Moral Pluralism." *Environmental Ethics* 12 (Summer 1990): 99–124.
Carrese, Joseph A., and Lorna A. Rhodes. "Western Bioethics on the Navajo Reservation: Benefit or Harm?" *Journal of the American Medical Association* 274, no. 10 (13 September 1995): 826–29.
Castiglione, Arturo. *A History of Medicine.* Translated and edited by E. B. Krumbhaar. New York: Alfred A. Knopf, 1941.
Chao Chu, Bhikkhu. "Buddhism and Dialogue Among the World Religions: Meeting the Challenge of Materialist Skepticism." In *Ethics, Religion, and the Good Society,* ed. Joseph Runzo. Louisville, Ky.: Westminster/John Knox Press, 1992.
Chaucer, Geoffrey. "The Parson's Tale," *The Canterbury Tales. In The Works of Geoffrey Chaucer,* ed. F. N. Robinson. Second edition. Boston: Houghton Mifflin 1957.
Cheney, Jim. "The Nep-Stoicism of Radical Environmentalism." *Environmental Ethics* 11 (1989): 293–395.
Cochrane, Donald. "Prolegomena to Moral Education." In *The Domain of Moral Education,* ed. Donald B. Cochrane, Cornel M. Hamm, and Anastasios C. Kazepides. New York: Paulist Press, 1979.
Cook, John W. *Morality and Cultural Differences.* New York and Oxford: Oxford University Press, 1999.
Crawford, Cromwell. "Hindu Ethics for Modern Life." In *World Religions and Global Ethics,* ed. Cromwell Crawford. New York: Paragon House, 1989.
Crosby, Donald A. "Civilization and Its Dissents: Moral Pluralism and Political Order." *Journal of Social Philosophy* 21 (1990): 111–26.
D'Arcy, Eric. *Human Acts: An Essay in Their Moral Evaluation.* Oxford: Clarendon, 1963.
Das, Veena. "The Debate on Abortion." *Seminar* (November 1983): 31–35.
Dennis, Marie. "For a Dignified Life: the Worldwide Movement for Debt Relief is Rooted in Debt Relief." *Sojourners,* May–June 1998, 30–34.
Dolan, Maura. "Jury System Is Held in Low Regard by Most." *Los Angeles Times,* 27 September 1994.
Donnelly, Jack. *Universal Human Rights in Theory and Practice.* Ithaca: Cornell University Press, 1989.
Dorff, Elliot N. "The Covenant: The Transcendent Thrust in Jewish Life." In *Contemporary Jewish Ethics and Morality,* ed. Elliot N. Dorff and Louis E. Newman. New York: Oxford University Press, 1995.
Ebersole, Frank B. "Where the Action Is." In *Things We Know.* Eugene: University of Oregon Books, 1967.
Ellis, Ralph D. "Moral Pluralism Reconsidered: Is There an Intrinsic-Extrinsic Value Distinction?" *Philosophical Papers* 21 (1992): 45–64.
English, Jane. "Wrongs and Rights." *Canadian Journal of Philosophy* 5 (1975): 233–43.
Ewing, A. C. *Ethics.* New York: Free Press, 1953.

Faruqi, Isma'il R. al. "Islamic Ethics." In *World Religions and Global Ethics,* ed. Cromwell Crawford. New York: Paragon House, 1989.
Ferrara, Alessandro. "Universalism: Procedural, Contextualist, and Prudential." In *Universalism vs. Communitarianism: Contemporary Debates in Ethics,* ed. David Rasmussen. Cambridge, Mass.: MIT Press, 1990.
Foot, Philippa. "Moral Relativism." Reprinted in *Relativism: Cognitive and Moral,* ed. Jack W. Meiland and Michael Krausz. Notre Dame and London: University of Notre Dame Press, 1982.
Freuchen, Peter. *Book of the Eskimo.* New York: World Publishing Company, 1961.
Gauthier, David. *Morals By Agreement.* Oxford: Clarendon Press, 1986.
Gelven, Michael. *War and Existence: A Philosophical Inquiry.* University Park: Penn State University Press, 1994.
Geertz, Clifford. "Anti Anti-Relativism." Reprinted in *Relativism: Interpretation and Confrontation,* ed. Michael Krausz. Notre Dame: University of Notre Dame Press, 1989.
Gilligan, Carol. *In a Different Voice: Psychological Theory and Women's Development.* Cambridge: Harvard University Press, 1982.
Gostin, Lawrence O. "Informed Consent, Cultural Sensitivity, and Respect for Persons." *Journal of the American Medical Association* 274, no. 10 (13 September 1995): 844–45.
Gustafson, James M. *Theology and Christian Ethics.* Philadelphia: United Church Press, 1974.
Harbour, Frances V. "Basic Moral Values: A Shared Core." *Ethics and International Affairs* 9 (1995): 155–70.
Hardin, Garrett. "Lifeboat Ethics: The Case Against Helping the Poor." *Psychology Today* magazine (1974). Reprinted as "The Error of Famine Relief. In *Ethics for Modern Life,* ed. Raziel Abelson and Marie-Louise Friquegnon. New York: St. Martin's Press, 1995.
Harman, Gilbert. "Is There a Single True Morality?" Reprinted in *Relativism: Interpretation and Confrontation,* ed. Michael Krausz. Notre Dame: University of Notre Dame Press, 1989.
———. "Moral Relativism." In Gilbert Harman and Judith Jarvis Thomson, *Moral Relativism and Moral Objectivity.* Cambridge, Mass.: Blackwell, 1996.
———. "Moral Relativism Defended." In *Relativism: Cognitive and Moral,* ed. Jack W. Meiland and Michael Krausz. Notre Dame: University of Notre Dame Press, 1982.
Harré, Rom, and Michael Krausz. *Varieties of Relativism.* Oxford: Blackwell, 1996.
Hatch, Elvin. "The Good Side of Relativism." *Journal of Anthropological Research* 53 (1997): 371–81.
Herodotus. *History of Herodotus,* Bk. 3, Chap. 38. Adapted from George Rawlinson trans. In Ethical Relativism, ed. John Ladd. Belmont, Calif.: Wadsworth, 1973.
Herskovits, Melville J. "Cultural Relativism and Cultural Values." Reprinted in *Ethical Relativism,* ed. John Ladd. Belmont, Calif.: Wadsworth, 1973.
Hick, John. *An Interpretation of Religion.* New Haven: Yale University Press, 1989.
———. *Problems of Religious Pluralism.* New York: St. Martins, 1985.
Hill, Thomas E., Jr. "Self-Respect Reconsidered." Reprinted in *Autonomy and Self-Respect.* Cambridge: Cambridge University Press, 1991.
———. "Servility and Self-Respect." Reprinted in *Autonomy and Self-Respect.* Cambridge: Cambridge University Press, 1991.

Hoffman, Frank J. "The Concept of Focal Point in Models for Inter-Religious Understanding." In *Inter-Religious Models and Criteria*, ed. J. Kellenberger. New York: St. Martin's, 1993.
Huntington, Samuel P. *The Clash of Civilizations and the Remaking of World Order.* New York: Simon & Schuster, 1996.
Hussey, J. M., ed. *The Cambridge Medieval History, vol. 4, The Byzantine Empire,* pt. 2, *Government, Church, and Civilization.* Cambridge: Cambridge University Press, 1967.
Jarvie, I. C. *Rationality and Relativism.* Boston: Routledge and Kegan Paul, 1984.
James, William. "What Pragmatism Means." In *Essays in Pragmatism,* ed. Albury Castell. New York: Hafner, 1954.
Kant, Immanuel. "Metaphysical Principles of Virtue." Trans. James W. Ellington. In Immanuel Kant, *Ethical Philosophy.* Indianapolis, Ind.: Hackett, 1983.
Kasulis, Thomas P. "Hypocrisy in the Self-Understanding of Religions." In *Inter-Religious Models and Criteria,* ed. J. Kellenberger. New York: St. Martin's, 1993.
Kekes, John. *The Examined Life.* Lewisburg: Bucknell University Press, 1988.
———. *The Morality of Pluralism.* Princeton: Princeton University Press, 1993.
Kellenberger, J. *Relationship Morality.* University Park: Penn State University Press, 1995.
Keown, Damien. *The Nature of Buddhist Ethics.* New York: St. Martin's, 1992.
Kluckhohn, Clyde, "Ethical Relativity: Sic et Non." Reprinted in *Ethical Relativism,* ed. John Ladd. Belmont, Calif.: Wadsworth, 1973.
Korsgaard, Christine M. "Personal Identity and the Unity of Agency: A Kantian Response to Parfit." Reprinted in *Creating the Kingdom of Ends.* Cambridge: Cambridge University Press, 1996.
———. "The Reasons We Can Share: An Attack on the Distinction Between Agent-Relative and Agent-Neutral Values." Reprinted in *Creating the Kingdom of Ends.* Cambridge: Cambridge University Press, 1996.
———. *The Standpoint of Practical Reason.* New York: Garland, 1990.
Ladd, John, ed. *Ethical Relativism.* Belmont, Calif.: Wadsworth, 1973.
———. "The Issue of Relativism." In *Ethical Relativism,* ed. John Ladd. Belmont, Calif.: Wadsworth, 1973.
LaFleur, William R. *Liquid Life: Abortion and Buddhism in Japan.* Princeton: Princeton University Press, 1992.
Larrabee, Mary Jean, ed. *An Ethic of Care: Feminist and Interdisciplinary Perspectives.* New York: Routledge, 1993.
Linton, Ralph. "Cultural Relativity." October 1951. Mimeographed.
———. "The Problem of Universal Values." In *Method and Perspective in Anthropology,* ed. R. F. Spencer. Minneapolis: University of Minnesota Press, 1954.
Lipner, Julius J. "The Classical Hindu View on Abortion and the Moral Status of the Unborn." In Harold G. Coward, Julius J. Lipner, and Katherine K. Young, *Hindu Ethics: Purity, Abortion and Euthanasia.* Albany: State University of New York Press, 1989.
MacIntyre, Alasdair. *After Virtue: A Study in Moral Theory.* Second edition. Notre Dame: University of Notre Dame Press, 1984.
Macklin, Ruth. "Universality of the Nuremberg Code." In *The Nazi Doctors and the Nuremberg Code,* ed. George Annas and Michael Grodin. New York: Oxford University Press, 1992.

Mandelbaum, Maurice. "Subjective, Objective, and Conceptual Relativisms." In *Relativism: Cognitive and Moral,* ed. Jack W. Meiland and Michael Krausz. Notre Dame: University of Notre Dame Press, 1982.
Mastnak, Lynne. "Diary." *London Review of Books,* 21 August 1997, 28–29.
Matilal, Bimal Krishna. "Ethical Relativism and Confrontation in Cultures." In *Relativism: Interpretation and Confrontation,* ed. Michael Krausz. Notre Dame: University of Notre Dame Press, 1989.
Meiland, Jack W., and Michael Krausz, eds. *Relativism: Cognitive and Moral.* Notre Dame: University of Notre Dame Press, 1982.
Messer, Ellen. "Pluralist Approaches to Human Rights." *Journal of Anthropological Research* 53 (1997): 293–317.
Miles, Jack. "Blacks vs. Browns." In *California Dreams and Realities: Readings for Critical Thinkers and Writers,* ed. Sonia Maasik and Jack Solomon. Boston: Bedford Books/St. Martin's, 1995.
Mill, John Stuart. *On Liberty.* Edited by George Sher. Indianapolis, Ind. Hackett, 1978.
———. *Utilitarianism.* Edited by George Sher. Indianapolis, Ind.: Hackett, 1979.
Mortimer, Robert C. *Christian Ethics.* London: Hutchinson's University Library, 1950.
———. *The Elements of Moral Theology.* New York: Harper & Brothers, n.d.
Moser, Shia. *Absolutism and Relativism in Ethics.* Springfield, Ill.: Charles C. Thomas, 1968.
Nagengast, Carole. "Women, Minorities, and Indigenous Peoples: Universalism and Cultural Relativity." *Journal of Anthropological Research* 53 (1997): 349–69.
Nagengast, Carole, and Terence Turner. "Introduction: Universal Human Rights Versus Cultural Relativity." *Journal of Anthropological Research* 53 (1997): 269–72.
Nussbaum, Martha. "Non-Relative Virtues: An Aristotelian Approach." In *The Quality of Life,* ed. Martha Nussbaum and Amartya Sen. Oxford: Clarendon Press, 1993.
———. *Women and Human Development: The Capabilities Approach.* Cambridge: Cambridge University Press, 2000.
O'Neill, Onora. "Justice, Gender, and International Boundaries." In *The Quality of Life,* ed. Martha Nussbaum and Amartya Sen. Oxford: Clarendon Press, 1993.
———. *Towards Justice and Virtue: A Constructive Account of Practical Reasoning.* Cambridge: Cambridge University Press, 1996.
Page, Clarence. "An Entire Deck of Race Cards." *Baltimore Sun,* 5 October 1995.
Plato. *Crito.* Trans. Hugh Tredennick. In *Plato: The Collected Dialogues,* ed. Edith Hamilton and Huntington Cairns. Bollington Series 61. Princeton: Princeton University Press, 1961.
Popper, Sir Karl. "The Myth of the Framework." In *The Abdication of Philosophy: Philosophy and the Public Good,* ed. Eugene Freeman. La Salle: Open Court, 1976.
Premasiri, P. D. "Ethics of the Theravada Buddhist Tradition." In *World Religions and Global Ethics,* ed. Cromwell Crawford. New York: Paragon House, 1989.
Quinn, Philip L. "Relativism about Torture: Religious and Secular Responses." In *Religion and Morality,* ed. D. Z. Phillips. New York: St. Martin's, 1966.
Rasmussen, David, ed. *Universalism vs. Communitarianism: Contemporary Debates in Ethics.* Cambridge, Mass.: MIT Press, 1990.
Read, K. E. "Morality and the Concept of the Person Among the Gahuku-Gama." *Oceania* 25 (June 1955): 233–82.
Redfield, Robert. "The Universally Human and the Culturally Variable." Reprinted in *Ethical*

Relativism, ed. John Ladd. Belmont, Calif.: Wadsworth, 1973.
Richmond, Ray. "Immense TV Audience Tunes In, Hears 2-Word Outcome." *Los Angeles Daily News,* 4 October 1995.
Rorty, Amélie Oksenberg. "Relativism, Persons, and Practices." In *Relativism: Interpretation and Confrontation,* ed. Michael Krausz. Notre Dame: University of Notre Dame Press, 1989.
Rorty, Richard. "Solidarity or Objectivity?" In *Objectivity, Relativism, and Truth: Philosophical Papers,* Vol. 1. Cambridge: Cambridge University Press, 1991; and in *Relativism: Interpretation and Confrontation,* ed. Michael Krausz. Notre Dame: University of Notre Dame Press, 1989.
Ross, W. D. *The Right and the Good.* Indianapolis, Ind.: Hackett, 1930.
Runzo, Joseph. "Reply: Ethical Universality and Ethical Relativism." In *Religion and Morality,* ed. D. Z. Phillips. London: Macmillan; New York: St. Martin's Press, 1996.
——. *World Views and Perceiving God.* London: Macmillan; New York: St. Martin's Press, 1993.
Saddhatissa, H. *Buddhist Ethics.* London: George Allen & Unwin, 1970.
Salmon, Merrilee H. "Ethical Considerations in Anthropology and Archaeology, or Relativism and Justice for All." *Journal of Anthropological Research* 53 (1997): 47–63.
Sartre, Jean-Paul. *Being and Nothingness.* Trans. Hazel E. Barnes. New York: Philosophical Library, 1956.
Schulweis, Harold M. "Judaism: From Either/Or to Both/And." In *Contemporary Jewish Ethics and Morality,* ed. Elliot N. Dorff and Louis E. Newman. New York: Oxford University Press, 1995.
Scott, Johnie H., and James Dennis. "'Rush to Judgment': A Mediated Analysis of the Politicizing of the O. J. Simpson Murder Trial by the American News Media." Paper presented at the annual convention of the National Association of African American Studies, Houston, Texas, February 1996; and at the Ethics and Values Colloquium, California State University, Northridge, April 1996.
Sen, Amartya. "Human Rights and Asian Values." *New Republic,* 14–21 July 1997, 33–40.
Shrage, Laurie. *Moral Dilemmas of Feminism.* New York: Routledge, 1994.
Shweder, Richard A. "Post-Nietzschean Anthropology: The Idea of Multiple Objective Worlds." In *Relativism: Interpretation and Confrontation,* ed. Michael Krausz. Notre Dame: University of Notre Dame Press, 1989.
Shweder, Richard A., and Edmund J. Bourne. "Does the Concept of the Person Vary Cross-Culturally?" In *Culture Theory: Essays on Mind, Self, and Emotion,* ed. Richard A. Shweder and Robert A Levine. Cambridge: Cambridge University Press, 1984.
Siddiqi, Muzammil H. "Global Ethics and Dialogue Among World Religions: An Islamic Viewpoint." In *Ethics, Religion, and the Good Society,* ed. Joseph Runzo. Louisville, Ky.: Westminster/John Knox Press, 1992.
Singer, Marcus George. *Generalization in Ethics.* New York: Alfred A. Knopf, 1961.
Singer, Peter. *Practical Ethics.* Cambridge: Cambridge University Press, 1979.
Stace, W. T. *The Concept of Morals.* New York: Macmillan, 1962.
Stackhouse, Max L. *Creeds, Society, and Human Rights.* Grand Rapids, Mich.: Eerdmans, 1984.
Stefánsson, Vihjálmur. *My Life with the Eskimo.* New York: Collier Books, 1962.
Sterba, James P. *The Demands of Justice.* Notre Dame: University of Notre Dame Press, 1980.

Stevenson, Charles L. *Ethics and Language.* New Haven: Yale University Press, 1944.
Stone, Christopher D. *Earth and Other Ethics: The Case for Moral Pluralism.* New York: Harper & Row, 1987.
Tachibana, S. *The Ethics of Buddhism.* London: Oxford University Press, 1926.
Taylor, Charles. "Explanations and Practical Reason." In *The Quality of Life,* ed. Martha Nussbaum and Amartya Sen. Oxford: Clarendon Press, 1993.
———. *Philosophy and the Human Sciences: Philosophical Papers,* Vol. 2. Cambridge: Cambridge University Press, 1985.
Taylor, Paul W. "Social Science and Ethical Relativism." In *Ethical Relativism,* ed. John Ladd. Belmont, Calif.: Wadsworth, 1973.
Thompson, Judith Jarvis. "A Defense of Abortion." *Philosophy and Public Affairs* 1 (1971): 47–66.
Tillich, Paul. *My Search for Absolutes.* New York: Simon & Schuster, 1964.
Tseng, Timothy, and David Yoo. "The Changing Face of America." *Sojourners,* March–April 1998, 26–29.
Turner, Terence. "Human Rights, Human Difference: Anthropology's Contribution to an Emancipatory Cultural Politics." *Journal of Anthropological Research* 53 (1997): 273–91.
Walzer, Michael. *Spheres of Justice.* New York: Basic Books, 1983.
———. *Thick and Thin.* Notre Dame: University of Notre Dame Press, 1994.
Warren, Karen J. "The Power and Promise of Ecological Feminism." *Environmental Ethics* 12 (Summer 1990): 125–46.
Wasserstrom, Richard. "Is Adultery Immoral?" Reprinted in *Philosophy and Sex,* ed. Robert Baker and Frederick Elliston. Buffalo, N.Y.: Prometheus Books, 1984.
Williams, Bernard. "Internal and External Reasons." In *Moral Luck.* Cambridge: Cambridge University Press, 1981.
Winch, Peter. "The Universalizability of Moral Judgments." In *Ethics and Action.* London: Routledge and Kegan Paul, 1972.
Wisdom, John. "Philosophy and Psycho-Analysis." In *Philosophy and Psycho-Analysis.* Oxford: Blackwell, 1964.
Wogaman, J. Philip. *Christian Moral Judgment.* Louisville, Ky.: Westminster/John Knox Press, 1989.
Wolgast, Elizabeth. *The Grammar of Justice.* Ithaca: Cornell University Press, 1987.
———. "Moral Pluralism." *Journal of Social Philosophy* 21 (1990): 108–16.
Womack, Mari. "Studying Up the Issue of Cultural Relativism." *NAPA Bulletin* no. 16 (1995): 48–57.
Wong, David B. *Moral Relativity.* Berkeley and Los Angeles: University of California Press, 1984.
Young, Iris. *Justice and the Politics of Difference.* Princeton: Princeton University Press, 1990.
Zechenter, Elizabeth M. "In the Name of Culture: Cultural Relativism and the Abuse of the Individual." *Journal of Anthropological Research* 53 (Fall 1997): 328–30.

Index

abortion, 122–32
absolutes versus universals, 45, 50
Achebe, Chinua, 223
adultery, 117–19
agreements between persons (as morality's basis), 70–74, 105–6
Alberuni (al-Bīrūnī), 211
Aquinas, Saint Thomas, 36, 63, 65–66, 134 n. 25
Arisaka, Yoko, 163
Aristotle, 23–24, 66, 94, 95, 118
Austen, Jane, 24
Austin, J. L., 55 n. 22
autonomy, 119–22

Baker, Robert, 120, 150, 181–83
Beauchamp, Tom L., 120
Benedict, Ruth, 18, 140, 198
Bentham, Jeremy, 83
Billy Budd, Foretopman, 100–102
Boas, Franz, 141, 215–16, 217, 222
Booth, Wayne C., 165–66
Bourne, Edmund, 160, 189
Bradley, F. H., 3
Brandt, Richard B., 25, 27, 33, 40, 43, 46, 57, 187–88, 191
Bringa, Tone, 138 n. 35
Buddhism, 35–36, 47–48, 64, 66, 67, 85 n. 25, 125–29

Callicott, Baird J., 76–77, 92–93, 92 n. 3, 157, 158
The Canterbury Tales, 23
Card, Claudia, x
Chao Chu, Bhikku, 35–36, 64
Cheney, Jim, 157
Childress, James F., 120
Chinese culture, 180
Christianity, 36, 47–48, 63, 66, 67
Clinton "scandal," 134–35
Cochrane, Donald, 169
Confucianism, 38
contractarianism. *See* agreements between persons (as morality's basis)
Cook, John W., 104, 141, 184, 191–92, 222
Crawford, Cromwell, 37
Crito, 40, 73, 106
Crosby, Donald A., 77, 80, 84, 109–11

D'Arcy, Eric, 55 n. 22
Das, Veena, 124
Dennis, James, 205
dharma, 36–37, 123
Dinka culture, 52–54, 59, 84–85
Divine Command Theory, 64
Donnelly, Jack, 142–43, 148–49
Dorff, Elliot, 64

Ebersole, Frank, 56

Ellis, Ralph D., 26 n. 57, 77
English, Jane, 111 n. 29
environmental ethics, 77
Eskimo culture, 51–52, 57–58, 59, 97, 172–73
ethical relativism. *See* moral relativism
ethonocentrism, 20–22
Ewing, A. C., 191, 214–15

Faruqi, Isma'il R. al, 37
female genital mutilation, 149–54
Ferrara, Alessandro, 24
Foot, Philippa, 27
Franklin, Benjamin, 24
Freuchen, Peter, 51–52, 52 n. 19

Gahuku-Gama culture, 160–64
Geertz, Clifford, 5, 20, 176, 178
Gelven, Michael, 164 n. 84
Gilligan, Carol, 92
Gowans, Christopher, x
group rights, 142–44, 147

Harbour, Frances, 33, 45, 46–47, 49, 61, 97, 99, 129
Harman, Gilbert, 4–5, 12, 28, 40, 44, 71–73, 166–68, 198
Harvey, J., x
Hatch, Elvin, 45, 140
Herodotus, 2, 46, 188, 223
Herskovits, Melville J., 17–18, 20, 26, 27, 50, 140, 191, 198
Hick, John, 15–17, 36
Hindu culture, 123–24
Hinduism, 36–37
Hobbes, Thomas, 70, 74, 159
Hoffman, Frank J., 50
Hopi culture, 40, 58–59
human nature (as morality's basis), 66–67
human relationships, x n. 2, 9, 91–112, 188–89, 220–22
  and moral principles, 212–14
  See also person/person relationship
human rights, 25, 41, 42, 139–54
Hume, David, 159

Huntington, Samuel P., 32–33, 38, 202–4, 223

Inuit culture. *See* Eskimo culture
Islam, 36, 37–38, 66
Islamic societies. *See* Muslim societies

James, William, 5–7, 175, 199
Japanese culture, 126–29
Jarvie, I. C., 18
Judaism, 64, 172

Kant, Immanuel, 14, 15–16, 76, 82, 120, 136, 159, 213
Kasulis, Thomas, 47–48
Kekes, John, xi, 25–26, 29, 34, 41, 48, 49, 52–54, 67, 69, 76–89, 107–9, 111, 129, 154–56, 173–74, 179, 184, 218
Kenyatta, Jomo, 150
Keown, Damien, 35, 67, 85 n. 25, 172
Kluckhohn, Clyde, 19, 33, 46
Korean-American culture, 121
Korsgaard, Christine, 74 n. 41, 92–93
Krausz, Michael, xi, 12, 14, 18

Ladd, John, 18–19, 141, 192, 194–95
LaFleur, William R., 126–28, 157
levels of description of action, 55–58, 190–95
Linton, Ralph, 46, 69
Lipner, Julius J., 123–24
Locke, John, 159

MacIntyre, Alasdair, 23–24
Macklin, Ruth, 180, 216–17
Mahābhārata, 123
Maslow, Abraham, 68
Mastnak, Lynne, xi, 138–39
Matilal, Bimal Krishna, 27, 36–37, 50, 67, 68, 69, 73, 168
Maudūdī, A. A., 66
Meiland, Jack, 12, 14, 18
Messer, Ellen, 142, 147
Mexican-American culture, 121
Miles, Jack, 209

Mill, John Stuart, 28, 76, 82, 83, 136, 158, 179, 212
moral absolutism, 28, 45, 65, 67, 68, 176–78, 198–99
moral diversity, 1–2, 8, 91–104, 115–32, 139–54, 201–14, 223–24
moral duties to oneself, 135–39
moral indeterminacy, 132–35
moral monism, 81–83
moral pluralism, 76–81, 154–58
moral progress, 81, 87–88, 214–22
moral relativism, 1–2, 22, 67, 68, 83–86, 171–76, 178–86, 197–99
  definition, 28–29, 44–45
  forms of, 23–27
  problem of, 2–7
Mortimer, Robert C., 63, 66, 67
Moser, Shia, 68, 69, 70
Muslim societies, 96, 131, 138–39

Nagengast, Carole, 151–52
Native American Church, 146
natural law (as morality's basis), 63–66
Navaho culture, 40, 120–21
needs (as morality's basis), 67–70, 107–8
Niebuhr, H. Richard, x
Nussbaum, Martha, 151, n 68

Oglala Sioux culture, 146
O'Neill, Onora, 74 n. 41, 152 n. 69

Page, Clarence, 204, 205
Paul of Aegina, 151
Paul, Saint, 63, 65
person/person relationship, 114–70, 183, 184, 186, 213–14, 220–21, 222, 224
Plaskow, Judith, x
Plato, 83
Popper, Sir Karl, 13
Premasiri, P. D., 125–26
Principle of Ascent, 44, 50–60, 186–90, 197
  its small paradox, 59, 195–97
privacy, 180–83

projection error, 110 n. 27, 191–92
Protagoras, 2

Quinn, Philip L., 132–33, 165–66, 177, 179, 186

Rain, Dr. Leo, xi
Rashdall, Hastings, 66
Rawls, John, 70
Read, K. E., 160–62
Redfield, Robert, 172–73, 187–88
religious pluralism, 15–16, 76
relationships
  human. *See* human relationships
  to nonhumans, x n. 2
relativism
  cognitive, 13, 22
  conceptual, 13–15, 22
  cultural, 17–19, 22
  moral. *See* moral relativism
  religious, 15–17
rights
  human. *See* human rights
  in rem, 148
Rorty, Amélie Oksenberg, 6–7, 173, 175, 176, 177, 199
Rorty, Richard, 20–22, 25
Ross, W. D., 57, 66, 79, 94
Ruether, Rosemary Radford, x
Runzo, Joseph, 13–14, 15, 27, 133–34, 175

Salmon, Merrilee H., 140–41, 150, 152
Sartre, Jean-Paul, 27
Scott, Johnie H., 205
Schulweis, Harold, 64, 172
Sen, Amartya, 38, 41, 211
Shrage, Laurie, 118–19
Shweder, Richard A., 20, 160, 189
Siddiqi, Muzammil H., 37, 66
Simpson, O. J., his murder trial, 204–8
Singer, Marcus George, 136–37
Singer, Peter, 105–6
Socrates, 73, 74, 106
social-self concept of person, 159–66
Stace, Walter, 25, 45

Stackhouse, Max L., 49, 70
Stefánsson, Vihjálmur, 51
Stevenson, C. L., 27
Stone, Christopher, 76–77, 83

Tachibana, Shundo, 125
Taylor, Charles, 74 n. 41, 159
Taylor, Paul, 45, 69–70
Thatcher, Sanford, xi
thin and thick morality, 33, 49, 98–99, 204, 206
Thompson, Judith Jarvis, 111 n. 29
Tillich, Paul, 13
torture, 132–34
Tseng, Timothy, 39
Turner, Terence, 141–42

United Nations Universal Declaration of Human Rights, 140, 145, 148

values
 Asian versus Western, 38–39, 42
 pan-human, 45
 primary or basic, 26, 33–34, 41, 46, 48, 49, 69, 78, 87–88
 secondary, 26, 47, 48, 49, 78, 87–88
 transcultural, 129–32
virtue, 23–24

Walzer, Michael, 24, 49, 98–99, 107, 129, 130, 204, 206
Ward, Keith, 211
Warren, Karen J., 144, 160, 161, 163
Wasserstrom, Richard, 117–19
Winch, Peter, 100–102
Wisdom, John, 3, 5
Wolgast, Elizabeth, 77, 83, 100–102, 159–60, 161, 163, 219–20, 222
Womack, Mari, 17, 141
Wong, David, 28, 169, 171, 198

Yagisawa, Takashi, xi
Yeats, William Butler, 223
Yew, Lee Kuan, 38, 39
Yoo, David, 39
Young, Iris, 144, 149, 160, 161, 163

Zechenter, Elizabeth M., 104 n. 20, 151, 153

www.ingramcontent.com/pod-product-compliance
Lightning Source LLC
Chambersburg PA
CBHW031549300426
44111CB00006BA/228